Sex and the Single Beer Can

"Walter Brasch is the most informed, opinionated, witty, and delightful commentator on the media scene today."
—John Noonan, Aspen Media Review

"Skewers the American media [in a] satiric romp [that is] hilariously funny and deadly serious. You will never read a newspaper or magazine, listen to the radio, or watch a movie or TV in the same way again."
—Sally Mattero, Koen Books

"Outrageous and Irreverent, but always on target. Better than most of what passes as commentary in the daily press."
—Donald Bird, Chair, Department of Journalism, Long Island University

"Exposes some of the most common journalistic foibles, and the impact they can have on the way the rest of society sees the world around them. Nothing is safe or sacred."
—Jane Alison Havsy, *American Reporter*

"Humorous, straight-forward, and laced with good old-fashioned logic."
—Pat Trosky, Wilkes-Barre *Citizens' Voice*

"A delightful read, as interesting and provocative as the writer himself."
—Dave DeKok, *Harrisburg Patriot and News*

"Brasch Illuminates the dark, and often absurd, sides of society and the media with a style that invites laughter and encourages the reader to look beyond reality to the truth."
—Nancy Baumgartner, *Williamsport Sun-Gazette*

"Insightful, readable and tightly written."
—R. Thomas Berner, head, journalism program, Pennsylvania State University

"Brasch keeps the readers entertained not just through his poignant satire, but with his ability to tell a good story first. He always displays a solid point and makes it a fun ride getting there."
—Bill Kohler, Standard-Journal newspapers

"A dynamic journalist in the tradition of Andy Rooney."
—Gil Bratcher, WYSP-FM, Philadelphia

"Wonderfully wacked."
—Bob Batz, *Pittsburgh Post-Gazette*

"Entertaining, informative, and fun for everyone."
—Rob Ervin, producer, "The Gary Burbank Show," WLW-AM, Cincinnati

"Wonderfully humorous essays."
—Lee Lawrence, WFPR-AM, Hammond, La.

"Walter Brasch has a wonderful way of cutting through the media hype to clarify the 'real' culture and media in a manner that can be understood by all."
—Jack Holcomb, WEEU-AM, Reading, Pa.

"A pleasant respite from the overly academic dissections of media events that allows the reader to learn through laughter. A great book of readings for students who are trying to learn how to tell it like it is."
—Pat Heilman, chair, Department of Journalism, Indiana University of Pennsylvania

"Excellent demonstration of the art of newspaper column writing, filled with the compassion and humor missing from many of today's papers."
—Robert Jones, Dept. of Journalism, University of Texas

"Effective and powerful. In Dave Barryesque fashion, Brasch weaves sights, sounds, feelings, and attitudes into clever, playful, entertaining essays. Brasch provides an excellent guide for students trying to learn the art of writing. For a teacher, this collection offers models of tone, dialogue, description, narrative voice, and point of view."
—Beverley Pitts, associate provost and professor of journalism, Ball State University

"Satire is a dying art [but] Brasch has rekindled some and direvted it against the media. For those seeking an insider's look at the media with the irreverence of the public, this is, above all, a book to enjoy."
—Jeff Inglis. Burlington, Vt., *Mountainview*

Also by Walter M. Brasch

A Comprehensive Annotated Bibliography
of American Black English
(with Ila Wales)

Black English and the Mass Media

Columbia County Place Names

Cartoon Monickers:
An Insight Into the Animation Industry

The Press and the State:
Sociohistorical and Contemporary Issues
(with Dana R. Ulloth)

Forerunners of Revolution:
Muckrakers and the American Social Conscience

A ZIM Self-Portrait

With Just Cause:
Unionization of the American Journalist

Enquiring Minds and Space Aliens

Betrayed:
Death of an American Newspaper
(forthcoming)

Joel Chandler Harris,
Uncle Remus,
and the American Social Conscience
(forthcoming)

Sex and the Single Beer Can
Probing the Media and American Culture

by Walt Brasch

Mayfly Productions
Elmwood, Illinois 61529

Copyright © 1997 by Walter M. Brasch

All rights reserved
This book, or any part,
may not be reproduced in any form,
including electronic transmission,
without permission of the author.

Publisher: Bill Knight
Typesetting and Cover Design: Marilyn Franklin
Copyeditor: Louise D. Palmieri
Printer: Thomson-Shore

Mayfly Productions
P.O. Box 380
Elmwood, Illinois 61529

Publisher's Cataloging-in-Publication

Brasch, Walter M., 1945–
Sex and the single beer can: probing the media and American culture
by Walter M. Brasch. — 1st ed.
  p. cm.
ISBN: 0-9624613-6-9
1. Mass media and culture—United States.
2. Popular culture—United States.
   I. Title.
P94.65.U6B7 1997   302.23'0973   97-73436
               QBI97-40696

This book is printed on acid-free paper
PRINTED IN THE UNITED STATES OF AMERICA

Dedication . . .

. . . This book is dedicated to Rosemary Renn Brasch who provided inspiration for many of the columns, and encouragement for all of them. Her ideas and suggestions are always good, her social conscience a model for others to emulate.

. . . And, as always, to my parents—Milton and Helen Haskin Brasch—who provided the inspiration to challenge injustice and stupidity while still being part of the greater community of mankind.

Contents

Critical Acclaim	ii
Dedication	vii
Acknowledgments	xiii
Introduction	xv

Information

Accuracy

Enquiring Minds and Space Aliens	3
Cockroach Hormones and Politician Promises	6
Creating Historical Fiction	9
The Case for Sensationalism	11
The Press Meets the Afo-a-Kom	14
War in the Gulf: Lessons of an Obsession	17
All the Beautiful People	21
Only a Part of the World	24

Language

Down for the Count	25
Linguistic Larceny	27
'Local Reporter Cops Lexicon Story'	31
Personages of the Mind	34
Driven by Ignorance	35

Editing

Editing the 12 Commandments	39
Fewer Words, Less Filling	40

Politics

Promises, Promises	43
Electing the News	45
Dead Air at the Convention	47
A Dam(n) for the Home Folks	50
President Sneezes, Film at 11	52

Broadcast Journalism

Blood on Their Lenses	54
The Only Alternative for KFAD	56
A Television Snow Job	58
Eyewitless Promotion	60
TV News 101: Introduction to Makeup	62

Ethics
Long Island Lolita Meets the Journalistic Low-Life	65
For Sale: Justice—O.J. Style	67
The Write Stuff	69
Compliments of a Thief	71
Stripping Off Their Royalties	73
Politically Incorrect Weather	75
A Major Conflict of Interest	77
The Intruder	79

The First Amendment
Make Mine Media Rare	81
Stealing the First Amendment	84
Thrown Out of the Game	86
Free Speech on Death Row	88

Obscenity
An Obscene Story	95
Of Matrons and Movies	97

Research
Playing the University Grantsmanship Game	98
Cellular Research	100
A Nation of Polls and Predictions	102

Crime and Violence
Withdrawing from an O.J. Overdose	104
Oh Joy, O.J. Every Day	106
Reel Violence	109
Escalating an American Paranoia	111
Labels of Violence	114
An American Triangle: Violence, the Media, and Individual Responsibility	116

Technology
America's Ding-a-Lings	119
The Beeper Cacophony	121
The Impersonal Society	122
Scanning an American Life	125
Windows Not of the Mind	127
Curbing the Paperless Explosion	129

Labor and Economics
The $6 Million Journalist	131
Patriotic Unemployment	133
Traded for Two Rookies, an Editorial Clerk, and a Future Draft Choice	135
Downsizing Baseball's Problems	137

Laying Off Marshbaum ... 138
An Unequal Competition ... 140
An Hour a Day ... 142
'We're Management; We Don't Have to Tell You Anything' ... 145

Intermission

Selling Out America by the Yard ... 150
Confusions ... 151

Persuasion

A Medal for the Army ... 154
Chicken Advertising ... 156
Missing in Atlanta ... 158
Jeanetics and the Cool 'Wannabe' ... 161
Sex and the Single Beer Can ... 164
The Stupid Season ... 170
Tanness, Anyone? ... 172
Cramping Up for Health ... 174
Death by Healthy Doses ... 176
Mixing a Bitter Pill for America's Drug Companies ... 179

Intermission

Dysfunctional Thoughts ... 181
Wonderings of an Idle Mind ... 183

Entertainment

Three Nights a Week ... 187
Sounds of the Concrete City ... 189
Voices of America ... 191
The Monday Night Football Game ... 198
Out of the Closet, and Into the Living Room ... 201
Swifter, Higher, Stronger . . . Greedier ... 208
Conventional Fund Spending ... 210
For Casinos, 'Six-Hour Visitors' Make a Full House ... 212
There She Is, Miss-representing America ... 217
The Day the Circus Came to Town ... 220
'And Now a Word From Your Local Sponsor' ... 222
Kernels of Truth ... 223
The Hustle ... 225
Creating a Best Seller ... 227
Liner Notes on an American Future ... 232
Fantasy Week at Walt's ... 234

Acknowledgments

During the past three years, I have been especially fortunate to have an excellent administrative assistant who has done everything from filing routine correspondence and helping with research to assisting with book promotion. Words and a pittance of a salary aren't enough to repay Jennifer T. Boscia for her time, energy, and loyalty.

Mark Steinruck, Marilyn Franklin, and Louise Palmieri provided significant help in the preproduction process.

Clerical assistant Beth Shultz made sure that now and then I could actually see my desk beneath a layer of notes, messages, and photocopied articles.

Every writer also needs an editor, although we often wonder why. With more than four dozen editors over the past five years, the frustration could have become immense. Fortunately, I have found editors who have provided valuable advice and friendship, even if now and then they have to edit or cut a column. I am sure that many of the columns may have caused them to hide behind bunkers, awaiting the volley of controversy that results. I am especially pleased to recognize and thank editors Nancy Acitelli, Wayne Bauer, Jacob Betz, Jim Burchik, Rita Cellucci, Carl Christopher, Shawnee Culbertson, Jim Curtis, Vivian Daily, Sharon Falkowitz, Jim Gallagher, David Gilmartin, Ann Marie Gonsalves, Bekki Guilyard, Bill Kohler, Rich Lewis, Leland B. Mather, Holly Matthews, Diane Mazonis, Marie McCandless, Wiley McKellar, Dave Monaghan, John Moore, James Oliver, Mitchell Olszak, Harold Prentiss, Michael Regan, Ray Saul, Joe Shea, Charles Schenk, Ed Schreppel, Troy Sellers, Linda Seligson, Joseph P. Shaw, Joe Sukle, Lynn Vanderberg, Eileen Winter, and Jack Yoset.

Another editor who helped is one I never met, nor had a chance to meet, but he helped shape my thought process more than any professor or editor. Horace Greeley (1811–1872), editor/publisher of the New York Tribune and one of the most influential people in the history of our country, showed just how good journalism can be when it's done well. He believed in integrity, followed a strict code of ethics, was unafraid to take forceful stands on many unpopular issues, including believing that the nation should eliminate slavery and give women the right of vote, and vigorously supported the working class.

Art Buchwald, Tom Lehrer, Jim Murray, Mark Russell, Michael Moore, Joseph Heller, and the Capitol Steps follow in the tradition of master satirists Horace, Juvenal, Rabelais, Cervantes, Moliere, Swift, Addison, Twain, William Gilbert, Sinclair Lewis, and James Thurber. They prove just how powerful humor and satire can be in making people think and better understand their lives and their society.

To my publisher, Bill Knight, I owe a special thanks for being a colleague and friend—and for paying royalties on time.

Finally, but most important, a special thanks to all my readers, especially those who take the time to write or call, even if they disagree with my views. The strength of our society shall always be in the foundation that allows many views to be heard.

Introduction

Hardly anyone admits reading the supermarket tabloids, but someone—other than movie star publicists who "leak" information to the tabloids to create controversy—must be reading them because the combined circulation for the six major weekly newspapers is more than 10 million.

I admit I am the someone who reads the tabloids, although it has been quite awhile since I read all 10 million copies in one week. Usually, I read The National Enquirer and, occasionally, one of the other tabs. I seldom read the *Weekly World News* because in the *USA Today* world of splashy color and flashy graphics, the black-and-white *Weekly World News* front page just doesn't measure up.

Nevertheless, it was a hot August afternoon when I went into the local air-conditioned supermarket to cool down and, perhaps, to find a few of the 30,000 advertised items that could translate into dinner for six, including two German Shepherds. (The pot-bellied pig came later.) Apparently, I wasn't the only one that afternoon who figured out how to get free air conditioning. The checkout lines were longer than a politician's lies, so there was only one thing to do.

I guessed I'd be able to get through most of the 15 magazines and six newspapers in the "you-gotta-buy-this" point-of-purchase racks by the time it was my turn. I also figured that my two sons would have graduated from college, moved out of the house, although still needing weekly "loans," and had grandchildren by the time I finished checking out.

Thus, it was in the checkout line that I learned from the *Weekly World News* that a space alien had come to earth to advise presidential candidate Bill Clinton. The alien had already advised President Bush and Ross Perot early in the Summer, but had to wait until after the Democratic convention to find out which of the donkeys was going to run.

Being the alert reporter I am, I was upset that a competitor had scooped me on what could have been the most important news of the week. Just a couple of weeks earlier, I had covered the first Clinton–Gore bus tour of America when it came into

Pennsylvania, and no one mentioned anything about an alien. Obviously, the Secret Service had covered it up once again.

That evening, Rick Renn, my nephew from Georgia, called. He had just read the space alien article, and knew I would be interested. The evidence was overwhelming. There were now at least two people who recognized good journalism. It was time to act.

For a few years, usually when I had too much time and not enough sense, I thought about writing a weekly newspaper column. It would be a great catharsis of what I proudly knew to be a warped mind, fertilized now and then by my wife. With only 23,000 other columnists trying to pitch their own catharses, I figured there was room for another 700–800 words a week, especially since newspapers appeared to be desperate for features. How else could anyone explain why they publish gossip columns and capsule summaries of soap operas?

Thus was born "Wanderings," a weekly column that probes a small particle of society. Sometimes it's biting satire; sometimes a wistful essay. Sometimes it looks into politics, other times the environment, health care, recreation, or whatever needs to be probed that week. About half the columns have a media focus. Occasionally, the media are the central focus, sometimes a supporting player, often an extra. But the media are always there—lurking; annoying; but most importantly, informing, persuading, and entertaining—just as in real life.

Sex and the Single Beer Can is a compilation of many of those media-related columns. Most of the columns have been revised for book publication. After all, newspaper columns stay around a couple of days, while books remain on the shelves, unread, for decades.

Read the columns. A few now; a few later. No one will rat on you if you read them out of order or if you fall asleep while reading the one column that has the secrets of the universe. Many may wonder where the sex and beer are that the title promises. It's a logical question—after all, the Introduction talks about the origin of the column and its relationship with the tabloids; the first column in the book is that first "enquiring" column.

Like tabloid headlines, book titles are meant to grab readers; more than half of all paperback books are sold on the basis of the title and cover design. In this case, the title is meant to grab two specific readers—my sons, Jeffrey and Matthew Gerber, wonderful children who have yet to read one of my books, but are fond of what the book title promises. Let them search this book, hopefully reading every column until they find what the title promises. For the rest of my readers, there really *is* a discussion about sex and beer; more important, it is a key discussion about what has happened to the media during the past three decades.

For 30 years I have been proud to be a journalist. I believe in the American media, and in the people I am pleased to call my colleagues and friends. For the number of obstacles business, government, and public institutions put into their paths, the media overall do a splendid job.

But, like any institution, the media have their problems, some inherent within the foundation. As a media critic, and especially as a satirist, I have a responsibility to examine the media, hoping that by bringing the excesses and problems to light—something every journalist strives to do—the media will do an even better job of helping Americans better understand their own lives and issues that affect them.

While reading this book, I hope you find yourself not only informed, persuaded, and entertained, but mentally stimulated and ready to act against the stupidity and injustice in this world.

"I write for the great mass of intelligent, observant, reflecting farmers and mechanics; and, if I succeed in making my positions clearly understood, I do not fear that they will be condemned or rejected."

—Horace Greeley

INFORMATION

Enquiring Minds and Space Aliens

When I don't believe I'm getting all the news from the nation's 1,570 daily newspapers, 7,417 community weeklies, 11,500 radio and TV stations, 12,000 magazines, or 50,000 new books published every year, I turn to the supermarket tabloids for the truth. After all, it was the 3.1 million circulation *Star* which first revealed the existence of Genifer Flowers, Bill Clinton's alleged prepresidential playmate.

Since most of the tabloid reporters have journalism degrees, worked on major daily newspapers, and are now earning $60,000 to $100,000 in their new assignments, I place great credibility in what is being reported in the six major tabloids, all of them published in Boca Raton or Lantana, Florida, and which have a combined circulation of about 10 million.

From the tabloids, I can monitor where Elvis is this week, learn first about who is being seen with whom, and which TV series is planning to replace which megastar, and more than anyone ever needs to know about soap stars, none of this reported by our usually vigilant local press.

I also know everything there is to know about Elizabeth Taylor, the Kennedys, the British royal family, Big Foot, and why taking coffee bean baths can perk you up.

I have also learned about monkey-faced boys, dog-faced girls, human-faced pigs, an 8-year-old who gave birth to twins, a woman who gave birth to a litter of 12 children, a 28-year-old grandmother, a man who was pregnant, and a tribe in South America that found a cure for cancer.

From the 350,000-circulation *Sun*, in one week alone, I learned that a survivor of the Titanic spent 20 years on an iceberg, that there really is a flying elephant with jumbo ears who lives in Zaire, that a woman is turning into Marilyn Monroe, that scientists in Jerusalem found Goliath's mummified head, and that miracles occur near a Florida tree that has the face of Christ. The establishment media also don't report much about house hauntings, psychic revelations, reincarnations, and extraterrestrials. However, all are conscientiously reported by the tabloids, and all for a buck or so a week.

In just one issue of the 722,000-circulation *Weekly World News*, in August 1992 I learned that condoms cause breast cancer, that a 7,000-year-old gargantuan shark patrols Lake Superior, that Hitler was really a woman who survived World War II and died in 1992 in Buenos Aires at the age of 103, and that a spaceship (with 14 perfectly preserved extraterrestrial corpses) was found in the Gobi Desert.

More important, I learned that a friendly space alien, not too unlike E.T., declared his (her? its?) support for Bill Clinton. A photo on Page 1 showed the smooth-skinned, large-headed, long-fingered, unclothed alien shaking hands with the Democratic presidential nominee after a 40-minute super-secret visit in Madison Square Garden during the Democratic National Convention.

It wasn't the first scoop for the *News*. In May, the newspaper had reported that the alien visited George Bush at Camp David; in July, it reported the alien stopped by Dallas for a chat with Ross Perot who, apparently taking the alien's advice, soon dropped out of the race. Pictures also accompanied these articles, thus proving the alien's existence.

We learned that the alien—who came from the most successful planet in the universe—gave Gov. Clinton advice on health and environmental issues as well as how to turn the economy around. The alien's mission—other than to evaluate and recommend a candidate for the confused American masses, most of whom would vote for the alien over any of the presidential candidates—was to seek "trade concessions that would benefit his home planet," according to reliable sources who talked with the *Weekly World News.*

However, a few of my more cynical journalist colleagues, obviously jealous they were scooped on the biggest news story of the decade, called the story a hoax. To get to the truth, I made a few phone calls. A member of the White House staff said she believed that the president made several light-hearted comments about the visit of the alien, but referred me to another office for confirmation. An official spokesman for President Bush at first indicated he didn't know what I was talking about when I asked about the space alien. After informing him of this late-breaking news, he said he didn't think the president made any comments about "that alleged meeting." He then informed me that "as far as we're concerned," there was no meeting, thus confirming my belief that if the White House says it didn't occur, it probably did occur.

On to Bill Clinton's team. The Governor had previously acknowledged that he discussed certain issues with an alien, and was pleased to receive the alien's support, an indicator that the Clinton–Gore team was broadening its base. At least that's what a few media reported.

But, being the hard-hitting investigative journalist that I am, I had to get actual confirmation, if not from the Governor, certainly from an official spokesperson. Did you ever try to find an official spokesperson when you need one? After three days of phone calls, all I had was a lot of conversations with a pack of confused but obviously arrogant campaign officials who couldn't or wouldn't confirm or deny anything. Obviously, the Clinton team was more impressed with themselves and in not revealing the truth.

To clear up the confusion, I finally contacted Eddie Clontz, editor of the *Weekly World News.* Eddie is a pleasant fellow and an excellent journalist who worked for the Associated Press, then for several years as a reporter and news editor of the *St. Petersburg Times.*

"We had been working the story for a year," says Eddie who revealed that the newspaper received the tip from "some of our people in the military." He says that credible sources "often don't call regular newspapers because the dailies take it as a joke or will treat it as such," thus confirming my suspicions that daily newspaper reporters are more concerned with trivial things like crime and city council meetings than they are with news of interplanetary consequence. The photos, Eddie says, were submitted by one of the newspaper's sources. A true journalist, he wouldn't reveal a confidence. He did confirm that the newspaper plans to follow the alien's travels through the country, but probably won't be tracking either George Bush or Bill Clinton.

"We don't get into political coverage unless it has to do with a space alien," the newspaper's editor slyly said. Now, for the big question. Does Eddie Clontz, editor of a newspaper with larger circulation than all but the top five American dailies, believe in the alien? "I really don't think so," he said, noting that although "the photographs look real to me, as a skeptic I'd say it's not true." Actually, he also called the existence of the alien "preposterous."

In every political campaign, there is always something to break the tension, something to lighten up a campaign that tires out candidates, staff, reporters, and voters. This year, it's the alien's visit with the candidates. Next campaign, maybe it will be coverage of the alien's race for the presidency.

Cockroach Hormones and Politician Promises

Michael Born just wanted to be involved with the television industry—and make several hundred thousand dollars. The TV industry just wanted some exclusive video footage; it didn't care of what, as long as it was exclusive "bring-home-the-ratings" footage.

Among the 32 videotapes Born sold to the German networks were footage of a Klan rally, some men shooting a cat, and drug dealers sneaking into Germany. The only problem was that Born staged the events. A German court called it fraud and sentenced him at the end of 1996 to four years in prison.

Journalists pietously proclaimed that people who commit fraud should be jailed. Born claimed the networks salivated all over his videotape, didn't check out the stories, and may have even known some of the stories were false.

A few months earlier, Britain's Independent Television Network broadcast an 80-second video allegedly showing sex scenes of Princess Diana and a riding instructor known to have been her lover at one time. The *Sun* took still photos from the video, recast them into blurry black and white images, and splashed them across five tabloid pages. The only problem— other than a massive invasion of privacy and a medium's voyeuristic quest for ratings—was that the scene was a hoax; the "princess" and the "riding instructor" were look-alike actors. A mysterious "American lawyer," acting on behalf of an equally mysterious man known only as "the Sergeant," had sold the tape to the *Sun,* which slobbered all over the offer before parting with a few thousand British pounds.

Hoaxes in journalism aren't new. In 1835, Americans believed life existed on the moon because a reporter for the *New York Sun* reported that astronomers with a powerful telescope saw winged creatures and vegetation. The modern tabloids have the aliens on earth, usually breeding with vestal virgins.

Author Clifford Irving, armed with forged letters, got a $750,000 advance in 1969 to write the official biography of reclusive billionaire Howard Hughes. Janet Cooke of the *Washington Post* won, then lost, a Pulitzer Prize in 1981 when it was revealed her story about a child born with a heroin addiction was as phony as her resumé. TV shows sponsored by Ford in the 1960s and 1970s either shot away from New York City's Chrysler Building, or electronically eliminated the building. The *National Geographic* digitally altered the pyramids for "aesthetic" reasons for one of its covers. NBC-TV broadcast a story about fish that were supposedly killed on government land; but it was footage of a different forest, and the fish weren't dead. To demonstrate that a GM truck could easily burst into flames, NBC's "Dateline" rigged the truck with an explosive. FOX-TV obliterated the distinction between news and hucksterism when it "interrupted" its coverage of the 1997 Super Bowl with a "special report" by news anchor Catherine Crier. The breaking news? The Blues Brothers "escaped" and were about to headline the halftime show.

However, most media-perpetuated hoaxes aren't the result of deliberate lies by the media, but sloppy reporting. In spite of their image as cynical, reporters often buy official statements dished out by official sources. One day the media report that oat bran is the "be-all, cure-all" of all life's problems; a few days later, they report there may be no effect of oat bran in the diet. One day, Vitamin C is the cure for cancer; the next day, it's Selenium. Sometimes, it's a new cancer-killing drug; the next, it's an admission that the drug still needs to be tested. If you believe the supermarket tabloids, it's a cancer-killing drug made of oat bran that was brought to earth by space aliens who plan to marry Madonna in a group ceremony in Fresno.

An Iowa farmer in 1868, upset about his pastor's constant

7

proclamation about Biblical giants, arranged for a block of granite to be carved into an exact likeness of a 10-foot man, then buried it in his field. When the "fossilized" man was accidentally discovered, the media jumped all over the story, quoting innumerable "experts" who declared the man was real.

In Minnesota 30 years later, the Kensington Stone, with purported Viking writing and the date of 1362, titillated the American public and media. In 1908, the skull of what became known as the Piltdown Man, believed to be the 250,000-year-old "missing link," was discovered in England. Although cynics doubted the authenticity, the media spent five decades quoting innumerable sources who had placed the skull in archeological history. In 1955, the newly-developed Carbon-14 dating method placed the skull at 700 years old. But, C-14 wasn't even necessary—additional studies proved that the jawbone was that of an orangutan.

In 1983, a Biblical scholar and archeologist led the media into a trap to show the public how gullible the media were when he arranged for an actor to feign discovery of a piece of pine wood from Noah's Ark. Sun International created a two-hour film, sold it to CBS-TV, which hyped it and ran it as a two-hour prime-time special. The news media, without investigating, devoted large chunks of their "news hole" to perpetuate the fraud. It took only a simple C-14 test to prove the wood was recently dipped in chemicals, but the media didn't ask.

C-14 dating in 1990 also put an end to thousands of media stories that the Shroud of Turin had been on the body of Jesus.

In 1981, the media first reported that crop circles and designs in England's fields may have had an extraterrestrial origin. For the next decade, new circles and headlines appeared each growing season, baffling scientists and giving "proof" that UFOs existed. Finally, in 1991, two artist/farmers gleefully admitted they created the circles and for more than a decade watched the media reactions.

During the daily "5 O'Clock Follies" during the Vietnam War, military officers discussed that day's operations, as well the body count. The reporters, having an official source and apparently thinking that body counts were a good way of quantifying the war, much like scores quantify athletic contests, included the numbers in their daily stories. By the end of the war, if readers believed the media, they would have learned that every North Vietnamese and Viet Cong civilian and soldier was killed at least twice.

During the Gulf War, reporters blamed the military for not

giving them more information, but seldom challenged Pentagon claims of how many Iraqi SCUD missiles were destroyed or how effective the American Patriot anti-missile missiles were. The media also bought the official versions of what happened at Wounded Knee, Ruby Ridge, and the Branch Davidian compound, all scenes of what many later claimed was FBI "overkill."

White House correspondents, and most of the country's news media, bought President Nixon's version of what became the Watergate conspiracy until the evidence became overwhelming. Local reporters often buy statements by well-dressed executives over the statements of the impoverished, unemployed, or the "whistleblower." And, certainly, the media publish every politician's campaign promise or company's press release that later prove to be as phony as Jenny Jones claiming in court she had no idea what happens on her own TV sleaze show.

Prankster Joey Skaggs has proven how easy it is to fool the media. Disguising himself as innumerable scientists, Skaggs titillates the media first by news releases, then by elaborate follow-ups. The media fell for the claim that cockroach hormones are the basis of super vitamins and that there really was a "Solomon Project" that developed a voice-stress computer test which proved O.J. Simpson was guilty of murder. Among the media that reported his innumerable pranks as truth have been *The New York Times*, the *Washington Post*, the *Philadelphia Inquirer*, *USA Today*, CNN, and the three major TV networks.

And that's the real problem. It's no longer the supermarket tabloids that have a credibility problem, but virtually all the media.

Creating Historical Fiction

A few years ago, I tried to tell my younger son that some passages in his ninth grade history book were incorrect. He refused to believe me. After all, there it was, written in print and paraphrased in lecture by his teacher. Even if he believed me, he knew he'd lose points on the next test if he didn't answer the way his teacher and textbook expected.

Even in the most meticulously-researched and written text, errors of fact are inevitable. However, because many public school social science texts are little more than well-designed cut-and-paste jobs from other texts, and often put together by committee, the errors in one are often compounded in the next. Nevertheless, errors of *commission*—a wrong date, the wrong name, an interpretation not based on facts—can usually be fixed either by an addendum, circular to teachers, or in the next edition.

Errors of *omission*, however, are more serious because they can't be verified as easily, and may have been caused by author, editor, or publisher bias, ethnocentrism, or just plain lack of knowledge of an area. Until recently, textbooks routinely omitted significant references to contributions of persons other than white males to the development of the country. Also missing from public school texts was almost anything that cast a negative image of American values, the school boards possibly reasoning that those "darling impressionable minds" couldn't handle all that conflict.

Thus, it isn't surprising to learn that textbooks fail to report that Revolutionary War patriots, even long after the Constitution was adopted, routinely violated the principles of the libertarian revolution by significant abuses of civil liberties and of continued violations of freedom of speech and of the press . . . or that both the Mexican–American and Vietnam wars had massive protests of American foreign policy . . . or that the government systematically and maliciously violated due process and civil rights during the McCarthyism witch hunts of the 1950s.

The reality is that the majority cultures write the histories, and their texts often reflect their biases and political agendas. During the latter 20th century, Japanese texts overlooked the slaughter of thousands of Chinese civilians; Soviet texts failed to mention America's massive economic and humanitarian assistance to that country; and the texts of all countries reported little about the Holocaust. Publishers in America, trying to reap the widest possible financial benefit by not offending anyone, often force authors to overlook significant social trends.

To establish standards for the study of history in the public schools and to correct some of the nation's textbook wrongs, the National Endowment for the Humanities, under congressional mandate, gave $1.75 million to UCLA's National Center for History in the Schools to bring together a wide range of academics to study the problems and to recommend a model text that would present history as it was, rather than what we hoped it was. The concept was good; the execution was abysmal.

The Center rightly determined that texts were sugar-coating and distorting American history, that there was an overemphasis upon a recitation of facts and in recounting the deeds of a few people, mostly white males, but far too little discussion about major trends and social issues that define the American republic.

However, in its recommendations, the Center did exactly what it condemned. With a political and social ideological agenda, the Center staff presented a 271-page document at the end of 1994 that discounted the Western European influence in the formation of the United States, and presented a distorted overview that the formation of the country was a convergence of Islamic, African, and European influence. It claimed the nation's continuing history is little more than struggle, conflict, and the abuse of the rights of people. It barely discussed the historic role of a free press and of free speech, mentioned the Gettysburg Address only briefly, and relegated the complexities of the Cold War as merely a "quarrel" among imperialistic nations.

The committee's proposed guidelines, although rightly adding many civil rights leaders, left out Eli Whitney, Thomas Edison, and the Wright Brothers, among many other scientists; it overlooked Daniel Webster and other major diplomats and politicians; and it gave few lines to innumerable creative artists. However, the emperor of an ancient African civilization is praised, as are numerous individuals, often female or of minority cultures, who were merely footnotes in America's 300-year history.

In historiography, as in journalism, the better writers not only research the facts, but also analyze and interpret them to help the people better understand the critical issues that affect them. It is not acceptable for the writers of public school social science and history texts to distort the reporting of history by creating fiction.

The Case for Sensationalism

During spring 1994, almost every American newspaper, news magazine, radio, and TV station hurled stories at the public about Streptococcus-A, a flesh-eating killer infection which can cause death within a couple of days. It's a story the media love, just as they love stories about sex, violence, and the extramarital affairs of film stars.

The critics claimed the story has been overplayed, accurately pointing out that the incidence of the killer infection, which acts as a toxin to the body's muscles, was no greater that year than any other year. They said the media were pandering to the public's worst fears in the hope of gaining higher readership; the critics said that exaggerated and sensationalist reporting would cause a panic that would result in physicians and hospitals being jammed with people who may have no more a problem than a mosquito bite.

All the criticism is probably true. But it was a historical precedent that helped set the base for the public's right to know, even if the media do occasionally enter the "gray area" of reporting.

It was 1834, and the upstart *New York Sun* was causing trouble for city politicians and fellow journalists. While other newspapers charged 6 cents an issue, made their readers buy a subscription, and their advertisers an annual contract, the *Sun* sold each issue for just a penny and allowed advertisers to purchase their ads whenever they wished. The other papers scorned such outrageous business practices.

The more established papers, targeting the city's business class and the elite as their readers, accepted bribes and favors from politicians and the public to keep their names out of the paper or to print "dirt" on some opponent. Naturally, they never reported that judges, police, and politicians also routinely took bribes, some from the newspapers themselves. But, *Sun* publisher Benjamin Day and newly-hired editor George Wisner, with a slate of police and court news, looked to the city's lower and middle classes for their support; their policy was that the *Sun* would print all the news or none. In response, the other journalists brazenly told Day and Wisner they were upsetting accepted practices that didn't seem to hurt anyone, yet helped fellow reporters and editors make a respectable wage.

While other newspapers kept their reporters in Manhattan, Wisner hired "stringers," community-based people in different parts of the city to report news when it happened, earning the ridicule of journalists who thought it was a waste of time and people.

Soon, the *Sun* attacked filth in hospitals and prisons, lashed out against slavery, opposed monopolies, and argued that an artificial increase in the price of flour was nothing more than greed.

The establishment press retaliated by demanding a grand jury investigation of the *Sun* on charges of inciting trouble for business. That demand, as well as numerous suits for libel, were usually thrown out of court.

Less than a year after becoming editor, Wisner learned that a New York City resident had died of cholera, an extremely debilitating illness that attacks quickly and, at that time, had a relatively high mortality rate. The cause could have been in the city's water supply or in tainted food sold in grocery stores or in restaurants. Wisner knew if there was one case, there had to be others. But, the public health department said there was no problem with cholera, certainly no epidemic.

Distrusting bureaucrats as much as he did the competing newspapers, Wisner asked his stringers to do a little bit of "leg work." When they reported there were other cases, Wisner went to the health department, which again denied any problem. After some badgering, Wisner got the health officials to admit there "may" have been a problem. But they said if the *Sun* published the story, there would be a panic that would lead the public to needlessly tie up doctors and hospitals. Besides, said the health department, the more "responsible" newspapers, knew about the potential epidemic, and had kept quiet because it was, said the health officials, in the public's best interest.

The public's best interest is to know all the facts, said Wisner who published the story and suggested the health department was negligent in detecting the disease in the first place. The other media attacked him for being irresponsible. But that aggressive "irresponsibility" led to the people knowing what was happening in their society and their lives.

Slightly more than a decade ago, the media were asleep when the first reports were made about an infection that had no known cure, had the potential for epidemic proportions, but was confined to a small group sociologists and the media called "deviant," but most of the public called "perverted." The infection became known as AIDS.

Had the media understood George Wisner's philosophy of journalism, the people would probably have known about AIDS a half-decade earlier, and may have been able to take evasive measures that would have saved thousands of lives.

Perhaps there was media overkill on the Strep-A story. But, mankind is largely rational, and it's better to have all the facts than to live in ignorance at the mercy of things unknown. If the media hype helped save one life, if it caused thousands of people who didn't have Strep-A to become scared enough of suspected symptoms to see their physicians who may have diagnosed and treated other less serious illnesses, it was worth the ink.

Although the media can rightly be accused of pandering to the public's fears, maybe it's permissible for there to be some "sensationalist" reporting now and then.

The Press Meets the Afo-a-Kom

The return of a ritualized and functional royal throne figure of African heritage from a New York City art dealer to the Kom people of Cameroon was widely but poorly reported by the world's media in late 1973. Not much has changed since then in either the worlds of art or journalism.

The Kom story was part of the budgets of virtually all American and several overseas wire services. News and feature articles were soon appearing in most of the world's media, including *The New York Times, Washington Post, National Geographic, Die Bunde Illustrierte, Ebony,* and *Esquire,* as well as the three major American television networks. The Afo-A-Kom even became the answers to questions on a number of television quiz shows, including "Jeopardy." The story was hot, and the media knew it.

Depending on what was read at the time, the Afo-A-Kom, a 100-year-old statue, was either a god . . . a phallic symbol . . . an icon . . . or a symbol of tradition, unity, and harmony. It was either "as sacred as" two other Kom statues . . . or the most sacred of all. It was either a national shrine of the Cameroon . . . or a part of the Kom people. It was 5- or 5½-feet tall, or 62-, 62½-, or 64-inches tall. It was made of ebony . . . wood . . . iroko. It was covered either by red beads . . . or reddish-brown and blue beads . . . or brown and blue beads. The beads were coral . . . plastic . . . semi-precious stones.

It was stolen from the people of Kom in 1966 . . . or 1967. It was taken from a storage hut that was loosely guarded . . . or not guarded at all. The original thief—there were many—was the son . . . or the nephew . . . of Fon (King) Law-Aw . . . or Al-Aw . . . who died shortly thereafter . . . or who died before the theft. The thief was ostracized . . . punished . . . not convicted. The Fon himself was powerful . . . or not-so-powerful . . . or had no power.

Aaron Furman, a New York City art dealer who had either an unblemished reputation . . . or was a scoundrel . . . purchased the Afo-A-Kom in Cameroon . . . or Paris . . . or somewhere else. In 1967 . . . or 1968. . . . It was brought to the United States, with Furman apparently believing that it was legitimately purchased . . . or knowing it was stolen. It was valued, by American standards, at $30,000 . . . $51,000 . . . $60,000 . . . $65,000 . . . $80,000. Furman eventually sold the statue for "his expenses" . . . or "a substantial sum" . . . or $25,000.

According to the media, Kom is a series of villages . . . a tribal enclave . . . Shangri-La. But, no matter what it is, Kom is located, according to the popular media, in West Cameroon . . . or East Cameroon; in the Federal Republic of Cameroon . . . or the United Republic of Cameroon. As for the people of Kom, that remote Cameroonian kingdom, they number 3,000 . . . 35,000 . . . 40,000 . . . 81,000 or 92,000. No one was really certain. The Kom, stated the media, are also primitives . . . savages . . . or trapped by modern civilization.

The first story about the Afo-a-Kom broke in the October 25, 1973, issue of *The New York Times,* after one of its correspondents had learned from two Peace Corps workers of the Afo-a-Kom's theft. Within hours, the other national media jumped on the story and became overzealous, rewriting and compounding errors. Even the *Times,* which published 15 stories (about 700 column inches) over a two-month period, committed numerous errors of fact and interpretation.

When the media weren't bungling the facts, they were locked in a trap of ethnocentrism. The majority of articles that came from the American media showed a basic lack of understanding of cross-cultural communication, as well as a certain lack of understanding of the people whose beliefs, world views, languages and cultures are not those of certain Americans.

Not untypical of the views were those of a writer for *Esquire* who apparently overdosed on Tarzan movies. Armed with experiences of less than a half-day in Kom, a place she never knew existed prior to her desire to suddenly write a "definitive" study of the Kom people. She claimed she had been "to the edge of the earth." She admitted, reflecting the views of many reporters, "I wanted to go to Kom. I wanted to see the Fon's 50 wives and half-naked slaves and all the pomp and panoply of great African kingdoms, where the people would receive us white bwanas, bowing low or maybe even casting themselves to the ground and throwing dust on their heads. I've heard of things like that. Also I wanted to see the Fon ride out on his legendary pure white horse to greet us, followed by ten servants carrying calabashes of palm wine and his umbrella and his chair." She worried whether the salad was safe to eat, called the flora of Cameroon "strange plumy vegetation," and called Kom's history "bloody murder, war, witchcraft, fire, famine, and flood," without recognizing that the history of the Kom is no different than the history of any people, including the Americans.

The *Times,* with numerous reporters parroting its reporting, inaccurately claimed, "The women of Kom are completely subordinate to their men. They are expected to work hard, bear many children and not complain. The women do all the farming, cooking, cleaning, child raising, and most of the market selling. . . . Many women say they like polygamy because it lessens the very heavy work burden." The Kom, however, are a matrilineal society, and there are clear cut distinctions in Kom society between sexual, biological, and sociological wives.

In contrast, some of the media, especially the BBC and the *National Geographic,* were relatively accurate, taking the time to verify facts and evaluate the sources of information.

Why the major media gave the story such heavy play probably is a reflection of Americans' fascination with "exotic" lands, crime and conflict, and what we thought was a work of art that carried a price tag. Johnson Ndimbie, cultural affairs officer at the Cameroon Embassy to the United States and Canada, believed the story received the coverage it did because not only were the media trying to find stories about Africa, but the media are "more concerned, or more capable, of covering the bizarre and sensational. They seemed to be more interested in coups and conflicts because it makes good reading."

In contrast to the exploitation of the story by the larger media, the smaller papers usually spiked the wire service copy. Most newspapers argued, "Well, you know that there's a newsprint shortage and we really don't have the room. Also, no one is interested in things happening in Africa. It's just too far away."

And that's the problem, but it isn't solely one caused by the media; they merely mirror society.

War in the Gulf: Lessons of an Obsession

With flags flying, Buck Rogers technology, and an allied army of 500,000 from more than two dozen countries, led by a charismatic teddy bear general, we sounded forth the trumpets, declared we believed in democracy, and systematically decimated Iraqi forces in a one-month air and artillery barrage, then Hail Mary-ed them in a four-day ground assault in February 1991.

When it was over, and 25,000 to 50,000 people lay dead, and another 150,000 to 200,000 injured, thousands of them critically, we proudly declared we defeated not only the "Butcher of Baghdad," but dictatorships and territorial aggression as well. So, let's see what we learned and what has happened since the United Nations Memorandum of Understanding of April 18, 1991, ended the Persian Gulf War.

Shortly after the Iraqi invasion the previous August, many Kuwaitis, including most of the royal family, fled to Cairo, London, and other capital cities where they took their wealth, complained about Iraqi atrocities, partied, and waited for the coalition to hand them back their country. There is little question that Iraq committed atrocities, not only against its own minorities, but also against Kuwaitis. But, the Kuwaitis aren't exactly saints. A Human Rights Report issued by the U.S. Department of State at the end of 1993 pointed out there were "continuing reports of torture and of arbitrary arrest, as well as limitations on the freedoms of assembly and association."

Four years before the Iraqi invasion, Kuwait's royal family dissolved parliament. Under American pressure, the al-Sabah royal family, safely in exile and promising anything to the coalition, agreed that once the war was over it would permit elections. In October 1992, the amir finally restored a 50-man parliament, but political parties are still banned. The "democracy" we fought to preserve is for the 90,000 or so voting citizens of Kuwait. More than 550,000 Kuwaitis—including women, servants, and laborers—have no voting rights. Only males older than 21 who can trace their ancestors to having lived in Kuwait prior to 1920 may vote.

The Kuwaiti Constitution, suspended in 1962, still hasn't been reinstated. Freedom of the press was curtailed in 1985, then barely restored after the war. Although prior restraint on the media has been abandoned, the media and people still face severe restrictions. A Department of Censorship exists. The people and the media may not criticize the amir, the Kuwaiti government, or the Islamic religion.

Seventeen reporters went to Saudi Arabia in August 1990 at the beginning of Operation Desert Shield. By the end of the month-long Operation Desert Storm at the beginning of the next year, almost 2,000 reporters were crawling all over themselves to be first on the air or in print with the latest in war news. The reality was that CNN and the BBC usually had the latest and most comprehensive coverage; most of the others had rumors.

In a month of saturation bombing, Americans were subjected to saturation media coverage. We learned that although many reporters excelled under extreme difficulty, most of the on-site reporters didn't have a clue of how to cover a war, asked dumber questions than freshmen after an all-night beer party, and allowed themselves to be manipulated by one of the most efficient public relations operations ever devised in American history.

The military told us, and the media reported, that Iraq had, and was likely to use, chemical, biological, and possibly nuclear warfare. In contrast, the American military piously proclaimed that we, noble warriors all, would never use those weapons. But, the media either didn't know, or they didn't report, that during the war, the coalition had limited nuclear weapons in Saudi Arabia, driven as much as 500 miles from the ports to the front by American Marines.

From the war, we learned that our military intelligence wasn't as precise as we needed. While the media parroted almost daily official statements that precision bombing by the coalition had destroyed all of Iraq's SCUD missile bases, the SCUDS somehow kept popping up, often against Israeli targets. We also learned that the highly-touted U.S.-built Patriot anti-missile missiles were about one-third effective.

We learned that the military bunker in Baghdad we bombed really did hold hundreds of frightened women and children. Our military and press claimed Saddam had deliberately put them there as hostages. Saddam declared, with some justification, that they were in a heavily defended bunker to be safe from American attacks. The baby milk plant we destroyed, then said was a front for weapons manufacturing, really produced baby milk.

Fortunately, this was a short, easily-managed war, unlike the seven years the United States was bogged down in Vietnam's rice paddies and jungles.

In the Vietnam War, the American government realized, perhaps too late, that it needed to win the "hearts and minds" of the enemy. In the Gulf War, the American government realized it had to win the "hearts and minds" of Americans, especially since this war, unlike any other war, could be reported live anywhere in the world.

The Pentagon quickly and efficiently established two Joint Information Bureaus in Saudi Arabia, and set up two briefings a day to provide as much information as most reporters could handle—and, possibly, to make sure that the reporters would be so bogged down in certain information that they wouldn't have time to find anything else.

The Pentagon didn't want pictures of body bags being prepared at Dover Air Force Base, Delaware; there weren't pictures of body bags. The Pentagon didn't want reporters to talk with the military, private through general, or Arab civilians unless an "escort officer" was present; the media didn't do 1-on-1.

To assure the media didn't overstep its boundaries and jeopardize the security of the troops, the Pentagon established media pools, selecting a few reporters, mostly from the "major" organizations, to accompany the troops and to provide coverage that all media could take and disseminate. "Pools rub reporters the wrong way, but there is simply no way for us to open up a rapidly moving front to reporters who roam the battlefield," said Pete Williams, assistant secretary of defense for public affairs. He claimed the use of the pools got "reporters out to see the action . . . guarantees that Americans at home get reports from the scene of the action, [and] allows the military to accommodate a reasonable number of journalists without overwhelming the units that are fighting the enemy." It also assures that there would be fewer stories, and that only acceptable viewpoints of "establishment" media would be heard.

Nevertheless, said Williams, "Our goal is to get as much information as possible to the American people about their military without jeopardizing the lives of the troops or the success of the operation." It was a decidedly different military philosophy than the one in Grenada which Williams readily acknowledged as "a journalistic disaster." As a result of complaints against the military's refusal to allow media coverage of its mini-invasion of a Caribbean island, apparently to make the world safe for American medical students, the Pentagon created a quick-strike media pool which, said Williams, "could be called upon on short notice to cover the early stages of military missions."

We also learned a lot about propaganda and public opinion. In October 1990, two months after Iraqi troops invaded Kuwait, a 15-year-old girl testified before a Congressional committee that she was a hospital volunteer who saw Iraqi soldiers enter a Kuwaiti hospital and "take the babies out of the incubators, and left the children to die on the cold floor." Several members of Congress said her testimony helped them decide to support what became Operation Desert Storm less than three months later.

Within months of the end of the war, we learned that the 15-year-old wasn't a volunteer, but the daughter of the Kuwaiti ambassador to the United States, and that there may not have been an atrocity at all. We learned that her testimony was orchestrated by the New York PR firm of Hill & Knowlton which received a large chunk of more than $20 million that Kuwait paid to establish two American-led front groups whose missions were to convince the American government—and, of course, American business—that there was overwhelming support by the American people for war against Iraq to preserve what we thought was democracy, but was probably America's obsession with oil for energy.

At the end of the war, we reported we destroyed the Iraqi military, then were surprised when Saddam, apparently with little opposition, launched attacks upon Shiite and Kurdish populations within Iraqi borders.

And, finally, what we didn't report is more of an indication of how impotent or culpable the media have been. Although thousands of combat troops, even five years after the war, were reporting health problems that didn't occur before the war, the media accepted official Pentagon explanations that the illnesses were not the result of combat activities. The media had reported that because of the danger from chemical and biological weapons, Americans were getting all kinds of vaccinations. But it wasn't for five years until the establishment media reported that the Pentagon required soldiers to take experimental drugs to reduce the effects of possible nerve gas attacks, that the Americans and allied troops became ill from the drugs, and that no nerve, chemical, or biological weapons were ever launched by Iraq. It wasn't until five years after the war that we reported that 5,000 troops may have been exposed to sarin nerve gas when they destroyed a weapons depot. We reported that we used strong pesticides to rid the desert of insects, but didn't report that the pesticides we used were probably more dangerous than the life we sought to eliminate. We reported that Americans were exposed to the Kuwaiti oil fires that blackened the sky, but we didn't report that thousands of soldiers and Marines were reporting health problems that were probably related to the fallout from burning oil.

And it all came down to the reality that oil fueled this war. For that, we sent in hundreds of thousands of Americans to kill, and to be killed, by hundreds of thousands of Iraqis, and to pretend we were fighting to preserve a democracy that never did and probably never will exist.

All the Beautiful People

From a pool of almost six billion contestants, the divinely-inspired *People* magazine editorial staff have once again chosen the 50 most beautiful people in the whole wide world, and duly etched them into the public mind by large color pictures and cutesy capsule biographies.

And, once again, it's also time for my annual *People* debunking. So, let's see if the people who put out *People* have learned anything in a year that saw wars, famine, and O.J. dominate the news.

Two years ago, the geniuses who make up *People*'s editorial staff decided that 23 of the world's 50 most beautiful people (46 percent) were actors or actresses. Last year, *People* decided actors and actresses were still 46 percent of all the beautiful people. This year, beauty explodes all over the screen as 18 actresses and 11 actors, 58 percent of all beautiful people, made the list.

Two years ago, *People*'s editors decided that seven singers were among the world's most beautiful list. But last year, there were only three, and this year only four, three of them men.

Models also lost position on the "elite 50." Two years ago, *People* decided that six models, all women and no men, were among the whole world's 50 most beautiful. Last year, there were still six women on the list, but now there were two men, apparently for gender balance. This year, it's one man and two women. Thus, almost three-fourths of the beautiful people are in the entertainment industry, leading me to believe that appearance counts more than raw native talent in American life. Or, at least, we commoners demand people in the entertainment industry to be beautiful. Interestingly, almost three-fourths of the full-page ads in the section feature "beautiful women."

Two years ago, five athletes (one woman and four men) made the list. Last year, six athletes (two women and four men) made the list. This year, only three athletes—all of them men—made the list.

For the fourth year in a row, celebrity lawyer John F. Kennedy, Jr., is a beautiful person. Perhaps the editorial staff could just give him a loving cup and let him retire as an undefeated beautiful person.

The first year I compiled the list, I complained that no journalists or teachers were selected to be beautiful. Apparently, that message got through to *People's* New York–Hollywood mentality. There are now beautiful journalists on the list. Last year, *People* selected former journalist and current Vice President Al Gore. In addition to our vice president, the beautiful people last year included a husband–wife documentary film team, an NBC "Today" show news anchor, and an ABC "Wide World of Sports" interviewer. Of course, some cynics might suggest that the two network beauties are really entertainers not journalists. So this year, possibly hoping to avoid my probing pen, *People* actually found a real journalist, 61-year-old Gloria Steinem, who should be honored to be recognized for being beautiful, but embarrassed by being included in a racist, sexist list. Nevertheless, for balance, *People* selected a male correspondent from NBC's "Today" show.

Teachers, alas, still didn't make the cut this year. But they need not worry about it. Neither did Miss America, Miss USA, Miss World, or, for that matter, Miss Crustacean—Ocean City, New Jersey's, tribute to beauty. Personally, I would have selected fat and balding Charles Kuralt as one of the world's most beautiful people. His words and truth are far more beautiful than all the vacuous heads who made up the list that takes up 60 full pages of a national magazine.

The elderly were finally recognized last year as beautiful. Of course, *People's* idea of elderly were 69-year-old Paul Newman, 57-year-old Barbara Babcock, and 53-year-old youngster Faye Dunaway. This year, the "elderly" included Steinem and 51-year-old Queen Silvia of Sweden.

For the first time, *People* tried to reflect reality last year by selecting 5-foot-11-inch, 180-pound-size 14 model Emme as a beautiful person, and pointing out she is a top star in the "burgeoning large-size modeling industry." Here's a shock, *People* editors.

Size 14 isn't fat! More than half of America's women are at least a size 14! If *People* wanted to highlight the reality that beauty comes in all sizes and shapes, it might have selected plump actress Shelly Winters. Nevertheless, apparently not wanting to set a trend by letting us commoners think beauty comes in all sizes, there are only modishly thin and ultrathin selectees this year.

Now, let's look at racial and gender balance. About a half billion people in the world are Black; about 1.9 billion are Asian. Two years ago, *People* could find only nine beautiful people in the entire world who weren't Anglo-Saxon white, and eight of them were Americans, most of whom photograph as light-skinned. Last year—what a surprise!—only nine of the list, eight of them Americans, also weren't white. This year, in a leap into almost social relevancy, *People* found all of 13 who weren't White. Interestingly, the ethnic distribution in each of the professions is also almost identical, including the reality that the previous two years, the only Asian represented each year was an actress, each of whom was born in China.

This year, in a major shift to recognize that there may be parts of the world other than Manhattan and Hollywood, *People* claims that a quarter of the most beautiful are "international." But, most of them are American residents, and all but two are from western Europe. Obviously, there aren't any beautiful people living in five of the world's seven continents.

At least there's gender equality. For each of the past three years, as if some quota was etched into *People*'s pancake-and-cream supply, there have been 26 women and 24 men, about the U.S. average.

To its credit, *People* editors, probably as an afterthought, might have been concerned about why no common people made the list. So, two years ago, the editors went "cutesy," and found two cities in Kentucky—Lovely and Beauty—and awarded "booby prizes." Perhaps the editors prefer to think of it as "honorable mention," but "booby prize" seems more appropriate. Last year, *People* found no "commoners," so this year, they searched their loading docks and found nine UPS drivers—mostly men from New York City, Los Angeles, and Florida—to feature in the "booby prize section."

Nevertheless, Lovely, Beauty, and UPS aside, we can only conclude that *People* editors believe almost all the beautiful people of the world are upper-class White entertainers from America, almost all of whom have entourages of at least a publicist, business manager, and agent.

Like all people, we in journalism tend to report about, be attracted to, and understand people and ethnic groups that are like our own. And, for the most part, we are White middle-class, sometimes even upper-class, college graduates who talk a lot about equality, but look, act, and dress as if we are part of the establishment we report about. In fact, until the 1960s, most reporters were white males. If we see only certain groups of people all the time—and *People*'s editors apparently see only certain groups of people—then we will report only about those people, leaving everyone else as invisible as the billions of beautiful people all over the world who didn't make the list. [*May 1995*]

Only a Part of the World

She quietly walked into the classroom from the front and stood there, just inside the door against a wall.

The professor continued his lecture, unaware of her presence until his students' eyes began focusing on her rather than him.

"Yes?" he asked. Just "yes." Nothing more.

"You shouldn't have done it," she said peacefully. He was confused. So she said it again, this time with a little venom.

"Ma'am," he began, but she cut him off. He tried to defuse the situation, but couldn't reason with her. She pulled a gun from her purse and shot him, then quickly left. He recovered immediately. It took less than a minute.

The scene was yet another exercise in the professor's news-writing class. His assignment was for the students to quickly write down everything they could about the incident. What happened. What was said. What she looked like. What she was wearing. Just the facts. Nothing more.

Everyone got some of the information right, but no one got all the facts, even the ones they were absolutely positively sure they saw or heard correctly. And, most interestingly, the "gun" the visitor used and which the students either couldn't identify or misidentified was in reality a . . . banana; a painted black banana, but a banana nevertheless. The actual gunshot was on tape on a hidden recorder slyly activated by the professor.

It was a lesson in observation and truth. Witnesses often get the facts wrong, unable to distinguish events happening on top of each other. Sometimes they even want to "help" the reporter and say what they think the reporter wants to hear.

Reporters are society's witnesses who record history by interviewing other witnesses, and they all make mistakes, not because they want to, but because everyone's life experiences and perceptions fog reality. Put 10 reporters into a PTA meeting, court trial, or the Whitewater hearing. No matter how well reporters pay attention to the proceedings, there will be 10 different stories.

Of the infinite facts and observations that occur during a meeting, reporters must select a few. Which few they select, which thousands they deliberately don't select—and, more important—which parts of a meeting or of society itself they don't even know exist—all make up a news story, usually written under deadline pressure. Thus, it isn't unusual for readers to wonder how reporters could have been in the same meeting as they were since the published stories didn't seem to reflect the reality of the meeting.

The New York Times arrogantly and stupidly proclaims itself to be the "newspaper of record," that it publishes "all the news that's fit to print." CBS News, however, is more honest. At the end of the newscast, we learn that we have seen just "a part" of today's world.

Down for the Count

I'm tired of reading, seeing, and hearing about the British royalty. The media believe that by shoveling the dirt on us, we won't notice that they didn't dig out the truth behind a politician's latest lies, or wade through piles of records in the courthouse to learn about tax reform issues.

The typical American doesn't know who England's prime minister is, and if asked to name three Canadian provinces probably comes up with North Michigan, Yuccatan, and Sasspittoon. Ask that same person to name which Royal got her toes sucked, and you have instant response. The prince and princess of Wales are divorced; I just wish we could divorce the American media from its royal fetish.

The British royalty of the Middle Ages and Renaissance had far more scandal than today's mentally-challenged blue bloods. But the newspapers didn't publish any of it. Not only did the editors know they could lose their heads for revealing gossip, they also knew there were more important things to report than who Henry was fooling around with.

Americans have always had a fascination with royalty. Although we organized a revolution to overthrow the monarchy's hold, and created a president not a king as head of State, we have spent more than two centuries trying to regain a royal image.

Our fast-food restaurants are called Burger King, Dairy Queen, and Pizza King. We have prom queens, homecoming queens, and even a Rose Bowl queen. The media, of course, are part of the royal awe.

Within weeks, *TIME* magazine alliteratively crowned four different singers—Barbra Streisand, Whitney Houston, Debbie Gibson, and Japanese superstar Seiko—as a "pop princess."

Just about any young ice-skating star is known as an "ice princess," but the media in 1989 derogatorily dubbed Deborah Norville an "ice princess" when she took over for popular Jane Pauley on NBC-TV's "Today Show."

Princess Cruises may have the "Love Boat," but there was no love lost when Donald Trump sold his 282-foot Trump Princess for about $100 million after he, Marla, and Ivana had formed a "Menage a Tabloid."

Among googobs of movie princesses have been Leia who helped Han Solo, Luke Skywalker, and that giant furry thing make the world safe for high-tech special effects; and a Lion King that made Disney rich enough to devour all other media companies, and take on the corporate shape of Jabba the Hut.

TV's "Queen for a Day" required contestants to be women who could sob a good story and get a washing machine to help them do the laundry for their 17 handicapped foster children. A spin-off was "The Prince of Tides," the story of a psychologist and her washing machine.

The greatest baron, until he was shot down by Snoopy, was Manfred von Richtofen, the Red Baron. However, for some reason the media prefer to use the title "baron" to refer to evil "kingpins"— as in "drug baron," "robber baron" and, understandably, "media baron."

The music industry abounds with royalty. Bessie Smith was the Empress of the Blues; Roger Miller was King of the Road. Among other kings are those of Ragtime (Scott Joplin), Blues (W. C. Handy), Swing (Benny Goodman), Rock and Roll (Elvis), Pop (Michael Jackson), and Waltz (composer Richard Strauss or bandleader Wayne King). One of the best singers was Nat

"King" Cole. Among others in the King family singers are Alan, B. B., Billie Jean, Carole, Don, Larry, Martin Luther, Stephen, and prodigal son Rodney.

Aretha Franklin may be the Queen of Soul, but James Brown is the Godfather of Soul; cross him, and you could find a broken treble cleff on your pillow in the morning. Rap singer Queen Latifah may think she's royalty, but British rock group Queen truly has a better shot at sitting in Buckingham Palace than she does.

Among singing princes are the Fresh Prince of Bel-Air, and the singer-with-the-unpronounceable symbol, formerly Prince, who has the ability to predict purple rain.

The most famous duke is the "Duke, Duke, Duke of Earl, Earl, Earl, Duke of Earl" who proved in the late 1950s that anyone can grow up and write song lyrics. Other less royal dukes have been baseball great Duke Snider and musical genius Duke Ellington who, had he gone to baseball games, would have had to sit in segregated seating in most ballparks. Upset there are no more "colored" seats, drinking fountains, and rest rooms is David Duke who once cornered the market on pointy white hats and dull-witted Whites.

Babe Ruth was the Sultan of Swat. But no royal monikers were attached to Roger Maris, who broke the one-season record, or to Hank Aaron, who broke Ruth's lifetime record, and had to put up with numerous racist comments.

Really, the only royalty that matters are the Counts—Tolstoy, Dracula, and Basie. As for the rest, perhaps the media might dump the nomenclature and then dump stories of the British royalty in favor of stories that matter.

Linguistic Larceny

A government investigation of Chicago's Veterans Administration Hospital (VA) in 1992 revealed that many of the resident physicians were poorly supervised, and that there were substantial instances of crucial diagnostic mistakes and inappropriate surgery. Sometime while all this was going on, six patients died in the operating room, and the VA was forced to make some rather large cash payments to the families of those individuals. According to an official explanation, each of the deaths was a "surgical misadventure." Sort of like "Adventures in Paradise," or even "Pee-Wee's Big Adventure." Maybe the VA thought it was on a camp out, and nothing worse occurred than the tent fell during the rain.

But, the VA isn't the only one to use the great linguistic coverup. A few years ago, a Colorado state legislator proposed a plan that would clean up Denver's polluted atmosphere, at that time well within the nation's "Bottom 10." Instead of spending millions to clean up the air, the legislator suggested a little language manipulation would solve the problem. "Hazardous air" would become known as just "poor air." "Dangerous air" would be "acceptable," and "very unhealthful air" would be "fair air." As for just "unhealthful air," it would be "good air," so pure that smoke-puffing industries would just have to bottle it and sell it as distilled. Even the Environmental Protection Agency has helped make American air safer by simply reclassifying acid rain as "wet disposition."

Because truth is the first casualty of war, we willingly accept the great linguistic coverup. Our Civil War wasn't a revolution, but a "war between the states." World War I, which we obtusely believed was "the war to end all wars," was the "Great War." Fortunately, no one labeled World War II the "greater war." At the beginning of the 1950s, we peace-loving Americans learned that a "police action" in Korea looked remarkably like a war and that peace was a "cold war."

A decade later, we were in an "undeclared war" known as the "Vietnam Conflict" where "military advisors" helped direct "preventive air strikes." The use of Agent Orange to defoliate the countryside was merely employing a "resources control program," and we learned that to "exterminate with extreme prejudice" meant that someone was going to be killed. About this time, the Pentagon, feeling its linguistic superiority, tried to slip a "radiation enhancement device," a neutron bomb, past Congress.

During the Vietnam War, Gen. William Westmoreland, commanding about a half-million troops, declared that the reason the military wasn't giving the American people the truth was because "without censorship, things could get terribly confused in the public mind." From linguistic manipulation in the Persian Gulf War, we learned that "foul ups" that caused injuries and death to our own troops were "accidents as the result of friendly fire." Our soldiers learned that exposure to nerve gas could result not in death but in "immediate permanent incapacitation." Warplanes were really "weapons systems" which were merely "visiting a site." If the pilots succeeded in "cleansing," "neutralizing," or "sanitizing" that site, they could report they "were successful in servicing their intended targets." If they over bombed or missed entirely, wiping out civilians and their houses, the pilots merely reported a lot of "collateral damage." A missile that went astray would be an "anomaly."

Of course, we are well aware that many of the Arab Coalition allies believe that sand fleas are more important than women. But, did we really have to accept the Saudi Arabian demands not to include women in combat units then agree that among the half million coalition troops in Operation Desert Storm about 40,000 were "males with female features?"

"Post Traumatic Stress Syndrome"—known as "shell shock" in World War I, and "battle fatigue" in World War II—has become the universal way to explain actions not only of persons traumatized by war but also the actions of spouse abusers and mass murderers as well, even if their only combat was changing typewriter ribbons in an air-conditioned HQ. In Bosnia–Herzegovena, the Serbs didn't murder, rape, or pillage, they merely went on a campaign of "ethnic cleansing." It's only time until the Serbs will probably declare themselves "victims of society," and will experience a massive attack of "post–traumatic stress syndrome" if there ever is another Nuremburg trial for war crimes.

In Somalia, the Sudan, and Mozambique, the starving masses are "nutritionally deprived." In the United States, we are loathe to admit that we also have starving masses or homeless people living on our streets, so we reclassify them as "individuals without permanent structural domiciles." During the Reagan–Bush era, "the Great Communicator" told us about a "revenue enhancement" program that looked suspiciously like we were going to have to dip into an "equity recovery program," or a second mortgage, to be able to afford the new taxes. And for reasons probably best left forgotten, when it came to nutritionally-balanced meals, the administration declared that ketchup is a vegetable.

Although some students spend their academic years vegetating, even they have a coverup. Students who don't get good grades are "socially or culturally disadvantaged," but there are fewer bad grades now than ever. Grade inflation lets students believe they actually learned something when they have a 3.0 average, and that no one will be the wiser when half the class graduates in the top 10 percent. Naturally, if they can find a job, they'll soon learn that an evaluation of "competent" roughly translates as "does the job, but with no great ability."

The 1966 plans for Hampshire College in Amherst, Massachusetts, probably written by a PR person who may have been a journalist but was edited by a committee of pseudo-intellectual cretins, called for the new college's mission to center around "a social structure [that] should be optimally the consonant patterned expression of culture . . . that higher education is enmeshed in a congeries of social and political change . . . that the humanities offers a surfeit of leeching [and] the exquisite preciosities and pretentiousness of contemporary literary criticism. [Further,] a formal curriculum of academic substance and sequence should not be expected to contain mirabilia which will bring all the educative ends of the college to pass."

From a plethora of psychobabble, often originating within the colleges, have come phrases meant to let us believe all of us aren't "at the margin of mental health." So, we merely need "our space" to avoid "feeling so vulnerable," the result of having had an "emotional disturbance" with our "significant other," and forcing us even more into a state of either being "hyperacidic" or "inner directed" when we should all just "mellow out." To keep our "warm fuzzy" instincts alive, a pharmaceutical chain recently mailed its advertising flyers not to "occupant" or "resident," but to "valued friend." (By the way, you can thank me now for "knowing where you're coming from," "feeling your pain," and for "sharing" that information with you.)

To make sure we all have a "feeling of self-worth," we have changed job titles, but not responsibilities. Mechanics are "service technicians" or "performance maintenance specialists" who often work on "preowned vehicles." Trash collectors are "waste management specialists"; movers are "relocation service representatives"; gardeners are "horticultural technicians"; cabbies in the big city are "urban short-run transportation specialists"; and waiters and waitresses are "beverage delivery consultants" or, in the era of being politically-ambiguous, "waitrons." Sort of like what Buck Rogers might have for a pet.

In business, we look to the "bottom line" to "maximize profit" so we have a better "cash flow" and achieve a "high degree of liquidity." Helping business avoid clear language are the legions of PR people, some of them former journalists, who have invented their own secret language to justify their existence. PR textbooks often inform future "strategic planning analysts" or "consulting image enhancement specialists" how to determine behavioral and attitudinal objectives to better "target" the "multitudinous publics," while taking "proactive" stands. To accomplish their mission, the "practitioner" must be able to anticipate, analyze, and interpret; counsel, research, and evaluate; plan, implement, and organize their multifaceted campaigns in order to provide an "intensification of existing positive behaviors" and a corresponding "reversal of negative behaviors."

If for some reason, business must "reorganize," "shift responsibilities," or even "go back to square 1," we should realize that they are only in "a state of temporary incapacitation," possibly caused by a "negative economic growth." But, if it continues, then business cites the "bottom line" and the need for "maximizing profits" as justifications for "downsizing" and "restructuring" which, naturally, has caused "a realignment of the work force" and subsequent "involuntary severance." Since 1992, Sears "involuntarily severed" 48,000; General Motors "involuntarily severed" 85,000 to 100,000; and IBM "involuntarily severed" 125,000. (Somewhere in Bangladesh, thousands of 12-year-olds earning $5 to 12 a month are making clothes for distribution to Americans who have been involuntarily severed when their companies "restructured" to "maximize profits," and went overseas.) Of course, the only ones who aren't being involuntarily severed by American business are the bosses (pretentiously known as chief executive officers) who caused all the problems to begin with.

'Local Reporter Cops Lexicon Story'

About 24 centuries ago, Hippocrates said, "The chief virtue that language can have is clearness." It's too bad the great physician's words haven't yet made it into American media.

Almost every day, we read or hear about a "spectacular fire" or "spectacular accident" where (pick one) (a) a car, (b) a truck, or (c) a fleet of skateboards "careened out of control." Nonsense! Fireworks on the Fourth of July are spectacular. A "fatal fire" (reporters love alliteration) or a traffic accident in which three people are killed are *not* spectacular.

And, where else but in the media can we hear about some psycho with a high-powered assault weapon holding "police at bay"? Sometimes, "shots rang out" to let us know that police were "forced to hit their mark" after being attacked. When the battle is over, we are likely to learn that "the community is buzzing" about the attack by the "perp"—who used to be a criminal before the debut of TV's "Hill Street Blues"—was "racked by guilt." And, since racked is such a popular piece of "journalese," we also learn there are people in our society, maybe even criminals just before their sentencing, who are also "racked by pain" and "racked by anguish." All this, of course, leaves most readers being "mental racks."

Has anyone else noticed that if a young lady is "brutally murdered" (as if some murders aren't brutal?) the lead often reads, "A pretty 27-year-old woman was killed late last night." Does anyone recall reading, "An ugly 27-year-old was poisoned early this morning?" How about men who are killed? Do we identify them as "A 27-year-old Greek god hunk with rippling muscles was stabbed yesterday afternoon while pumping iron in his West Catcall basement?" So far, reporters haven't identified any murder victim as having been "drop dead gorgeous," a term used by the media to apply to numerous living actresses and models.

Should there be an "eyewitness," apparently someone more alert than just a plain ordinary witness, we might learn that the criminal or victim was last seen "exiting the building at approximately 11 p.m." Apparently, "leaving the building about 11 p.m." doesn't sound as menacing.

To pretend we are covering all possible law suits, we drop in "alleged" now and then. Thus, if one "alleged" is good, then several of them apparently protect journalists from suits even more, as in "the alleged burglar was arrested by police who charged him with allegedly committing the alleged crime." One Denver TV reporter claimed "several alleged shots were fired," and a Bloomsburg, Pennsylvania, newspaper, apparently believing that everything must be attributed to someone, splashed a headline: "Stabbing victim dies, police say."

On coverage of labor issues, the media often report that both sides are "eyeball-to-eyeball," a condition that leads either to a "strike-bound condition" or a visit to an optometrist. Often, the negotiations "hit a snag," which should leave someone terribly upset by that injury. Nevertheless, following these "tense moments," both sides "come to terms" and are now in the "process of hammering out a contract"—just as soon as they "nail down the clauses."

<u>Sportswriters</u> seem to believe language was invented so they could butcher it. Athletes no longer exist; they're booters and gridders, tankmen, grapplers, and hoopsters. As for the teams themselves, they don't defeat an opponent, they maul, extermi-

nate, pulverize, crush, annihilate, and devastate them. Check out the headlines and see "cop" become a verb, as the "locals cop a victory." In baseball, pitchers no longer throw fast balls; they're flame throwers who "toss the pill" or, even worse, "throw with velocity." A sports editor I once worked with wrote about a high school player who, with a few seconds left in the game, brought victory to his team when he "hooped the brown spheroid through the draped iron doughnut." Naturally, in every contest, some sportscaster has to tell us that some team "came to play," as if it were an option.

Of course, the language of the sports reporter is no match for the language of government which has 15-page recipes for a simple fruitcake, labels a parachute an "aerodynamic personnel decelerator," and tells us a toothpick is a "wooden interdental stimulator."

From the nation's 700,000 professors have come so much incoherent babbling disguised as professional papers, journal articles, and books that banning what poses as academic scholarship would help save the rain forests. Unfortunately, much of the bad writing comes from professors of mass communication, few of whom ever worked more than a few months in a newsroom, and who believe that conducting pseudoscientific research will give them respectability, or at least tenure. The following are just parts of titles of what passed as scholarship in one recent convention of an association of journalism professors: "symbolic modeling and persuasive efficacy information on self efficacy beliefs," "heuristic perspectives," "contextualist cultural functionalism," "concept mapping," "conceptions of salience," "systemic methods of measuring free recall," "synchronous and asynchronous forums," "dyadic interaction," "news framing and audience framing," "structural pluralism," "discourse analysis," and "observations on a conundrum."

Indeed, most "mass communicologists" are more comfortable with running statistical analyses with two degrees of freedom, and in jabbering about channeling, cognitive dissonance, and content analysis than they are with leads, transitions, and conclusions.

Perhaps, that's why we're still wondering why many recent journalism graduates can't write.

'Personages' of the Mind

The *Riverside* (Calif.) *Press-Enterprise*, a 175,000 circulation daily newspaper, is looking for a "hip, groovy, experienced personage . . . to oversee weekly see and do tab."

The announcement in the weekly Job Bank of the 14,000-member Society of Professional Journalists (SPJ) also asks that the "personage should be creative, well-versed in music, movies, TV and have solid assignment desk and copy editing skills."

Not knowing what a "personage" is—I had been a newspaper reporter and editor, but never a personage—I called SPJ headquarters, thinking it might have been a "typo" in the ad. Heather Gilbert, who runs the Job Bank, checked the ad copy and reported that the *Press-Enterprise* was, in fact, looking for a personage. Next stop, Riverside.

"What does this 'personage' do?" I asked.

"Oversee a weekend tab," said Sally Ann Maas, assistant managing editor for features and the personage's boss.

"Did you write the ad?" I asked.

"Several of us worked on it," she replied.

"Including the managing editor?" I asked.

"He wrote the final copy," she said.

Obviously, the *Press-Enterprise* cares about accuracy, especially when several senior personages take time from reporting and editing duties to group-hug each other, feel their pain and suffering, know where each one is coming from, then share a 58-word ad with the rest of us.

"And this 'personage' has to be hip and groovy?" I asked.

"It was supposed to attract attention," Maas said.

"Could you have used another word than 'personage'?" I asked.

"The ad was meant to be unisex," she said.

"Wouldn't 'editor' have been appropriate?" I asked.

"Maybe it wasn't such a good idea," she reluctantly admitted after a couple of minutes of polite inquisition.

A lot of what passes as "linguistically politically correct" these days isn't a good idea. A kinder, gentler language often reveals little more than a life based in ambiguity.

In Massachusetts during the mid-1980s, I first saw job ads for "waitrons" which I assumed were emotionless space-age robots designed to take, deliver, and remove food orders from restaurant customers. I now see "waitrons" in many restaurants, all of them emotionless robots.

"Manholes" are now called "sewer hole entrances" or in a few places "personholes." I suppose the artist Edourd Manet, to really be nonsexist, should have changed his name to "Personet," and Thomas Mann might have become Thomas Person.

For many, "herstory" is supposed to be less sexist than "history," and "womyn" is seen as acceptable for "women." Had these "herstorians" done a little linguistic research, they might have learned that the root of "history" is the French "histoire," meaning "story." And, "women" is not "womb from men" as many believe, but actually from the Old English "wiffmon," meaning "wife of man." True, there was no equal "monnwif," but "womyn" is not unique. Since 1200, it has undergone changes, being spelled "wifman," "winman," "wooman," "wymman," "wymmon," and "whoman," as well as "wyman." If the "womyn" truly wanted to have a nonsexist name, they might invent a word that has absolutely no basis in "woman."

Certainly, "poetess" and "authoress," once common appellations, are sexist and unnecessary. And it's good we now have firefighters instead of firemen, and police officers instead of policemen. In many cases, creating a nonsexist lexicon isn't so difficult. But, many have tried to reduce or eliminate sexism by creating lunacy instead of reason.

The reality is that language is fluid. But, in the interest of clearness, let's not have any more personages, waitrons, herstories, and womyn.

Driven by Ignorance

Nonsense

It's now called ebonics (ebony + phonetics), after having been called colored speech, negro English, Black English, Black English Vernacular, and some abomination called Pan–African Communication Behaviors. It's identified as a slang, dialect, or language. But, whatever it is, ebonics is as controversial today as it was in 1855 when the first major linguistic study was done. At the center of the current controversy is a decision by the Oakland, California, school board to use ebonics in teaching.

Misinterpretation by reporters has led the masses to believe

Black English is "sloppy," "inferior," or "broken English," that Oakland's administrators want to replace Standard English with Black English, and that the 300 California schools and several hundred more in the nation's urban areas are condoning the students' use of slang.

The truth is that these educators, following long-established models for second language teaching, want to understand their students' own language in order to help them learn a different language—in this case, Standard English. A federal court in July 1979, after hearing several days of expert opinion on a civil rights case, had ruled that the Ann Arbor, Michigan, school district violated federal civil rights laws by not providing "equal educational opportunity" when it refused to accept Black English as a legitimate language of many of its students. The court ruled "no matter how well-intentioned the teachers are, they are not likely to succeed in overcoming the language barrier caused by their failure to take into account the home language system unless [they] recognize the language system used by the children . . . and to use that knowledge as a way of helping the children to learn to read standard English." In December 1996, the 6,000-member Linguistics Society of America declared that instruction in Black English is an effective way to get many Blacks to learn Standard English.

Nevertheless, innumerable columnists and cartoonists, almost none of whom studied linguistics, have had fun portraying "jive-talking" teachers and their Black students. However, most Blacks don't speak any of the varieties of Black English, nor is Black English restricted to the lower classes. Driven by ignorance and fueled by the media, the public argues that the nation's teachers are "dumbing down" their students by even allowing such "substandard" speech in the classroom. Richard Riley, the U.S. secretary of education, incorrectly stated that "elevating black English to the status of a language" wasn't acceptable, apparently believing that a dialect can be "elevated" to a language. *Washington Post* columnist William Raspberry, who for almost two decades has vigorously opposed Black English instruction, incorrectly claimed in 1996 that "virtually all" adult Blacks know ebonics and there are no texts for ebonics instruction. The National Association for the Advancement of Colored People (NAACP) called ebonics "a cruel joke," 25 years after declaring it was "a cruel hoax."

These well-meaning but largely ignorant critics claim that

because of cultural deprivation, Black English speakers have linguistic deficiencies, and that thought is restricted because Black English is a deficient, substandard language. Like all languages, Black English is composed of the lexicon (words), phonology (pronunciation), and syntax (grammar). The public and the media have focused upon the lexicon ("Hey, bro', slap me five!"), and only a couple of syntactic constructions, mocking such phrasing as "he be sick." They do not understand that Black English is based upon African language, most probably of the Hamitic and Bantu language families. Ship captains and plantation owners separated slaves from the same cultures to prevent them from talking to each other, and possibly planning escapes or overthrows. What the owners never realized was that many of the slaves spoke not only their primary language, but also Wes-Kos, a common trade language, composed of several African languages as well as British English.

Just as there are many varieties and dialects of Standard English, there are many variations of Black English, including the Gullah spoken off the Sea Islands of Georgia and South Carolina, which few Standard English speakers can even understand, and the mixture of several dialects of Southern Standard English and Urban American English spoken in Detroit.

During the past three decades, young Blacks searching for their own identities and cultural heritage, began using varieties of urban Black English as their own secret "codes," much like their slave ancestors used language and music as a way of secret communication.

In Black English rules, the Zero Copula—"He sick"—indicates that the person is sick at this very time. The "Invariant be"—"He be sick"—indicates that the person is sickly or has a long-term illness. Critics point out that some Black English phonology—for example, pronouncing "desk" as "des"—is sloppy speech, unaware that almost no African languages have consonant clusters in the final position, and that it is Standard English which has *added* such clusters, rather than the African languages *reducing* them. Black English phonology markers (including stress, pitch, timbre, and intonation) are closer to West African languages than to Standard English.

Even if all of this is true, argue the critics, Black English speakers must learn Standard English to survive in America. We arrogantly claim that Standard English is the "right" language for America, naively believing there is one correct language.

But, Standard English itself is constantly evolving as millions of immigrants brought their languages to America. The Standard English we use today, with its several hundred dialects, has little resemblance to that spoken by the Puritans.

During the Civil Rights era of the 1960s and 1970s, newspaper editors, most of whom faced all-White newsrooms, hired Blacks. But, Black reporters soon found that being the same color as their news sources wasn't the panacea their editors had hoped to achieve. Those Black reporters who, for the most part acted White and spoke Standard English, found that Black English speakers were just as closed to them as to the White reporters. But, those reporters who were able to code-switch—disguising their knowledge of Black English to their editors while using it within Black communities—found they could get stories others could not.

No one is suggesting that Black English should be the dominant language in education, commerce, or government. Nor is anyone suggesting that Blacks who don't communicate in Standard English can succeed in assimilated American society. Since children usually have an ability to learn new languages, perhaps the school districts could work with 5- and 6-year-old students in kindergarten and the first grade so they develop knowledge of the basics of Standard English, while retaining the rich cultural and linguistic heritage of their own home language.

American White society tried to destroy the slaves' religions, then forbidding them from entering White Christian churches; it denied them the vote or the right to own property; it kept them out of jobs and neighborhoods; it refused to air on radio stations Black music, then reluctantly embraced White rockers Anglicizing Black music in the early 1950s. Now it wants to destroy the vestiges of Black language, one of the most important indicators of cultural heritage. The failure of teachers and the public to understand the nature of a student's home language—whether Black English, Yiddish, or Pennsylvania Dutch, then to hold it up to ridicule—guarantees not only an inferior education, but also the trivialization of a culture.

Editing the 12 Commandments

Every writer needs an editor, although most writers sometimes wonder why. God and Moses faced the same problem 3,000 years ago. Fortunately, a reporter was present at that meeting on Mt. Sinai. Unfortunately, he could hear only Moses' side of the conversation . . .

Now, Yahweh, I really have to talk to you about those commandments. We have an economic crisis at the moment. You see, the price of stone tablets has gone sky high. That means we have to cut back on some of the commandments in order to save money. . . . Yes, I know you think 12 commandments are necessary, but it'll cost us more to use three tablets. . . . Yes, I guess you can just make more rocks.

But, Yahweh, there's this other matter. You see, your people have too many things to do to read all those commandments. Right now, they're down in the desert partying and watching a real cool comedy routine from Maimonides Seinfeld. . . . No, I don't think there's going to be a problem with the Jews acting like they were life members of a college fraternity since my brother Aaron is taking care of the people while I'm gone. But, Yahweh, your people don't have much of an attention span, so to hold their interest, we add a couple of charts and pictures, and float them into one killer page design. Of course, it means we'll have to cut some of the text. A few words here. A couple of paragraphs there. . . . I realize that the words are the most important thing, but work with me on this.

For starters, you gave me seven paragraphs just about you. Don't you think that's a bit egotistical?. . . . WO! Hey, Yahweh, could you lighten up with those lightning bolts? I'm just looking out for your own interest. I mean, Yahweh, you say you're the boss—The Big Kahuna. We all know that. But then you go ahead and say all that stuff about graven images and jealousy and vengeance and swearing. How about we just tighten it up a little? How's this sound?—"I'm in charge and don't you forget it." . . . Well, we can work on it.

Now, the next three paragraphs deal with taking a day off. That's good. Shows the people that you believe in the labor movement. But, three paragraphs? Why not just, "Don't overwork yourselves and others so you have time for reflection?"

Now, of the next six, isn't there any you could do without? . . . Oh, I see, it's commandments that the Jews can't do without. What about dumping the "don't kill" commandment? I mean, there's going to be a lot of killing in this world. What about a few exceptions? . . . I see. It's your world and you don't want people killing anything. No exceptions. Well, then, *you* deal with the National Rifle Association. Now, the commandment against that adultery thing could get a bit tricky. After all, a lot of your chosen people chose to go into the entertainment industry. . . . OK, so the commandment stands as you wrote it.

Maybe we could combine the commandments about not stealing and coveting? Seems a bit redundant. . . . Well, that's true. I guess some Philadelphia lawyer could claim that lusting for things isn't the same as stealing them, and some D.A. in the name of justice could tack two charges upon some thief so there's something to work with in a plea bargain.

Maybe we dump the false witness thing. . . . I see, you're saying that it's needed because of something known as an O.J., which won't occur for three millennia? Well, if you say so.

I suppose the clause about honoring mothers and fathers stays?. . . . Well, sure, if you have this covenant with Hallmark Cards, I'm not going to tell you to renege.

But, Yahweh, we still need to cut you back by half. . . . *Six Snappy Secrets to Success* is a better book title than your *The Daily Dozen.* . . . Yes, I know you have final right of edit. OK, here's the deal. Dump just two of the commandments, let me tighten up the writing on the rest, and I may even be able to get you a film deal; maybe even a big-name star. Add in some special effects, and we'll call it "Firestorms of Desire." . . . O.K., have it your way, but I'm telling you, "The Ten Commandments" just isn't sexy enough.

Fewer Words, Less Filling

It was a delightful show. All 37 Shakespearean plays, cleverly and humorously abridged to just two hours by the Reduced Shakespeare Co. Short of having a set of *Cliff's Notes*, source of innumerable student essays for more than a half-century, or a collection of Classics Illustrated comics, it was the least painful way to "learn" Shakespeare.

The condensation of the media probably began in 1922 with the founding of *Reader's Digest,* the pocket-sized magazine that keeps its 27 million subscribers happy by mulching articles from hundreds of other magazines. Books also aren't safe, as the *Digest* editors grind four books into the space of one, and call it a "condensed book." In 1996, the company entered the world wide web, doing what it does best. *Reader's Digest* World, a navigation system to search millions of home pages and documents, seizes relevant materials so anyone with a computer can download slices of knowledge.

Reader's Digest edits literature to allow readers more time to participate in society's more meaningful activities, such as doing sit-ups with Richard Simmons, watching the adventures of Luke and Laura on "General Hospital," or swapping useless lies with the folks at the country club. However, most media condense life solely to save money and improve corporate profits.

Once, for a buck, you could spend the entire afternoon at the movies, watching an "A" film, a "B"-quality second film, two or three six-minute cartoons, and a couple of "trailers" promoting upcoming films. Inflation now dictates a $6 to $8 admission, for which you get three or four trailers and only one film. Even the films themselves have been downsized. Once, "A" films ran at least two hours. Now, with few exceptions they tend to be about 100 to 110 minutes, long enough to fit into comfortable two-hour cycles that allow theater owners 10 or 20 minutes to rewind the film and clear a theater before showing the same film again.

At one time, television was divided into four 13-week blocks a year. Three of the blocks were for original programming; the fourth block was for summer reruns. However, network executives figured that even with reduced advertising rates and union-mandated requirements to pay residual fees to numerous creative personnel each time the same episode is aired, it would be less expensive to schedule reruns than to order new programs. The result is that the networks have reduced original programming to 22 shows a year, plus occasional "specials."

In radio and TV news, the seven-second sound bite is now standard, forcing news sources to become terse and witty, though superficial. News stories themselves average about 30 seconds, topping out at 90 seconds, down considerably from the era when journalists, not talking heads and image consultants, were responsible for what appeared on air.

During the past 30 years, the print media have downsized

not only the quality of paper, but the size as well. Page sizes of 8½ by 11 inches are still the most common magazine size, but several hundred major national magazines are now 8 by 10½ inches, a 10 percent reduction. Newspaper page width has dropped to 13½ inches, from almost 15½ inches during the 1950s; many Sunday color comic sections are now being printed in 12½ inch widths.

To fit onto abbreviated pages, publishers demand shorter manuscripts, then to save even more costs squeeze more type onto a page than ever before, sometimes photographically compressing type to save a few bucks. Book publishers, which have been swallowing up each other for the past decade, have even figured out how to do a *Reader's Digest* number for people who don't like to read or think they don't have time. During the past two decades, publishers have condensed more than 25,000 books onto two-hour cassettes, suitable for shoving into a car's tape system, allowing the driver to digest words while weaving among traffic jams.

USA Today, the *Reader's Digest* of newspapers, condenses the world into four sections. Publishers of community newspapers, citing both *USA Today*'s format and nebulous research about reader attention span, impose artificial limits on stories—15 inches is a common measure for most stories—while throwing color and graphs at the readers.

Of course, newspapers have been in a free-fall for most of the past three decades. There were 1,763 separate daily newspapers in 1946; by 1980, there was a net loss of only 18 newspapers. However, by the end of 1996, there were only 1,520 dailies. Weekly newspapers dropped about 13 percent, from 8,174 in 1960 to only 7,176 in 1994.

Although the population increased 10.3 percent from 1985 to 1995, newspaper circulation, which peaked at 62.8 million subscribers in 1985, dropped 7.3 percent to 57 million in 1996, according to the Newspaper Association of America. More alarming, readership dropped from 77.6 percent of all adults who had read newspapers daily in 1970 to 64.2 percent in 1995, according to Simmons Marketing.

Also dropping is the media's work force. During the early 1990s, television networks cut their news operations and dumped thousands of news staff. Although local radio has increased news staff, about 70 percent of all stations have only one reporter, with 97 percent having five or fewer full-time staff, according to the Radio and Television News Directors Association. Magazine and book publishing companies now assign much of their work to independent contractors. Newspapers, TV, and radio stations have increased the use of "stringers," part-time reporters who often work almost a full-time load, but are paid significantly less than full-time staff and have no benefits.

Layoffs and job eliminations of full-time staff by newspaper publishers dropped total newspaper employment from 542,000 in 1989 to 468,000 in 1996, while employment throughout the United States was increasing about 25 percent. As news quality diminishes, about the only things that seem to be increasing are advertising revenue (from $2.1 billion in 1950 to $38.2 billion in 1996 for newspapers) and publisher profits, which are among the highest in all types of businesses.

Promises, Promises

With less than a month before the election, Marshbaum was campaigning furiously.

"A chicken in every pot! Free health care for everyone! There's light at the end of the tunnel!"

"Marshbaum!" I commanded, "you can't make those kinds of promises."

"You're right. I don't want to offend the health care industry. There's a lot of campaign money there. I'll just make up something else."

"You just can't make up campaign promises."

"Sure I can. It's easy. How about vote for Marshbaum and win a date with Bette Midler?"

"You don't even *know* Bette Midler."

"I like her movies," he said casually."

"It has nothing to do with her movies," I said.

"Think someone doesn't like her singing? I sure don't want to offend anyone. I could make it a date with Natalie Cole. How about Pat Boone for the women? The media will report anything I say."

"Marshbaum!" I screamed. "Get reasonable!"

He thought a moment. "You're right. Nat and Pat are probably supporting someone else. How about 'Elect Marshbaum and you'll never pay taxes again!' "

"That's ridiculous," I said. "No one will believe you."

"They will if the media say it's so."

"But the media may not believe you."

"Doesn't matter if they do or don't; they'll be so afraid of being scooped they'll report anything I say."

"But you'd be lying to the people," I said.

"It worked for Sen. Packwood," said Marshbaum smugly. Not long after Bob Packwood of Oregon was elected to his fifth six-year term in 1992, he admitted he had lied during the campaign when he denied he had made numerous improper sexual advances to members of his staff during the previous 20 years. A group of voters had petitioned the Senate to overturn the election on the basis that Packwood had lied. The Rules Committee thought about issues of the greater public good, then they remembered their own campaigns, and unanimously declared that lying to the people during a campaign wasn't strong enough grounds to overturn an election. "There's got to be some law that prevents politicians from lying," I said.

"Even for being a journalist you're rather dense," said Marshbaum. "Not only is history written by the victors, but Hitler himself said that the victor will never be asked if he told the truth."

"I doubt that quoting Hitler is going to get you very far," I said.

"It's not *who* said it," said Marshbaum smugly, "but the truth of *what* he said. Besides, the FCC says it's OK to lie."

"The Federal Communications Commission gave its approval?" I asked skeptically.

"Section 315. The FCC says that radio and TV stations can't refuse to run political ads even if the station management knows the ads are outright lies."

"Most people don't believe most of what they see on TV anyhow," I sniffed.

"Try the Supreme Court," said Marshbaum.

"The Supremes said lying to the people is acceptable behavior?" I scoffed.

"OK, not the U.S. Supreme Court, but *A* Supreme Court."

"Which one? In Baghdad?"

"Albany. The New York Supreme Court."

"Not even New York's court could be that incompetent."

"Got it right here," he said, taking a wadded paper from his pocket. "You know, if it's in print, it's gotta be right. Case of *O'Reilly* v. *Mitchell*. Guy named O'Reilly sued a politician named Mitchell in 1912 and charged him with making promises that weren't kept."

"A promise is a verbal contract," I said. "I'm sure you read it wrong. The court undoubtedly *upheld* O'Reilly's claims."

"Wrong, Newsprint Breath," said Marshbaum smugly. "The court said that politicians lie all the time, that promises in a campaign are just that. Promises. No one believes them anyhow. Verdict for the politician. Case closed."

"But that occurred before World War I," I said.

"It's precedent," Marshbaum said. How about 'Vote for Marshbaum and he'll wash all your dirty laundry?'"

"Marshbaum," I said disgustedly, "you can do whatever you want, but just remember that some politicians actually tell the truth."

"Name one who did and got elected!" he demanded.

"Honest Abe," I replied.

[For the legal scholars, the case of *O'Reilly* v. *Mitchell* is cited as 85MISC176, 148NYS, 88 SUP, 1914.]

Electing the News

Days before the election, Picapole was fighting hard to retain his seat as editor of the *Daily Noise*. Challenging him was Leadshot, a law school graduate who had worked his way up from janitor to president of his father's gun manufacturing company.

The latest polls showed that in the two-county area the *Noise* served, Picapole and Leadshot were in a virtual dead heat, an additional 10 percent of the vote, mostly reporters, aligned against having any editor.

First elected in 1984 as a fresh candidate against trickle-down journalism, Picapole had been comfortably re-elected every two years since. But now, with the readers demanding change, Leadshot had charged from 15 points behind, and was on the verge of winning his first election since the sixth grade when he became assistant hall monitor.

"I'll vote for anyone running against Picapole," said a determined Marvin Blunderbuss of Porkbelly, Pennsylvania, who admitted he never read the newspaper, but defiantly insisted that anyone who spends more than four years as editor is part of the establishment and must be replaced.

In a slick TV ad campaign, financed primarily by the American Medical Gun Association, Leadshot charged Picapole with being soft on reporters, and blasted him for allowing two reporters to leave the *Noise* before their contracts expired. "These scumbags," said Leadshot, "are now writing award-winning stories for the *Morning Blab,* and are killing us with their constant scoops."

Picapole acknowledged it may have been a mistake to allow the reporters to break their contracts, but claimed that in the 10 years he was in office, the *Noise* efficiently picked up its reporters on the streets right after committing a journalism degree, and sentenced them to work slave-like conditions until the end of their terms.

Taking the offensive, Picapole charged that Leadshot himself was soft on reporters. Waving a sheaf of statistics, Picapole pointed out that for all his histrionic blustering, Leadshot allowed his own staff to be pummeled by reporters 88 percent of the time, and that if he were to be elected there would be "every evidence that he will continue to preach toughness yet be soft on news."

Leadshot countered that at least if he were elected editor the newspaper would run more good news stories. Picapole retorted that the media can't make up hard news when there isn't any.

Picapole then charged that Leadshot not only was a poor businessman, but that the readers shouldn't be swayed by anyone who never worked on a newspaper, never even took a journalism course, and wouldn't know the difference between a hole in news copy and a hole in his assets. In response, Leadshot scored points when he retorted that the biggest problem with journalism today is that it's being run by journalists.

Not letting up on his attack, Leadshot produced 8 by 10 glossies of a press party in which Picapole was seen standing near the editor of *The New York Times*. Picapole responded that although both he and the *Times* editor were members of the same party, they barely knew each other, and that he would never lower himself to ask for an endorsement.

"The economy is in a dumpster," Leadshot charged in a major speech in Hogswallow, Iowa, "and Picapole is responsible for it with all his spending on reporter salaries and expenses."

Picapole acknowledged that in the past 10 years he was responsible for increasing reporter salaries by 3 percent, bringing them just past the poverty line, but said he had no choice in the matter of buying wrist rests and nonglare computer screens since the newspaper lost a suit when 11 of its nearly-blind reporters with carpal tunnel syndrome won a class action suit in federal court.

In one of his more popular yet controversial planks, Leadshot also proposed that every reporter be required to carry a gun, a proposal that split the newsroom's loyalty. "You never know when your life will be threatened at a school board meeting," said a long-time reporter who asked that for matters of security he not be identified.

However, another reporter who also asked for anonymity since she feared retribution from the Leadshot faction, said she would oppose any reporter being required to carry a gun. "It'll just escalate problems," she said, then summarized a report that revealed that reporters who carry guns are five times as likely to be shot by their editors as are unarmed reporters.

Nevertheless, throughout the election the readers have been puzzled by the lack of substantive debate about issues of news design over substance, artificial limits on story length, the candidate's response to the lack of resources and personnel to cover the news, as well as a general lack of health, labor, and environmental reporting. A recent poll shows that 94 percent of voters are making plans in two years to repaginate whoever wins.

Dead Air at the Convention.

At the San Diego Convention Center, the Republican National Committee was finishing preparations for a four-day convention that would unanimously nominate Bob Dole for the presidency.

Nearby, Pat Buchanan, Dole's leading challenger in the primaries and whom the Republicans denied the right to speak to the convention in anything more than a 15-second videotape sound bite, was giving a major speech to a large herd of dissident Republicans and a few equally dissident Democrats.

Two hours north by freeway, at the Long Beach Convention Center, Ross Perot and former Colorado governor Dick Lamm, who, like millions of their followers, don't believe in the policies of either the Democrats or the Republicans, were giving major campaign speeches in the first of a two-part Reform Party convention.

Unless you were watching CNN, you probably missed hearing what they had to say. ABC chose to run the first of a two-part docudrama about the singing dysfunctional Jackson family. CBS ran a five-year-old two-star film. NBC ran a nine-year-old two-star film. FOX ran "Baywatch Nights." It wasn't much different two weeks later in Chicago at the Democrats' convention. Each of the networks scheduled only five to six hours of prime-time TV coverage for each of the two major conventions, a few minutes more each day on morning wake-up programs and the evening news. Even when the networks broadcast the convention, it was often anchors and correspondents talking to each other.

To get some of their message to the people, the Republicans created and staffed GOP-TV, and bought ten hours of prime time nightly from the Family Channel. USA cable ran highlights the following morning.

The Democrats put Bill Clinton on a 21st Century whistle-stop train tour from West Virginia to Chicago to guarantee headlines every night, while the media ran endless stories about the differences between the violent 1968 convention, hosted by Mayor Richard Dailey, and the 1996 packaged convention, hosted by Dailey's son who was now mayor. Even then, viewership dropped more than 12 percent over the 1992 convention.

"People know there's nothing really happening here," ABC News vice president Jeff Grainick told the *Chicago Tribune* about the Republican convention, then stated that the "meaningfulness of these conventions has declined." NBC-TV executive producer Jeff Zucker said he doubted any network would give much coverage to future conventions. Ted Koppel, calling the convention "more of an infomercial than a news event," pulled his 31-person staff away.

The media piously cite the "infomercial packaged convention" as a reason why they don't give more air time to the conventions, unable to understand that by restricting their own coverage they force political leaders to package and control the convention to meet limited time frames. Although the media and politicians complain that the other are manipulating them, they readily accept that manipulation. Much of the air time is devoted either to pandering to the politicians, with coverage of speeches and interviews with candidates and delegates dominating the coverage, or to anchors and correspondents chatting with each other.

The networks also cite figures to prove their case of why they shouldn't waste their time on coverage. Only about four million Americans at any time watched the 1992 conventions; the network marketing analysts figured fewer than 40 percent of Americans would watch even one minute of either convention in 1996.

In contrast, the equally quadrennial Olympics attracted about 25 million Americans at any time, with more than a billion worldwide watching at least one part of the 17-day event, spread over 171 hours of air time. Driven by ratings and advertising revenue, TV assumed that electing a president must be irrelevant when compared to watching emaciated squeaky-voiced girls doing flips on a four-inch wide piece of wood.

PBS and cable networks CNN, C-SPAN, and upstart MSNBC broadcast more complete coverage of the conventions, with CNN and MSNBC using the internet to feed additional information to the public. But, fewer than one-fourth of Americans have immediate access to those cable networks, and surfing through myriad menus is confusing and time consuming for the average citizen.

The media response to full convention coverage, like the response to a lot of important social issues, is a circular argument—the people don't watch it, so we won't show it. Of course, the people watch only what they're shown and, in our electronic age, if it isn't seen on TV, it doesn't exist.

Another part of the problem is the politicians' groveling recognition of the ubiquitous nature of television, and the medium's command of American lives. During the 1950s and 1960s, the political parties held their conventions, while the media watched, reported, interviewed, and analyzed. But, the politicians soon learned that television can have a powerful effect on the masses, and began structuring their conventions and political announcements to meet television needs. As television has become a greater force, the politicians lost sight of their mission, packaging their conventions like they have packaged their campaigns, with the delegates nothing more than ribbon-bedecked props. Speeches became shorter, with lines deliberately written to appeal to mass audiences. Politicians and delegates soon tripped over each other in a furious dash to find anyone with a microphone and get a few seconds of air time.

In an interesting piece of logic, the Republicans claimed the reason they couldn't give Pat Buchanan—or any of the candidates in the primaries—any time to speak at their 1996 convention was because there was limited "prime time" available, and all the slots were filled. The Republican-selected speakers, keyed to TV's attention span, gave speeches of only three to ten minutes; Bob Dole gave a 56-minute fourth night acceptance speech, although initial plans called for a speech half that long. Bill Clinton, a master debater, delivered an unofficial "state of the union" 69-minute acceptance speech.

Another problem is that media focus upon establishment politics. At both conventions, the media had hospitality suites and cozy relationships with the major political parties and lobbyists.

Time Warner/CNN, one of the nation's largest media conglomerates, even paid the Republicans $100,000 to become a Republican convention official sponsor. The parent corporation of the *Chicago Sun-Times* donated $100,000 to the Democrats, and threw a lavish rooftop party at the newspaper for the Mississippi delegation.

About 16,000 accredited media personnel—most of them support staff, the rest reporting what local delegate Aunt Matilda ate for breakfast—attended the Democratic and Republican conventions; only about 400 attended Part 2 of the Reform Party's convention in Valley Forge, Pennsylvania. And not many gave much credibility to consumer advocate Ralph Nader or any of the other so-called minor candidates who may have even better plans for America than do Bill Clinton, Bob Dole, or Ross Perot.

The media cover the primaries as if they were athletic contests, focusing the reporting on who's ahead in the polls. Thus, when the nominee is already known by the time of the convention, the media have lost interest.

What is lacking in coverage is the media's refusal, or perhaps inability, to report numerous stories related to policies, platforms, and effects, then to analyze how the political process affects individuals.

Campaigns today are being run on, and by, television. Most campaign funds—each major party received about 62 million taxpayer dollars after their conventions—were spent on TV ads, not in establishing an effective grassroots organizing campaign, the kind with candidates going into communities and talking boldly about America and the future, and not worrying about creating a seven-second soundbite that would "play better" on TV.

And that, more than the lack of substantive television coverage of the two major conventions and the packaging of the campaign, is why the American political process and the media need to be overhauled.

A Dam(n) for the Home Folks

With the arrival of the new TV season, it's only a matter of time until one of the TV networks buys out C-SPAN for the rights to prime-time coverage of "The Congressional Follies."

"Quiet on the set! House of Representatives, Monday session. Take 1."

Speaker: I'm Troy Calhoun, Speaker of the House and your host for "Congressional Follies." But first, a message from our sponsors.

Sponsor: Are you tired of people taking advantage of you? Upset that your views aren't heard? The Ace Lobby Service has direct access to some of the people who can improve your life. Whatever your needs, contact Ace Lobby Service. As always, prices are negotiable.

Speaker: Welcome back. With us today is Rep. Howard Sludgepump of Oklahoma with a bill he'd like to tell us about.

Sludgepump: Thanks, Troy. And it's certainly good to be here with all you wonderful people. As I tell my folks back home in Hushaby Holler, Oklahoma—some of the finest people in the world— this is a real honor for me to present their wishes to the Congress of the United States. In fact, just the other day—

Speaker: Forgive me for interrupting, Sludge, but the floor manager just gave me the speed-up sign. Please don't keep us in suspense. What's in your bill?

Sludgepump: Dams. A billion-dollar dam right in the middle of Hushaby Holler, Oklahoma.

Speaker: Well, let's hear it for Rep. Sludgepump's billion-dollar dam. *(A chorus of cheers.)* Now, ladies and gentlemen of the House, are there any questions you would like to ask Rep. Sludgepump? . . . Mr. Popoff.

Popoff: Thank you, Mr. Speaker *("How's my makeup. I hope they get my left front close-up. I look better that way.")* Mr. Sludgepump, according to the records of the Weather Bureau, Hushaby Holler hasn't had rain for 20 years. There are no rivers or lakes. And your district is the wealthiest in the nation because of all the oil you have. Why is that dam necessary?

Sludgepump: That's a very good question. And the folks in your home district of Wattabago, Iowa, can be assured that they've really got a good congressman looking out for their financial interests, especially since you convinced the Congress to open a federally-funded Museum of Corn in your district. Yes, sir, it's hard to find congressmen as concerned about the taxpayers' money as you are. So, all you folks in Wattabago, Iowa, make sure you vote the Popoff ticket in November. Are there any other questions I can answer?

Rep. Hotchkiss: Congressman, isn't a billion dollars a bit much for a dam?

Sludgepump: Not really, Mr. Congressman. After all, you have been doing a fantastic job for the large corporations in your district to help them find cheaper labor in Mexico, and know the importance of full employment. You, my most esteemed colleague, should be the first to realize that the billion dollars will be used primarily to feed underprivileged construction workers, PR people, and thousands of administrators who would be out on the streets penniless and starving if we didn't pass this bill. Certainly, a man as courageous as you are in helping the people of your district who will be given preference for work on this dam can see that.

Speaker: Well put, Mr. Congressman. I'm sure Bushneck folks know that Congressman Hotchkiss really cares about them. But, right now, we must break for a public service message from the New York Stock Exchange.

Sponsor: A lot of people say that big corporations are capitalistic conglomerates, bent on making profits at the expense of the people of this country. We don't have any great conspiracies, or plans to take over the country. We want to do only what's best for the country. And we want you to know it.

Speaker: Thanks, Dad. We're ready to vote. All those in favor of the dam bill, signify by removing your sunglasses. Those opposed, hit the miniature gong on your desk. . . . It appears we'll soon have a billion-dollar dam in Hushaby Holler. This is Troy Calhoun wishing you courage for another tomorrow.

President Sneezes; Film at 11.

Whenever the president sneezes, several dozen reporters file their stories. Because it's the president, and because it's easier to file a "Presidential Sneeze Story" than to root through the causes of the health care crisis, the reporters fall all over themselves trying to beat each other out to get the comprehensive coverage TV-News fans have come to expect.

Anchor: This is Clyde Barrow at the White House. The President sneezed about 2:45 this afternoon. We understand it lasted about three seconds. We now take you to the emergency room of the Bethesda Naval Hospital. Standing by is Lance Redux.

Lance Redux: The president has just arrived, and we'll be interviewing bystanders, orderlies, and maybe even a nurse or two. Security is extraordinarily tight, and only the 237 accredited reporters have been allowed into the ER at this point. Anticipating a presidential sneeze, and to give more room to the news media, every area hospital for the past week has been sending patients without health insurance to the Fumigate Center in Arlington. Back to you, Clyde.

Clyde Barrow: With me is Gatekeeper Jones, special assistant to the president for sneezing. Gatekeeper Jones, what does this sneeze mean to the American people?

Gatekeeper Jones: First of all, let me say that the President has made great inroads into understanding and responding to the needs of the American people. This sneeze was not only the result of his tireless efforts on behalf of the people, but also a declaration that he and the First Lady are going to extraordinary lengths to deal with health care issues in this great nation of ours.

Clyde Barrow: Thank you for that great insight. Now, to Susie Sweetwater with Sen. Porkbelly Pineapple at the Capitol.

Susie Sweetwater: Sen. Pineapple, we just heard that the President's sneeze was in sympathy with the plight of Americans everywhere. Do you agree?

Sen. Pineapple: While all of us Americans are concerned about the president's health, this particular sneeze was the result of a president who has disregarded the wishes of the people and the Congress, and who has thumbed his nose at the health care industry.

Susie Sweetwater: For an opposing view, we turn to Rep. Horace Sludgepump.

Rep. Sludgepump: While I don't wish to disagree with my esteemed and most distinguished colleague from the other side of the Capitol, I should point out that if it weren't for him and the other cretins from the opposition party who filibustered the death of so many of our great and glorious programs which were designed by our party to help the working class, we'd have a chicken in every pot in this glorious country.

Clyde Barrow (interrupting): Excuse me, Susie, but the President's personal physician is about to make an announcement. We now return to Bethesda Naval Hospital.

Dr. Alfred Chiu: After running a series of tests on the President's body fluids, examining X-rays of his nasal passages and respiratory system, and checking the results of the MRI-scan, we now believe the cause of the sneeze was a pollutant in the air. We have not yet identified that particular pollutant.

Reporter 1: Harry Hotlips, ABC Action News. Doctor, can you identify that pollutant?

Dr. Chiu: As I mentioned, we haven't yet identified that pollutant.

Reporter 2: Judy Jumpstart, CBS-TV. Just how serious is this pollutant?

Dr. Chiu: We can't determine how serious the pollutant is until we can identify it.

Reporter 3: Darla Dazzling, NBC-TV. Doctor, just exactly what kind of pollutant could that have been? And does it have long-term effects?

Dr. Chiu: I don't know, but we will try to find out.

Reporter 4: Sid Serious, CNN. Doctor, could you indicate what you believe would be the world consequences of this particular sneeze.

Dr. Chiu: I can't at this time, but I will ask the secretary of state to respond as soon as he completes his phone calls to the other world leaders.

Reporter 5: Polly Prattle, *New York Post*. Was the President sleeping with anyone other than his wife when he was polluted?

Clyde Barrow (again interrupting): I regret that we must temporarily interrupt our in-depth team coverage at this point. Right after these important messages from our sponsors, we'll return you to "General Hospital," already in progress.

Blood on Their Lenses

"If it bleeds, it leads" is local TV's aphorism which dictates its belief that violent crimes and traffic accidents lead off the nightly newscast. Focusing on broken body parts is more "visual" and easier to cover than the economy, Senate hearings, and the health care crisis. And if it isn't violence that grabs the viewer, it can usually be something so soft that no self-respecting newspaper would run it any higher than the bottom of Page 17.

But, now and then, it's hard to find an assortment of accidents, fires, and murders. And so it was that KFAD-TV's panicked station manager met with his news director late one afternoon to go over the final line-up for the "6 O'Clock Aren't-We-All-Happy?" news.

The station manager wasn't happy.

"What do you mean leading off the news with a report that some jokers at the Public Health Service found the cure for AIDS!

Weren't there any accidents? Fires? Murders?"

"Sorry, Boss, there's nothing out there."

"Nothing!? Is that 'Nothing' as in 'no accidents,' or 'nothing' as in 'I'm close to finding another job in the industry'?!"

"Boss, we really tried. I've got five camera crews running around right now."

"Think you can get two of them to run into each other? We'd pay the hospital bills."

"Boss, don't you remember? The union made us agree to a six-month moratorium on stories that involve us maiming our crews just for the sake of ratings."

"Some union," the station manager huffed. "Doesn't even want its members to get more air time."

"It's only for six months," said the news director. "After that, maybe we could cut the brake linings on Unit 3 and have Unit 4 cover it. But for now, the news scanner is dead."

"What happened to that fatality on Mulberry?"

"By the time we scrambled the chopper, the drivers had exchanged insurance numbers and left."

"Left?!" thundered the station manager. "No one leaves when there's a camera crew on the way!"

"Best we could figure out, it was just a few paint scratches."

"Any of the cars red? You guys get there faster and maybe it'd look like blood. Check the cops again."

"Sorry, Boss. Even Philly's not reporting any murders in the past 24 hours."

"Then go out and shoot someone!" the station manager demanded.

"Sorry, Boss, I can't do that."

"Yeah, you're right," said the station manager. "Tell Susie Sweetwater to do it. Her ratings are down. This oughta help."

"Susie's in the middle of her reading class right now, and you know how she hates to be disturbed when she's learning new words."

"Then Heartthrob! He's got the highest TVQ of any anchor in the country. Audiences salivate whenever he's on. The public would back him even if he had assault weapons and made welsh rarebit out of the Easter Bunny."

"It's an hour until air," the news director reminded the station manager. "Heartthrob's already in Makeup. They're darkening his hair tonight."

"Roseanne!" shouted the station manager. "She's always good for something. Think we can get her to kill someone?"

"We have two crews on her," said the news director, "but all she's doing is threatening a couple of writers and a producer or two. Besides, we've done that story 23 times this month."

"Check with the crew you have permanently assigned to Madonna. She's been quiet lately."

"Out of the country."

"Get me a fire! Forest. Trailer. Stove. I don't care what kind!" the station manager demanded, smashing his coffee mug against his desk, and cutting his wrist. "Blood!" he shouted. "We have blood!"

"It's only a scratch," said the news director.

"It's blood! And it's good for a grabber. Grab a producer. Come in with an extreme close-up full-frame, then pull back to a medium shot. Dissolve to some of the footage of the O.J. crime scene. Here's your lead: "Violence in California leads to national blood-letting." He paused a moment. "Make sure you run teasers on this every five minutes."

The Only Alternative For KFAD

The news rating of television station KFAD went out to lunch and didn't return. This, of course, caused great concern for the news director who didn't like the possibility of being exiled to a small 500-watt radio station in Hogshead, Iowa.

"What about story length?" the station manager snapped. "Haven't they been getting longer?"

"No, sir! We've never run a story longer than 90 seconds, and most of the stories are 15 to 20 seconds."

"Good. We're still using the local newspapers, right?"

"Oh, yes sir! My reporters know that the only way to get good television news is to rewrite from the local papers. That way we devote our energies to stories of real importance."

"Like that beauty pageant last week," said the station manager enthusiastically. "Real hard-hitting news coverage."

"It just lent itself to news film. I sure hated to miss the Senate investigation, though. But since they don't allow cameras in the chambers, there wasn't any sense in having a reporter there."

"Well," said the station manager reflectively, "there's nothing wrong with our basic news coverage, so it has to be our on-air personalities. How long has it been since Susie Sweetwater changed her hairstyle?"

"About two months, but I think we should let it stay that way another month or so just to increase viewer identification."

"In another month or so," said the station manager tersely, "we may be fourth in a three-station market. How's Susie handling the slump?"

"Remarkably well. Just yesterday, she had her fingernails manicured, and bought a new dress. I think she looks a lot better than Laura Landfill over at that other station. The technicians certainly have noticed."

"But, hasn't she presented a few special problems to your staff?"

"It's true our news writers are cramped writing scripts with no more than two syllable words, but someone saw Susie actually trying to read a newspaper last week."

"What about Heartthrob? You know the co-anchor is just as important."

"He's been putting on a little weight, so I sent him over to the spa. It'll boost his image immeasurably."

"How's our ethnic balance? You know how the FCC is. Can we get better ratings by adding another ethnic?"

The news director shook his head. "We already have two Chicanos, three blacks, an Alaskan, an Indian, two Laplanders, and a Southern Baptist on the news team. I don't think we can add any more right now."

"Maybe we can laugh it up more on the set. Maybe expand the Happy News format?"

"We're saturated now, and I don't think the viewers are ready to tolerate Susie giggling through another air disaster."

"What about the weather?"

"As you know, McDonald gave the weather once in a raincoat, and another time in a bikini. And remember the times she brought the chickens into the studio to apologize for laying an egg with the previous forecast? You can't do much more than that to get ratings!"

"Pack your snow shovel," said the station manager. "It looks like you're heading to corn country."

"Give me time," pleaded the news director, "I'll come up with some innovative way to boost the ratings." There was a moment of silence, then the news director blurted out his idea. "A journalist!"

"A what!?"

"A journalist! That could be the radical new way to boost the ratings. We could hire a journalist to give the news!"

The station manager was furious. "Don't be ridiculous! A journalist on TV would be a disaster!"

"No, Boss, I mean it. No one else has a journalist on the air. It could be the novelty that sells the station to the advertisers. Imagine our slogan—'Watch KFAD, the station that has the only journalist on the air.' It could be *big*!"

"Well," said the station manager thoughtfully, "we did have one journalist who applied for a job a couple of months ago. Claimed to have won something called a Pulitzer. I'm afraid I was rather rude to him. It lowers our image just to have them around."

"We're desperate, Boss, let's give it a try."

The station manager leaned back in his overstuffed chair, pushed away from his eight-foot conference table, lit an oversized cigar, and thought a moment. "A journalist . . . On TV . . . It's radical enough. . . . It's even revolutionary!" . . . Then, he turned on his personal TV to watch a rerun of "LaVerne & Shirley."

A Television Snow Job

During the Blizzard of '96, with heavy winds, subfreezing temperatures, and more than two feet of snow having fallen over much of Pennsylvania, the governor ordered all roads closed for 32 hours. The only vehicles allowed were for snow removal crews, emergencies, health professionals, and those of broadcast journalists whom he called "essential." Let's see what an essential broadcast that day looked like.

"I'm Harry Hansom. Susie Sweetwater just called in. Her car had slid into a ditch about eight miles from the studio. Fortunately, she had her three-speed bike in the car, and is pedaling furiously to get in so she doesn't lose a day's pay. We begin our extended and comprehensive team coverage of the snow emergency with chief meteorologist Flake Sepulveda who's at his command post on the roof."

"From on top of the 85th floor, I can report more accurately than any other weather person that the high was 25 today, with a low of 8. That's well off from the records. The record high, set in 1945, was 68 degrees. But, in L.A., today, it was a sun-drenched 87, and those babes in the Sunshine State must be catching some real cool rays. Here's a reminder. If you do get to California this week, always wear a good sunblock. That sunshine can really do some damage. The record low in our area was a bruising minus 11, set way back in 1981. Maybe you old-timers will remember that one. The nation's low today was set in Washington when the Congress and president still couldn't come up with a budget, but that's another story. We're currently tracking a low pressure system that may meet up with a high pressure front just north of Minneapolis and begin to move southeast at 25 miles an hour. However, one of our computers has it starting in San Francisco and cruising east along I-80 at 65 miles an hour. But our third computer says the only storm front at the moment is forming 30 miles east of Death Valley, with snow expected all over the Mojave Desert before coming out here where it may or may not drop anywhere from two inches to seven feet of sleet, snow, or acid rain."

"Flake, can you see what's happening right now?"

"Not with all these rooftop barriers, Harry. Let me fight the bruising wind and go to the edge and take a closer look. From the roof of the WFAD building, it appears . . . "

"We've lost communication with the roof. Let's check traffic with Barry Blades in HeliCam 2."

"It's real white out there. I can't see the road, but it looks like I'm up to my rear rotor in snow. I'm also running out of fuel. Back to you, Harry."

"For a ground-eye view, we go live to Polly Prattle."

"I'm standing in the middle of the Interstate. Because the Governor closed the roads, we haven't seen much traffic the past hour. Just a few snowplows which we'll let through as soon as we finish this vital and essential report. As you can see, there's nothing but snow all around me. If my dumb cameraman hadn't broken his leg trying to set up his 100 pounds of equipment, we'd have even better pictures of nothing."

"Thanks Polly. Now to Bob Covina, live at the mall."

"Harry, I'm standing live in the parking lot at the West Begonia Mall. There aren't any cars in the lot. Except ours, of course. There's a lot of snow and the mall is closed."

"Do you know when it'll open?"

"It's a little past 11 p.m. right now, so I guess it'll probably open tomorrow morning sometime."

"Thanks for that insightful report, Bob. Now, live on Second Street is Kiki Vertigo who's been interviewing residents about their response to the snow."

"With me right now, live on Second Street, is resident Homer Bigeloo who has a snow shovel. Homer, what are you doing?"

"I'm shoveling snow."

"Have you been shoveling long?"

"Yeah. I don't like snow."
"How long haven't you liked snow?"
"A long time, I guess."
"Thanks, Homer. I'm Kiki Vertigo, live on Second Street. Back to you, Harry."
"Another great interview, Kiki. We'll be back with our comprehensive team coverage right after this message from Menodcino Frozen TV Dinners."

Eyewitless Promotion

Once, when we were all naive, the media let the news speak for itself. However, several dozen consultants, aided by cowardly editors and news directors, believe the strength of a story isn't sufficient to carry audience interest. Newspapers explode with color, graphics, and duotone sidebars. Making room for the hype leads to fewer and shorter stories. But, nowhere has news embellishment become more developed than in local TV news operations, trumpeted by pretentious graphics and full-orchestral fanfare, as seen on a typical newscast at KFAD.

"NEWS right NOW! LIVE from KFAD-TV, the all-news and entertainment station that's taking the lead in news and entertainment. This is the Eyewitless 15 Action News Team with all the news and information in River Valley. And now KFAD-TV, the Number One source of all news and entertainment in all of River Valley, proudly presents Eyewitless 15 Action News at 6. The news starts RIGHT NOW!"

"Good evening. This is Harry Hansom."

"And I'm Susie Sweetwater. Tonight, we have TWO top stories. A fire in Potshot Township and the opening of a supermarket in East Rutabaga. But first, our BIG story. Harry."

"Thank you, Susie. Our BIG story concerns a family of six that's been wiped out in a hail of gunfire. And, here's the kicker, the cops went to the wrong house! We'll be back with that story and others, right after five minutes of these rapid-fire earth-shattering messages."

"We're back. But, first, this just in. LIVE on the Interstate is Eyewitless 15 Action News reporter Kiki Vertigo."

"Thanks, Harry. This is Kiki Vertigo LIVE with LATE-BREAKING NEWS on River Valley's premiere news and entertainment station. I'm LIVE on the Interstate, somewhere around Exit 35 or 36. Traffic is backed up almost a half-mile. Back to you, Harry."

"Kiki, do you know why traffic is backed up?"

"I didn't get any confirmation, but it appears the cause is more cars than the Interstate can handle at this time. This is Kiki Vertigo reporting for the Eyewitless 15 Action News Team."

"Thanks for that great LIVE report only on Eyewitless 15 Action News. At 11 tonight, Eyewitless 15 Action investigative reporter Polly Prattle tears open the previously untold story of the seamy underworld of Betsy Ross. And on Daybreak at 7 News tomorrow morning, Bob Covina begins his three-part in-depth probe of the annual Miss Nude New England contest. On tonight's 11 p.m. Action Report, chief meteorologist Flake Sepulveda will ask some useless weather question, tell us the history of temperature, then give the latest on the tornado that's heading east from Kansas and is expected to destroy all of Philadelphia. ONLY on Eyewitless 15 Action News. KFAD-15. But first, let's break for some messages of critical social importance about where to buy your next used car."

"We're back, and with sports for the Eyewitless 15 Action Sports Team is former minor league baseball reserve pitcher Boom-Boom Brannigan."

"Thanks, Harry. At the top of the sports news, a $5 million per year pro-basketball player has committed suicide. The National League announced plans to dissolve. And the Philadelphia Eagles will move to Bosnia next season. But, first, a sports EXCLUSIVE on KFAD-15, your Eyewitless News Action Team for all of River Valley. It's the second day of the season, and we have eight teams with identical 1-and-1 records. Now, how often do you think that happens? We'll be back with more sports right after these important messages."

"We're back with more sports. At 11 tonight, we'll give you all the details about the suicide, the dissolution of the National League, and the Eagles flying off to Bosnia. Back to you, Susie."

"Thanks, Boom-Boom. Straight ahead on Eyewitless 15 Action News KFAD is an EXCLUSIVE interview with Mayor Sammy Schmaltz who plans to announce a major building project for the Valley. Stay tuned to KFAD-TV 15, your Eyewitless 15 Action News Team. We'll be back and teasing you with even more stories right after these messages."

"Finally, on the news station that has more promotion than any other station, we have this cute little featurette from the network. A Kansas-bred lion that was sunning itself near City Hall was thrown into the air by the tornado that's heading our way, and landed on its feet in Indianapolis where it qualified 15th for the Indianapolis 500 Memorial Day race. At 11, we'll have an exclusive interview with the lion. For the Eyewitless 15 Action News Team, the best news in River Valley, this is Susie Sweetwater."

"And, this is Harry Hansom. Now to our disembodied baritone-voiced narrator and his full orchestra."

"You've been watching Eyewitless 15 Action News on KFAD-15, the all-news and entertainment station for River viewers in the River Valley. KFAD, your eyewitness to life, liberty, and the pursuit of ratings. Good Night. And good news."

TV News 101: Intro to Makeup

It was the first of 114 episodes of the critically acclaimed TV series "Lou Grant," and I eagerly awaited seeing it again, now in syndicated reruns. The first episode reintroduced Ed Asner to American television as the crotchety, hard driving, but cuddly journalist who once worked on a Detroit newspaper and had just been fired as news director of WJM-TV, Minneapolis—you know, the one where Mary Richards was a producer, and Murray Slaughter (before becoming the "Love Boat" captain) wrote copy for the bumbling Ted Baxter who was everyone's idea of the typical anchor. Lou was 50 years old and had $280 in the bank. Coming to his rescue was Charlie Hume, a once tough reporter now buried as a corporate leaning managing editor, who said Lou would be perfect as city editor of the *L.A. Tribune* as long as Mrs. Pynchon, the publisher, agrees. But, just one word of caution, said the editor, when meeting the publisher, avoid mentioning those years on TV—"she hates it."

"Then what do I tell her I've been doing the last ten years?" Lou asked.

"Tell her you were in jail," said Charlie.

And so it began. The first episode was directed by Gene Reynolds of "M*A*S*H" fame, from a brilliant script by Leon Tokatyan. During its four-season run, some of Hollywood's finest directors and writers worked on the series. In each episode were social and journalistic issues that made the one-hour show the best journalism classroom any student could imagine. But, I always remembered those early throw-away lines of cynicism between Lou and Charlie, that it was better to admit to having been in jail than to having worked in TV news.

The more I watch local TV news, the more I am convinced that even the worst of our local newspapers—and, certainly, the print media seem to have as many problems as there are lines of type—may be better than the average local newscast, most of which seem to be concerned more about appearance than content.

In December 1996, a reporter from a Wilkes-Barre TV station, a CBS affiliate, was punched out by a guy who declared, "So you think you're so pretty!" Station management, of course, would have maintained that the reporter, a hunk who sports a great winter tan, was hired on the basis of his competence not his looks. But, then management told the media the hunk was going to continue to report stories, but wouldn't be on air until his cut over his eye looked more presentable. The next time we saw him on air, he was wearing a hat and sunglasses.

The typical TV news room has about as many reporters as a small daily, but at least ten times the news to cover. To compensate for the lack of reporters, the station leases a helicopter to give it "a presence in the market," hires three meteorologists to tell us the weather in Muscogee, Oklahoma, and two or three washed-up or never-was athletes to pump the latest exploits of the local Wattabago Whales Single-A baseball team. But, the station doesn't give us stories about the environment, health, labor, or the economy. What it does give us is gore.

To lead off the news, local stations send what few reporters they have to fires and car crashes to get that "visual" and to shove microphones up someone's nose and ask, "How do you feel now that your house burned down and your only son died in the inferno?" The rush to "quickie news" now dominates the local newscasts.

"The locals use any old barn burning or jackknifed trailer truck, and pass that kind of thing off as news," former CBS anchor Walter Cronkite told *Women's Day* readers in 1995. Station executives, he says, "have probably costed it out and that even maintaining the satellite trucks to run around to crime scenes is cheaper than having enough people on staff who can understand the news and spend time reporting it."

Find good reporters—and TV news does have good reporters—and their station management limits them to about 90 seconds of air time, no more than about three paragraphs in the local newspaper, then restricts their budget to nothing more than covering the local Miss Petunia Pageant, while encouraging the sports reporters to chase college and pro teams all over the country.

Unable or unwilling to dig out stories of substance, the typical 30-minute newscast gives us eight minutes of commercials, five minutes of sports, four minutes of weather, a couple of minutes of nauseating happy talk banter broken up into 10-second bites, a minute or two of canned network cast-off news, a minute of teasers and "upcoming at 11" self-promotion, and no more than 10 minutes of local news. That, of course, leaves no time for local editorials, which is fine with management since it believes cordial relations with viewers and advertisers is preferred to journalistic integrity. In fact, the official CBS-TV policy is a very stark, "We do not take advocacy positions on controversial issues."

Behind all this are the ubiquitous "consultants" who are paid fortunes to tell station managers that stories about some starlet "accidentally" losing her bra in the surf is more substance than how the latest Senate hearings on health care reform will impact the local market, and that the station could squeeze another one-tenth of a rating point by lighting the set differently to highlight the anchor's "pool green" eyes.

It's not as if local television doesn't have any models. "60 Minutes," "Nightline," and just about anything on CNN can go one-on-one with the best newspapers and news magazines. But more Americans watch local news than the network news magazines. However, even the major players are noticing problems. Morley Safer, a "60 Minutes" anchor, said in March 1997, there "is generally a lowering of standards about what we see on the air," and Lesley Stahl admits she occasionally has been asked to report a story she hasn't thoroughly researched. "It's frightening," she says.

Charles Kuralt, one of the nation's most distinguished network correspondents, once explained what TV news has become: "Urgent electronic music plays, the lights come up, and an earnest young man or woman says to a camera, 'Good evening, here is the news.' This is said very urgently and with the appearance of sincerity most often by an attractive young person who would not know a news story if it jumped up and mussed his coiffure."

Andy Lack, NBC News president, is even harsher. "There's a generation of reporters coming along who are more interested in who their agent is or whether they're 'in play' at Fox than in going after the big stories," he charges. Because many of the reporters aren't willing "to invest in the homework that comes with really developing your skills as a first rate reporter," says

Lack, "there's very little emphasis on quality of work and a great deal of emphasis on compensation for it."

CBS anchor Dan Rather simply calls much of what passes as TV news "fuzz and wuzz."

However, actor Greg Kinnear best sums up what has happened to TV news. Kinnear says he was unsure of whether to be an actor or broadcast journalist when he entered the University of Arizona in 1981. A year later, his drama teacher told him that only 2 percent of actors made their living as actors. "I thought to myself, 'Geez, that leaves the news,'" Kinnear told the readers of *Parade* magazine in December 1996.

"Let's face it," says Kinnear, targeting what has happened to the profession, "the lines between entertainment and broadcast journalism were blurred way before I came along. The lines between news and publicity have been blurred. It's increasingly difficult for the viewer to discern between what is true and what's a lie. That's incredibly scary."

Maybe if the journalists, both print and broadcast, learned more about their profession by watching what happened at the fictional *L.A. Tribune,* then maybe Lou Grant could have admitted he once worked in TV news, and we wouldn't have thousands of journalism students begging for a chance to be the next million dollar anchor, and preparing for it by checking hair styles instead of courthouse records.

Long Island Lolita Meets the Journalistic Low-life

It was 6 a.m., Monday, when the phone rang, so I knew it was Marshbaum eager to involve me in his latest scam. I wasn't disappointed.

"Got any extra money?" he whispered.

"Not since I became a humor columnist," I replied.

"Too bad," said Marshbaum. "I'll just have to take it elsewhere."

"Take what elsewhere?" I asked sleepily.

"Revelations about my life with Amy Fisher."

"You had a life with the Long Island Lolita?"

"Actually, I once bought some fabric at the sewing store her parents own, but I figure what they told me about their daughter is worth a few thousand on the journalistic market."

"What'd they tell you?" I asked.

"Not so fast. It'll cost you. You been looking at the tabloids lately? They pay real good for my kind of news."

"Look, Marshbaum," I said, "the papers I write my column for are respectable and ethical. Usually. They don't pay for revelations."

"Everyone else is!" he said outraged. "Three hundred thousand to the woman who got shot and her husband who either was or wasn't Amy's pizza-eating pimp, Fifty thou to some boyfriend. A bundle to a triggerman. Quarter million to some hack to write a paperback about all this. Thousands to just about anyone who ever lived in the same county she does. Millions to produce the 'Amy Fisher Film Festival' on TV. Add in a half dozen tabloid TV shows, a few talk shows, and all the local news, and you have a billion dollar Amy industry."

"But, that's schlock entertainment," I said. "Newspapers have ethics."

"Yeah," he said sarcastically, "like the New York papers that had photographers staking out everyone's houses? Or, the battalion of reporters who invaded her upper-class hometown to talk to all the neighbors? What about the newspaper reporters who were paid by the entertainment industry to be 'consultants'?"

"I have no desire to write about sex-crazed teenagers on the prowl for body shop repairmen," I said. "Besides, every hour they take to report on this teenage prostitute with a fatal attraction complex is one hour less they can investigate corruption. Every inch they use in every paper is one inch less that can be devoted to stories about the economy and health care crises."

"What about a scoop on body shop repairmen who lure teenage girls into lives of crime?" he asked. "I can sell that one a little cheaper."

"He may have been a sleaze," I said, "but there's no evidence he suggested that his alleged lover killed his wife."

"Precisely," said Marshbaum. "There's no evidence of any of this, but TV has already devoted more air time to it than they did to the Gulf War. Besides, you're the only one who hasn't written about it. Aren't your editors concerned that you're not giving them the latest news? Sin sells papers. Publishers reward sinners by increasing their salaries. Frankly, you're well behind at the moment."

"OK, Marshbaum, what choice piece of trivia did you learn that'll save my career and get me the Pulitzer Prize for sensationalism?"

"Like I said, I'm no fool. This stuff's too hot to entrust to someone not willing to pay."

"I said I had ethics."

"Ethics don't pay the bill at Victoria's Secret," he said. "Besides, it's relatively simple. You get the scoop on why Amy's parents never thought it was unusual that their 16-year-old daughter not only had a beeper, but a nearly new usually dented Dodge Daytona with an automatic pilot to guide it into the body shop. You put it into your column. Some lowlife publisher or producer with a wad of bills calls you up, pays you even more. Everyone makes out."

"Everyone but the readers," I said.

"It's the readers who want this stuff," he reminded me. "They'll read your column before they'll read about poverty, the environment, and the health care crisis."

"That may be true," I said, "but I'll pass on this one. My readers will just have to remain ignorant of some of the significant events that affect their lives."

"Well, don't come crying to me when "Hard Copy" scoops you, and your editors replace you with someone known as 'a highly reliable source.'" I said I'd have to risk it. "By the way," Marshbaum said shortly before hanging up, "I'm sure you'll get a column out of this somehow. I'll send you a bill in the morning."

For Sale: Justice—O.J. Style

"Get your O.J. T-shirts, mugs, and witnesses here! All shapes, sizes, and colors! Get 'em while they're hot!"

Behind a stainless steel vendor cart on Manhattan's Avenue of the Americas was—who else?—Marshbaum, who was doing a brisk business.

"Marshbaum!" I shouted, "what are you doing selling witnesses in New York!"

"Because L.A. doesn't allow vendor carts on Sunset."

"That's not the point," I said. "You shouldn't be selling witnesses anywhere."

"Actually," said Marshbaum, "I'm just their agent. I put witnesses together with attorneys and editors, and get 15 percent commission."

"We got two forensic pathologists available! Bargain basement price. Only two thousand a day plus expenses. They go either way." Two attorneys opened their wallets and walked away with the discounted docs.

"Marshbaum, I don't know what scam you're working, but I think it's illegal."

"Hardly," he said snickering. "It's good old-fashioned American capitalism, and supported by the Constitution."

"The Constitution allows this?" I asked skeptically.

"Sixth Amendment," said Marshbaum smugly. "The right to capitalize on crime."

"Got a psychiatrist here. A little crazy, but does well on the stand. Take her at only three hundred an hour, minimum of four hours."

Almost before he finished his spiel, another attorney opened a large briefcase, gave Marshbaum $1,200 in unmarked bills, and bought the psychiatrist.

"You can't be selling justice like this," I said shocked.

"Who said it's justice?" he said. "I'm selling expertise to the lawyers, and information to the news media."

"But only the seedy media believe in checkbook journalism," I said smugly. "The establishment media would never pay a source."

"Got someone here who says he used to deliver diapers to the Simpson home. Only three thousand, and you get 80 minutes with him." A buyer who demanded anonymity put a brown paper bag with low denomination bills on the counter, grabbed the owner of Tidy Didy Diapers, and was last seen darting between traffic on her way back to Times Square.

"The *Times* bought a source?" I asked shocked.

"Can't tell you," said Marshbaum. "But this week alone, I've seen editors from 30 papers. The *Post* bought an exclusive to a witness who said she could prove aliens soaked up O.J.'s spirit and are using it to cure cancer."

"How long you been doing this?" I asked.

"A month. And if I don't keep hustling, the other agents will grab what's available."

"There's *other* agents doing this?"

"Of course there's other agents. Why do you think A. C. Cowlings turned down a million bucks? Why did Kato turn down a hundred grand? It wasn't because they're Boy Scouts. They got some smart agent on the West Coast holding out."

"O.K, folks, this one's a little tainted, but it'll wear just as well on TV. She says just before she was arrested for robbery and assault with a deadly weapon, she saw O.J. buy rubber gloves from the store she hit." Three editors tore each other apart trying to get the highest bid. When they were through, an ambulance

carried them away, but Marshbaum had $15,000—15 percent of it his commission—for the thief's guarantee that she'd tell the truth.

"That's terrible!" I said, still shocked by the display before me.

"You think that's bad," said Marshbaum, "two days ago, I had to have the cops clear the sidewalk when the staffs from "Inside Edition" and "Hard Copy" began fighting over a witness who says not only did he sell O.J. the white Bronco, but heard him say it's a killer machine."

"*Jurors! Live jurors! Get the exclusive story of what went on in deliberations! Only fifty thou apiece! Available only to the news media!*"

"That's ridiculous," I said. "They didn't even pick the jury pool yet. How can you be selling jurors?"

"They choose jurors from the voting lists," said Marshbaum. "In the past month, I signed exclusive letters of intent from every voter in L.A. County. Hundreds have been registering just in the past week alone. It's only a matter of time until the lawyers choose who they want on the panel."

"Is there anyone you don't represent?" I asked.

"Yeah. I don't represent lawyers. Even agents have ethics."

The Write Stuff

It was close to deadline, and I was hurriedly flipping through newspapers and magazines, trying to find a news hook upon which to hang this week's column. Marshbaum was on vacation; I didn't have time to read the *Congressional Quarterly,* source of innumerable columns; and every two-bit humor "wannabe" was mining the Bar Association for cheap lawyer jokes.

Dejectedly, I thumbed the classified ads—maybe there'd be a job for a washed-up columnist. My mind wandered over to the "literary services" section. There, in *Harper's,* one of the nation's most respected magazines, was my salvation. Among ads from vanity publishing companies promising to make me a star was exactly what I needed. Three companies said they'd write this week's column for me.

The first ad promised, "We write everything. Reports, papers, company books." The ad even claimed the company was "professional." Alas, it had only a mailing address, and I needed something in less than a day.

Next was a Los Angeles company with a "toll-free hotline." John, a polite young man eager to help, told me most of the previously-written term papers in the company's catalog were 6 to 20 pages, and the cost was only $7.50 per page. The company was even so concerned about its clients' finances that it never charged for more than 17 pages, and threw in the footnotes and bibliography for free.

"I'm on a deadline," I told him.

"No problem," he helpfully said, "we can fax it to you or send it by overnight mail."

I told him I really didn't need any of the advertised 19,278 term papers, but thought maybe there could be some "special" assistance he could provide. There was no problem there either. For only $20 to $25 per page, the company would custom make an "undergraduate level" report to my specific needs. For $25 to $45 per page, I could get a graduate or professional level report. It could be six pages; it could be 400 pages. My choice. "Of course," he said, "we expect you to put in some of your own opinions." Of course.

In exchange for this "fully written report," I'd have to sign a statement guaranteeing, "I understand this report is to be used for research purposes only." Right.

I opted for the professional level report, and was told to call another number and to talk with a Dr. Something-or-the-Other who was in charge of the researchers. Not wanting to lower the quality of my column, I first asked her about qualifications, and was told "every one" of the staff has at least a master's. I didn't have time to verify writing ability, subject knowledge, or even if the M.A.s were from the schools that advertise in the classifieds of supermarket tabloids. Alas, she said the company doesn't do fiction. "Try a grad student at a university," she suggested. "Someone in English might be able to help you."

A grad student? In English! Obviously, this woman had the artistic sensitivity of a drain pipe.

Time for my last contact. A kindly voice answered, "Research Services."

"Can you do a custom report?" I asked.

"Everything we do is custom made," he replied. He charged $12.50 per page, with a special rate of $200 for the first 15 pages. I'd have to supply the cover page, but he'd throw in footnotes and bibliography at no cost.

"Can you do satire?" I asked.

No problem, he answered. However, he explained that writing satire "is time consuming because there's no library research, and it involves creative writing." I said I understood.

"I'd like a foil in it if possible. You know, like Mike Royko uses Slats Grobnik, and this writer in Pennsylvania uses a guy named Marshbaum?" Still no problem. "I need it pretty soon," I begged. No problem there either.

However, if he were to do a good job writing a satire, he might need more time since "if you do it too fast, a good idea may come after it's in the mail." But, for $50 he'd do something relatively quick. Three pages. Even with a foil.

That's when I decided not to hire him. I spend all week perfecting my column. And he wanted only $50? For 800 choice words? It seemed awfully cheap. Besides, by then, I had my column.

Compliments of a Thief

They won't tell you their names, but they'll sell you a genuine knock-off Rolex for only $50. Too high? How about 40? 35? But they can't go any lower; why, it's almost a steal at that price. Don't want a watch? How about a pirated video from a $250 million a year industry? Pretend 14-karat gold necklaces and rings? Something nice for that special lady? Still not interested? Wait! Don't go! Nice jeans? A bandanna?

It's the street vendors. They're in almost all major cities trying to make a buck. Most don't make a lot of money, just enough to survive, enough for a seedy but overpriced walk-up; some clothes; a decent meal once a day. Many are immigrants, here in urban America to find the "good life." Most don't know, at least not "for sure" know, if their merchandise, provided by middlemen, is stolen or just purchased in large quantities at fantastic wholesale prices.

Like the street vendors, a few "needy" college professors also have something to sell. However, they're the amateurs, and their buyers are the pros. At the end of every semester, book buyers descend upon the college campuses to buy books from the professors. Not the used books that students sell back to the bookstore the day after their finals, but new books. Complimentary ones. Books supplied by publishers, often at the professor's request. The purpose of complimentary copies, sometimes as many as 5,000 per press run, is to entice the nation's professors to adopt the books for a course. No one knows how many of the nation's

700,000 professors sell comp copies, although good estimates are that of more than 100 million copies of college texts published a year, as many as half of the estimated one million complimentary copies may make it into paid distribution.

Almost everyone benefits. The professors make out well since they can sometimes make $300 to 400 in undeclared income merely for opening mail bags a few times a semester and occasionally thumbing through the merchandise.

The agents make out well since they buy $40 books for, maybe, $5. And the wholesalers and bookstores make out well since they buy books at far less than half the cost of new books.

Not making out so well are the publishers and authors. In 1986, the last time the Book Industry Study Group checked, authors were losing $10 million a year in royalties, and publishers were losing $80 million a year in sales to the comp book racket. Those figures, even with increased vigilance and enforcement by publishers, is probably double that of a decade ago. A few years ago, Karl J. Smith, a math professor at Santa Rosa (California) Junior College, quickly learned how bad the problem was; more than half the students in his class had "used books"—although the book he wrote had just been released three weeks earlier.

Professors, in rebuttal, say that many of the copies are unsolicited, so it's their right to sell them. They say even books they asked for may not, after inspection, be appropriate for the courses they teach. The publishers suggest sending back the unused books, and often include postage-paid coupons and mailers; they suggest the professor may place the books on department library shelves or even donate the books to charitable agencies. But, the comp copies are still being sold for "spare change."

To stop the sale of complimentary copies, publishers began embossing "Complimentary—Not for Sale" on the covers, and stamping the same message on the end of the pages. But, wholesalers have placed unremovable "USED" stickers on the covers, and sanded off the message on the pages. Many wholesalers even rebind some titles.

Many colleges have policies that forbid the professors to sell their comp copies. However, professors still find ways to circumvent the policies.

"We strongly suggest that stores don't buy comp copies," says Jerry Buchs of the 3,000-member National Association of College Stores. But, the association has no enforcement powers in its code of ethics. Nevertheless, says Buchs, "We keep addressing the issue."

Except for authors and publishers not receiving money for writing and producing books, and some ethical considerations swirling around professors who make money from books they had no part in creating, students wonder what the problem is. After all, they're getting new books at used prices. The problem is that the sale of complimentary textbooks to agents—not the sale of legitimately purchased used books the students sell back, but which also yield no income to authors and publishers—directly leads to higher list prices for all textbooks, says James Lichtenberg, vice president of the Association of American Publishers (AAP).

It's rare that a student doesn't complain about the high price of textbooks; they should be complaining about their greedy, unethical professors.

Stripping Off Their Royalties

He's there by 7 a.m. almost every Sunday except in winter to make money at one of the largest permanent flea markets in northeastern Pennsylvania. In three-foot long cardboard boxes he has an inventory of hundreds of paperbacks, all of them displayed spine up. Westerns. Romances. Adventures. Whatever you want. Three for a buck; 50 cents each. The books are virtually mint condition, and if you don't mind reading something without a front cover, it's a bargain, especially since paperbacks with the covers, sold at supermarkets, pharmacies, and bookstores, are now going for $5.95 each. The only problem is that it's illegal.

The sale of stripped books, says Patricia Peron-Polster of the Association of American Publishers (AAP), is a "significant and ongoing problem" that involves fraud, possible copyright infringement, and often federal interstate commerce violations.

However, Eric Raymond, an executive at Simon & Schuster, one of the nation's largest publishing houses, says that police departments and prosecutors often don't have the time, manpower, or resources to investigate and bring to court sellers of stripped books. "It's just not the thing prosecutors want to spend time with," he says. Nevertheless, because of the volume of lost sales, publishers have begun their own investigations and have been working with both local and federal law enforcement officials. The FBI refuses to discuss ongoing investigations.

To understand why the sale of stripped books is illegal, it's important to know a little about the nature of book publishing. Although the major book chains usually buy books on the basis of a book's cover and the promotion effort put out by the publisher, no one can predict which books will titillate American reading appetites. So, publishers of the mass market paperbacks—the kind with colorfully-embossed titles superimposed over pirates and scantily-clad women on slick $4^{1}/_{4}$ by $6^{3}/_{4}$ inch covers—order large print quantities to try to saturate American book stands. They sell these books to distributors for 50 to 60 percent of the list price, and hope a few titles bring in enough profit to carry the rest of the line.

Unique in the field of retail sales, booksellers can return to publishers for full credit any books they can't sell. Often, booksellers return to publishers as much as half the copies of a mass market book. However, publishers have no desire to pay shipping costs for books they probably won't redistribute, especially since there are another couple of dozen titles they're trying to push that month. And, neither bookseller nor publisher wants several skids of taxable inventory. So, distributors and publishers sign contracts that allow the bookseller to send only the cover back to the publisher, tack on shipping costs, and agree to destroy the rest of the book to prevent further sale.

The bookseller usually sends stripped books to a recycler who picks them up at no cost and makes his money by selling recycled pulp. Mass market paperbacks accounted for about $2.2 billion in sales in 1995, but about $844 million of that was credited for returns—most of them supposedly shredded and destroyed by booksellers—according to the AAP.

However, some booksellers "forget" to send some books to a debindery or recycler, either selling some in their own store or, more likely, selling books for pennies apiece to mini-distributors. But, even if the bookseller (who can be the owner of just about any kind of a business) plays by all the rules—and almost all major bookstores do—and sends the books to a recycler, that doesn't mean the books don't show up again. Some books may be stolen in transit or in storage. However, a few unscrupulous companies may file claims they have shredded 10 tons of what is now literally literary garbage, but have really gotten rid of just nine tons, throwing the coverless books into the streets, like leftover food for the cats. The cats, in this case, have pickups, and pay for the leftovers.

So, what's really the problem? After all, even though these transient booksellers probably don't pay taxes on their income, it's hard enough these days to make a buck. And certainly it's a break for the readers who are more likely to buy a 50-cent paperback than one costing ten times as much.

The problem is that when a reader buys a stripped paperback, the publisher doesn't receive any money. Since there's no income to the publisher, there's also no royalties to the author. Except for the few million dollar deals that make the headlines every now and then, we authors don't make a lot of money anyhow from meager royalties, which average 10 to 15 percent of the list price of hardcover books and 5 to 10 percent of paperbacks. So every stripped or stolen book that's sold means the author gets no money while a lot of people who had no part in the creative process are making money off of us. And, I really object to that.

Politically Incorrect Weather

A high-pressure front swept across the news room of KMJ-AM, Fresno, California, with a 100 percent certainty that it would leave a new low in its wake.

Depending on whom you believe, weatherman Sean Boyd was either fired for being accurate, or program director John Broeske had finally had enough of Boyd's insolence and refusal to be "a team player." Boyd, an independent contractor, had forecast weather as many as 20 times a day for 17 years at the station.

However, for at least the second time in two months, Boyd was politically incorrect, a sin for anyone in our society, but especially so for a weatherman whose continued employment may have been based on being meteorologically inaccurate. In March 1995, Boyd had determined there was a better than average possibility that it would be partly cloudy, breezy, and cool for a station-sponsored golf tournament. Boyd says he remembers his program director suggesting that it would be better if the forecast could say it was partly sunny, not partly cloudy. Actually, why not report it would be mostly sunny with highs in the 70s and "let people make their own decision," Boyd remembers Broeske telling him. Nevertheless, Boyd stuck by his forecast; the weather for the divot swingers that afternoon was, in fact, partly cloudy, breezy, and cool.

Two months later, Boyd again got into trouble. KMJ, which carries the Rush Limbaugh talk show, was sponsoring the Second Annual Dittohead Barbecue and Politically Incorrect Picnic, Saturday, April 15. Since it was already politically incorrect, it was apparently no big deal that it was also Easter and Passover weekend.

Four days before the Dittoheads were to meet, Boyd forecast a chance of showers, based on reports of the National Weather Service. Broeske possibly didn't think that anyone, including the clouds, had a right to rain on his plumped up sizzling raucous barbecued hot dogs. After all, the station, which sends 5,000 screaming watts of conservative thinking into one of the state's biggest media markets, had something of an investment in making sure thousands showed up to celebrate the Biggest Mouth That Roars, even if the Chief Dittohead himself had no plans to attend.

So, Broeske strongly suggested that Boyd revise the forecast. After all, you never know with California weather. It *could* have been a nice day in the neighborhood.

"Do you want me to change all the forecasts?" Boyd asked, then sarcastically suggested that the program director could just write down what he thought the weather should be, "and I'll tell it just the way you have asked." The program director might have thought about the temptation to move a few clouds but declined.

Boyd stuck with his weather report. About 3 p.m. that Sunday, rain began falling on the char-smoked Dittoheads. Boyd says he and Broeske had "meetings in the past about how he wanted me to do things." Boyd said the station manager even told him that the program director had once mentioned that dealing with Boyd was "like a Chinese water torture."

Ten days after the Dittohead Debacle, Broeske approached Boyd. The Arctic Clipper cold front came with more warmth. "You can say you resigned because of stress and long hours," Boyd remembers Broeske telling him.

Broeske has a different version of the events. "Everything he's saying is completely untrue," says Broeske. However, he cites "station policy" for reasons why he won't discuss the events further. "No comment" is the extent of Broeske's official version. Apparently, other media and their listeners don't have a problem with Boyd's personality or forecasts. Since 1988, Boyd has provided weather information throughout the day, including weekends when necessary, for the independently owned KAAT-AM/KTNS-FM stations in Oakhurst.

"Sean has been very responsible to us and to our listeners," says Larry Gamble, station manager and owner of the radio stations. He says that Boyd not only "provides the detailed information necessary," but also receives "very positive feedback from our listeners." Without question, Gamble is "very pleased" with the quality of the forecasts.

At KSEE-TV, an NBC affiliate in Fresno, news director Eric Hulnick also has no question about Boyd's competence. In the eight TV-station metro market, Boyd not only "has the most accurate forecasts in the Valley," says Hulnick, he's quite simply "the best forecaster in Fresno."

The best forecaster, unfortunately, now has a much smaller audience.

A Major Conflict of Interest

Like reporters everywhere, Keith Martin wanted to be where the action was, and during the first part of 1991 the action was in the Persian Gulf. Unlike the other reporters, Martin was a double agent. In fact, the other reporters at WBRE-TV, an NBC affiliate in Scranton and Wilkes-Barre, Pennsylvania, where Martin co-anchors the evening news, even proudly proclaimed his conflicting assignments—although they never mentioned the phrase "double agent." They didn't see it as a conflict.

Martin has been a TV journalist for more than two decades. He's also in the Pennsylvania National Guard. Not a grunt, but an officer. A *major*. And, he isn't just any officer, but a *public affairs officer*. Commander of the 109th Public Affairs Detachment. The military's very own flack.

Martin spent a week in February 1991 in the Persian Gulf reporting on the war and local units from northeastern Pennsylvania. He wasn't activated by the Department of Defense—apparently even the military have their limits on how many PAOs it can tolerate in combat zones. No, he was there as a journalist, although the distinction between flack and journalist blurred when on-air promotions and fellow reporters identified him as *Major* Martin. In addition to daily reports, Martin produced a one-hour special in which he interviewed 85 troops from Northeastern Pennsylvania.

Now with the war over, there are still stories to report. So, Maj. Keith Martin went to Fort Drum, New York, to report on the encampment of the 109th Infantry, a unit of the Pennsylvania National Guard. For the 6 p.m. newscast, he reported on the training the unit was getting so it can convert to being an armor unit by the end of the year. For the 11 p.m. newscast, he reported on the "excellent" safety record of the 109th.

Because Maj. Martin was on active duty at the time, a part of his 15-day a year commitment, he fed video and sound to all three stations in the Scranton and Wilkes-Barre market. Not surprisingly, only WBRE-TV aired his report. And, of course, he was identified on air as *Major* Martin. But that wasn't completely necessary since he was dressed, on air, in battle fatigues, complete with combat face paint.

The codes of ethics of the various journalism organizations are fairly clear about conflicts of interest. The Society of Professional Journalists states that journalists "must be free of obligation to any interest other than the public's right to know the truth. . . . Secondary employment . . . should be avoided if it compromises the integrity of journalists and their employers."

The Radio-Television News Directors Association (RTNDA) code states that "Broadcast journalists shall govern their . . . nonprofessional associations as may impinge on their professional activities in a manner that will protect them from conflict of interest, real or apparent."

The American Society of Newspaper Editors states that journalists "must avoid . . . any conflict of interest or the appearance of conflict."

And the Associated Press Managing Editors code declares that journalists "should make every effort to be free of obligations to news sources and special interests . . . Outside employment that conflicts with news interests should be avoided. Secondary employment by news sources is an obvious conflict."

So, what does Larry Stirewald, WBRE-TV news director, say about all this? Stirewald doesn't believe there is a conflict of interest. "We make it very clear that Keith is in the National Guard," says Stirewald, noting that "as long as you're straight forward with the people, it's all right." He says that all journalists have conflicts, and that "being a professional means compensating for whatever baggage you're carrying." Then he asks the question, "Why *shouldn't* journalists [be able to] serve their country in the National Guard?"

Journalists, if they choose, should be able to be in the Guard or any of the military reserves. Or even the Rotary Club, for that matter. They just shouldn't be reporting about them. *[The National Guard later promoted Major Martin to lieutenant colonel.]*

The Intruder

He came to the front door late one Saturday morning in April 1995 and knocked. When there was no answer, he knocked again, then began yelling "Hello," hoping someone would answer. When no one answered, he opened the front door, and walked into the house.

"I heard a man shouting 'Hello,' says Rachel Kerr, a 21-year-old speech pathology major at Bloomsburg University of Pennsylvania, and one of two women in the sorority house at the time, "but I didn't go down because I thought it was for someone else."

He walked up the first flight of stairs. Kerr, in her bedroom at the time, heard him, but didn't know if he was friend, repairman, or burglar.

"Hello!" he again shouted. No answer. So, he walked down to the living room, looked around, left, then returned to the other side of the house and looked around. At the top of the stairwell, alerted by a sorority sister who had just come into the house, was Michelle May, sorority president and a 21-year-old speech communications major.

Before he could identify himself as a reporter for WNEP-TV, Wilkes-Barre/Scranton, May sharply told him, "I know who you are. We have nothing to say to you."

He politely asked if there was anyone he could talk with. "I'm the president," said May sharply, "and we don't want to talk with you."

The reporter probably thought he was being fair, trying to get the other side of the story—or at least a decent 10-second "sound bite." After all, a 19-year-old pledge nearly died from alcohol overdose two days earlier in what was rumored to be a hazing incident.

"Can you at least tell me her name?" he asked. May refused, then snapped, "You can walk out of this house, just like you walked in." He walked out of the house.

Although reporters expect everyone to open up their life histories to them, this reporter says his station's policy is that its reporters may not talk to the media. Officially, he has "no comment."

The women of Chi Sigma Rho were frightened, upset, and acknowledge they weren't as courteous as they could have been. "We felt violated," said one of the women.

The reporter trespassed on private property, according to Bob Buehner, Jr., Montour County district attorney. The entry, he says, falls under the category of intentional tort—a civil action. However, Buehner also says there probably was nothing criminal about the reporter's entry, and if there was no damage, any charges would probably be dismissed in court. For there to have been a defiant trespass, says Buehner, the reporter had to be in the house after being told to leave. To be charged with burglary or breaking and entering, he had to be in the house with the purpose of committing a crime.

Nevertheless, the reporter's actions, although not criminal, violated the ethics and standards of the journalism profession. There is a universal implied consent for reporters to go onto private property when there is breaking news, such as a fire. Reporters also usually have access to privately-owned quasi-public institutions, such as malls. However, there are ethical limits.

"You just don't enter someone's house without being invited," says Reggie Stuart, assistant news editor for the Knight-Ridder News Service and president of the 14,000-member Society of Professional Journalists (SPJ). "If you do walk in," he says, "you should stay in the living room until you're recognized. You should never, under any circumstance, proceed to go through the house."

David Bartlett, president of the Radio and Television News Directors Association (RTNDA), agrees. "I don't think I would have gone into the house," he says, noting the reporter probably didn't exercise "very good judgment." Item 3 of the RTNDA Code of Ethics calls for reporters to "Respect the dignity, privacy, and well-being of people with whom they deal." Bartlett says the situation in which a reporter enters a house uninvited "might be construed as an invasion of their dignity."

The SPJ Code of Ethics specifically states that not only must the media "guard against invading a person's right to privacy," but that "Journalists at all times will show respect for the dignity, privacy, rights, and well-being of people encountered in the course of gathering and presenting the news."

During the next three days, the local media ran innumerable stories about the alcohol incident, many of the stories factually inaccurate, some based on the WNEP-TV reporting.

Four days after the media first reported the alcohol incident, a WYOU-TV reporter and his cameraman stood on the sidewalk before the house and, say witnesses, "taunted" sorority members following a university-wide meeting. "This is your chance to tell your side of the story," he said, a perfectly acceptable request, and important in the issue of fairness. But, say witnesses, he also kept taunting the women. "Tell us. Tell us," he kept saying over and over. "You look guilty if you don't say anything. Why don't you talk? This is your chance." He even told the women, "You need to take advantage of the media for your own good."

Three times the women asked the reporter to leave. That night on air, he identified Chi Sigma Rho as "the bad girl sorority," while the station aired footage of the women persistently yelling for the reporter to quit bothering them and to leave.

The public has a love-hate relationship with the media. They want the press to meet its obligations to make sure the public knows what's happening in society. But, they also hate the way the media go about their jobs.

Surveys show media credibility is at one of its lowest levels historically. The public is upset not only with factual, grammatical, and spelling errors, but also with the media's failure to admit mistakes. They are also upset with poor writing and editing, reliance upon unnamed sources, glorification of the criminal and of the bizarre. They don't like the media's failure to report on itself as well as it tries to cover other American institutions, and perceived unfairness, political bias, and conflicts of interest.

But most of all, they don't like ambush journalism" and the invasion of individual rights and privacies.

"We know we were wrong to allow a minor to drink," says May. But she and her sorority sisters also have every right to be upset with what the media may have done to them and to their own credibility.

Make Mine Media Rare

Whenever people get upset with the media, they often demand that reporters be licensed. When challenged that the First Amendment and America's libertarian philosophy forbid governmental bodies to determine who can and can't report the truth as they see it, these critics become upset. If reporters wish to be treated as professionals and be taken seriously, these critics whine, then they should meet certain educational, ethical, and professional standards, like lawyers, teachers, and beauty shop operators—all of whom must be licensed.

But, in this emerging era of Machiavellian democracy, the Constitution may get tattered a bit. And so it was that Sam Frattlebaum, a journalist for 25 years, was the first to be brought before the Court of Ultimate Decisions of the State Board of Journalistic Licensing.

The chair of the three-member court looked down upon Frattlebaum, and solemnly asked him how he pled to the charges of malfeasance, gross negligence, and reckless disregard of the truth.

"Not guilty," came the whimpered response.

"How dare you!" thundered the chair. "We wouldn't bring you here unless we were sure you were guilty! Now, stop wasting this court's time, and admit your guilt."

Once again, a frazzled Frattlebaum pleaded not guilty, forcing the chair to present the case.

"By 8 a.m. the day after the murders of Nicole Brown Simpson and that other guy whose name none of us remember 3,000 reporters were all over L.A. Where were you?"

"I was in Rwanda covering the massacre of the Tutsis," said Frattlebaum.

"No excuse," snapped the chair. "A half-million dead people in Africa aren't as important as one American football player. Where were you during the preliminary hearings?"

"I had to return to Bosnia to report about a new wave of Serbian ethnic torture."

"Don't you think O.J. is tortured by these charges? During six months of preliminary motions, you again deserted your country."

"Your Honor, I was in Japan to report about the earthquake that killed more than 5,000."

"Did you find any of Judge Ito's relatives? Maybe dig up some sex scandal?" Frattlebaum hung his head. "The record also shows you weren't even in L.A. when the most important trial of the millennium began."

"No, sir, I was in West Virginia to interview some hill people for a series about hunger in America."

"Don't you think O.J. gets hungry? What about the prosecutor's favorite foods? What's the judge's eating habits? What's the defense team's favorite restaurant? Since ice cream is such an important part of the trial, didn't you want to find out its flavor? Was it ice milk or frozen yogurt? How many ounces? What time did it melt? Certainly, you could have interviewed Ben and Jerry for a feature profile."

"I didn't think that—"

"It's obvious you didn't think," snapped the chair, continuing his inquisition. "You also didn't think about bribing lab techs to reveal the DNA results or to badger some cop down in Homicide."

He checked his notes, then actually smiled. "Ah, I see you did try to meet your responsibilities, and finally made it to Los Angeles."

"Yes, sir, I went there to report about the people left homeless by the floods."

The judge sighed deeply. "I suppose you didn't have the insight to realize that a flood could damage orange trees, lead to higher prices for orange juice, and affect the public's perception of O.J."

"No, Your Honor, but I did get a story about gang killings. Do you know that last week in L.A., 35 people were murdered, 12 of them children?"

"I don't care if the whole voter registration list was snuffed. None of them were TV sports commentators who run through airports huckstering rent-a-cars."

"I did try to get to the trial one day," said a sweating Frattlebaum, "but I tripped over some TV cables and had to go to the ER."

"Yeah yeah," said the chair throwing newspapers in the air. "While in the hospital, you didn't even steal O.J.'s medical file. When they let you out, did you at least try to interview a juror? Sneak into the O.J. compound for exclusive photos? Plant a hidden microphone in the judge's chambers? Find out if the judge wears briefs or boxers. The public has a right to know!"

"I'm sorry," said Frattlebaum, "but I had to leave to cover the story of a family who were being evicted after they exposed the worst case of corruption in Housing Authority history."

The chair sadly looked at Frattlebaum. "Your failure to report the important stories is killing our credibility. By your own words, you haven't lived up to the standards set by your peers."

And with that, he slammed down his gavel, and suspended Frattlebaum's license for one year. "Maybe in that time," said the chair, "you might develop a sense of what's expected of our profession."

Stealing the First Amendment

"Got a match?"

I didn't know where he came from, but there he was, right behind me—as usual. "You know I don't smoke," I told Marshbaum. "Come to think of it, you don't either. What's up?"

"Not much. Planning to roast some marshmallows and hot dogs. Burn some books."

"Marshbaum," I shouted. "You can't burn books."

"Sure I can. All I need is a match. See, first you—"

"Burning books is against everything this country stands for."

"Not when the books are evil."

"Marshbaum! Didn't you ever read anything Jefferson wrote? Our country was founded on the principle that all views must be heard."

"Sure, and my view is that we're going to burn some books to keep them from causing any more trouble."

I could have given Marshbaum a 10-minute lecture about John Milton's arguments that those who seek to destroy books destroy reason itself, and that mankind is best served when there is a "free and open encounter" of all ideas. Or, maybe, a few words from philosopher John Stuart Mill who stated, "We can never be sure that the opinion we are endeavoring to stifle is a false opinion, and if we were sure, stifling it would be an evil still."

Maybe a little bit of wisdom from Supreme Court Justice Oliver Wendell Holmes who told us that democracy is best served in a "marketplace of ideas." But, I knew Marshbaum wasn't in a mood to hear philosophy. So, all I said was a sarcastic, "I assume you plan to burn everything you think is evil."

"Just romances. Historical. Contemporary. Anything with a female byline and a cover of a woman with lust in her eyes and a torn dress on her bod."

"Why romances?" I asked.

"Because romances lead to crime."

"Most romance novels may be a crime against good writing," I said, "but that's still no reason to burn them."

"It's a case of numbers," said Marshbaum. "The major publishers put out more than 120 romances a month, three times more than 14 years ago. And, the average romance reader spends about $1,200 a year on the books." He smugly told me he got that information from the Association of American Publishers.

"Wasting money on syrupy nonsense still isn't enough of a reason to burn books," I said.

"Get away from your computer and see what's been happening to America," said Marshbaum. "In the past 14 years, the crime rate has tripled. It's a direct relationship. Where do you think those bored housewives get all that money to buy romances? You can't read just one romance. Once you're hooked, you need 10 or 20. You become addicted. You need more and more until one day your whole life is nothing but a long print-enhanced haze of bodice-rippers and sap. Eliminate romances, and you'll walk safer in Central Park at night."

"That's the most convoluted piece of logic I've ever heard! And even if it were true, you can't burn books!"

"The *Washington Post* says it's OK to burn books," said Marshbaum.

"I doubt the *Post* believes in burning books," I said eruditely. I was eruditely wrong.

"Maybe not books, but newspapers. Remember all the thefts of newspapers on college campuses?"

I remembered them vividly. At more than three dozen campuses a year, according to the Student Press Law Center, students who disagree with something in the student newspapers steal them from distribution racks and throw them into dumpsters or burn them. The culprits are often persons who think of themselves as liberals, but whose actions certainly suggest they spent more time in parties than in classes that discussed the founding principles of the nation.

"So, how does all this tie into the *Post*?" I asked.

Marshbaum pulled an editorial from his pocket. "Read this!" he commanded. According to the *Post* editorial, dated January 22, 1994, "scooping up copies of publications—whether to send a message or to protest one—may in itself be a form of free speech." It argued that proposed legislation in Maryland to ban the theft of newspapers is "neither a good idea [nor] a worthy pursuit." It was a shocking philosophy from a newspaper that screeches a national emergency almost any time a governmental agency doesn't yield all its secrets.

"Obviously someone kidnapped all the reporters and editors," I said.

"Obviously the *Post* has divine guidance to determine what

is truth," said Marshbaum. "Maybe *they* have a match I can borrow."

[Against the *Post's* advice, the Maryland legislature became the first state in the nation to declare it illegal to steal newspapers with the intent to prevent others from reading them.]

Thrown Out of the Game

On the morning of June 12, 1996, a three-judge federal panel in Philadelphia issued a 175-page decision that declared the Communications Decency Act unconstitutional. "The strength of our liberty depends upon the chaos and cacophony of the unfettered speech the First Amendment protects," wrote Judge Stephen Dalzell.

That afternoon, the owners of Major League Baseball, apparently having not read the First Amendment lately, declared the opinions of Cincinnati Reds owner Marge Schott to be an embarrassment, and ordered her suspended from day-to-day operations for two and one-half years.

In February 1993, Schott was fined $25,000 and banned for a year following remarks that the baseball owners thought were blatantly racist and anti-Semitic. This year, in an ESPN interview, she defended Hitler as someone who at the beginning of his career helped the people and accomplished much, although she did say he later "went too far." In a *Sports Illustrated* interview she insulted Asians, working women, and others. On opening day of the season, after umpire John McSherry died at the plate and the game was postponed, Schott told the *Cincinnati Enquirer*, "I feel cheated. This stuff isn't supposed to happen to us here."

Acting commissioner Bud Selig told the media that the ban was the "result of a succession of events," and declared the way Schott ran her team, including her tight-fisted financial control and her nauseous beliefs "quite frankly were not in anyone's best interest." National League president Leonard Coleman pointed out, "The message we wanted to send with this action is that we as a sport are sensitive to diversity and multiculturalism." Selig promised there would be even harsher action if Schott said anything else stupid or racist during her suspension.

This, of course, is the same sport that banned Blacks and Hispanics from its fields for more than a half-century, which didn't allow a Black to be a manager for another three decades, which still bans women, and for which the owners were at least half the reason why there was a strike in 1994.

Marge Schott may be an embarrassment. She says stupid things. She definitely does things to her club that enlightened owners probably wouldn't do. And, she may be a bigot, although she denies it. But, none of that should be sufficient for some owners to ban another owner. If all widget manufacturers decided they didn't like how the president of Acme Widgets ran his company, and wanted him to resign in the best interest of the industry, we would become suspicious of the other owners' reasons for their concern, wondering if a resignation would bring about less competition for the rest of the industry.

An inherent belief in America's capitalistic system is that in the absence of blatant violations of the law, capitalists should run their own companies the way they want. If they make dumb statements, stupid decisions, and exploit their workers, it's tolerated. If they spend wildly and charge excessive business expenses, as long as the board of directors approves, it's acceptable.

However, the supporters of Schott's ban argue that Major League Baseball isn't like any other business—it's *(trumpets and fanfare)* a national pasttime! As a national pasttime, it enjoys a special status—cities float municipal bonds for stadiums then issue eminent domain orders to tear away houses and fields; and the Federal government has waived anti-trust action against a sport that reeks of blatant disregard of the nation's laws against monopolies. And that brings us back to the First Amendment.

"Purists" rightfully claim that the First Amendment applies only to government infringement, and that private enterprise, such as Major League Baseball, can do what it wants. Because baseball willingly accepts extensive government assistance, it should be compelled to adhere to the tenets of the First Amendment. But even if the First Amendment doesn't apply to Major League Baseball, there are still critical social and philosophical issues.

The American revolution was built on a libertarian foundation that all views, even ones that may be blatantly stupid, racist, or obscene, must be heard. In *The Areopagitica* (1644), which Thomas Jefferson freely quoted from, John Milton had written that truth and falsehood must be allowed to compete in a free and open encounter, and that truth will eventually be known. Two centuries later, John Stuart Mill in *On Liberty* (1859) reaffirmed the essential freedom of America when he pointed out, "We can never be sure that the opinion we are endeavoring to stifle is a false opinion; and if we were sure, stifling it would be an evil still." And in 1927, Supreme Court Justice Louis Brandeis in *Whitney v. California* (1927), wrote that "the remedy to be applied [to evil and falsehood] is more [free] speech, not enforced silence."

By silencing Marge Schott, the owners of Major League Baseball, as American as apple pie and hot dogs, have shown how little they respect the foundation that is America.

Free Speech on Death Row

Usually, a five-minute radio commentary about fatherhood wouldn't be controversial. But Temple University decided that anything a death row inmate has to say shouldn't be broadcast on WRTI-FM, its 50,000 watt noncommercial radio station that has a range of more than 100 miles.

Not only did Temple pull the series of 13 commentaries in February 1997, it also pulled the one-hour daily "Democracy Now" program—a magazine-format show that includes news, features, and commentaries—and cancelled all of the Pacifica Network News programs.

George Ingram, Temple's associate vice president for university relations, and the man who ordered the programs cancelled midway through its $6,000 contract, says the decision had been "under consideration for some time," but acknowledges that the abrupt termination was "accelerated" by the commentaries. None of the station's executive staff had input into the decision.

Ingram says the new programming reflects more classical jazz and provides an opportunity for the university "to provide audiences with a window into the academic excellence and enormous educational resources that Temple University offers." Since the radio station is under control of the university's PR office, the university apparently believes airing diverse views isn't the proper image for an urban university, but that using a radio station as a PR vehicle is.

Steve Geimann, president of the 14,000-member Society of Professional Journalists (SPJ), called Temple's action "censorship." George Ingram emphatically states, "we can program what we want to program." Many legal purists agree with Ingram, claiming censorship exists *only* when the government tries to stop publication or broadcast. However, if the news and programming divisions of a station had no voice in the cancellation, as Ingram states, and if Temple University, which received almost $150 million of its $565 million budget from the Commonwealth in 1996–1997, made a decision while concerned about public funding issues and outside pressures, then no other word than "censorship" could apply.

At the center of the controversy is Mumia Abu-Jamal, 42, convicted in June 1982 of killing a Philadelphia police officer. He is on "death row" at the state's Greene County prison, still maintaining his innocence. According to undisputed facts, about 3:50 a.m., December 9, 1981, Philadelphia police officer Daniel Faulkner stopped William Cook for driving the wrong way on a one-way street. Shortly after that, Abu-Jamal, moonlighting as a taxi driver, drove past, saw his brother being beaten by a police officer and stopped. Not long after that, Abu-Jamal was in critical condition at a nearby hospital, having been shot by Faulkner; Faulkner, having been shot four or five times, was dead. It took police about 45 minutes to get Abu-Jamal to a nearby hospital. "They beat me on the street. They beat me in the paddy wagon," says Abu-Jamal.

At the time of his arrest, Abu-Jamal, who had that year won a Peabody award, the most prestigious award in broadcast journalism, was a Philadelphia radio journalist with no criminal convictions, nor any history of violence. In fact, he had been under both FBI and local police surveillance since he was almost 15 years old, the result of having been a member of the Black Panther party, a connection that the prosecution illegally and repeatedly used to discredit him. But, the prosecution couldn't find anyone who claimed Abu-Jamal was anything other than a gentle and caring individual who uses words not physical violence to make his points.

In contrast, the Philadelphia police at that time had a reputation for violence, something Abu-Jamal had frequently reported, and for which Abu-Jamal's attorneys say is why he was singled out for police revenge.

Even Abu-Jamal's "confession" is suspect. Gary Bell, Faulkner's partner, claims he heard Abu-Jamal, lying semiconscious on a hospital gurney following surgery, shout, "I shot the motherfucker and I hope he dies." But Bell didn't report the "confession" until two months later, and only after there were questions about police brutality the night of the murder. A corroborating witness who says she heard the same confession denied knowing Faulkner, until it was pointed out she had coffee with him several times.

The police never ran standard tests to determine if Abu Jamal had recently fired a gun, nor did they run ballistics tests on his own licensed gun. Even a cursory review of trial evidence reveals significant problems with the judicial system.

The prosecution used 11 of its 15 peremptory challenges to exclude Blacks from the jury pool solely because of their race (leaving a jury of 10 Whites and two Blacks in a city that was 40 percent Black), some prosecution "eye witnesses" may never have even been at the scene, those witnesses who were at the scene identified a heavy-set man with an Afro who stood over the officer's body although Abu-Jamal is thin and wore dreadlocks, and information favorable to Abu-Jamal's case was never given to his defense attorneys by the prosecution, a violation of court rules. Witnesses later claimed police and prosecutors harassed and intimidated them, threatening to arrest them if they testified for Abu-Jamal, but would overlook even felonies if they testified for the State.

Further, the judge who assigned Abu-Jamal an inexperienced attorney who constantly asked to be removed from the case, refused sufficient time to adequately prepare a defense, allowed only $150 expenses for investigations, quashed subpoenas for essential defense witnesses, kept a White juror who had said he couldn't be fair to both sides, violated acceptable trial procedures, suppressed conflicting reports, allowed improper cross-examination of defense witnesses, refused to grant a continuance so the defense could bring to court a police officer who was vacation at the time of the trial, and gave faulty instructions to the jury. He also answered questions intended for witnesses, injected his own opinions during testimony, and badgered defense attorneys. In an appeals hearing in October 1996, the judge, the same one who presided over the trial, declared that Abu-Jamal's brother would be arrested on outstanding warrants if he testified, then allowed New Jersey police to enter his courtroom to arrest another defense witness on a charge of having passed a bad check.

That judge is Albert F. Sabo, undersheriff of Philadelphia County and a life member of the Fraternal Order of Police before he was elected to the Court of Common Pleas. In his judicial career, he was "distinguished" only for having handed down more death sentences than any other active judge in the nation, condemning 31 persons, 29 of them black, to death between 1976 and 1991. Appellate and supreme courts have already reversed 11 of those cases.

"Sabo has long since abandoned any pretense of fairness. He's openly hostile to the defense and lavishly liberal with the prosecution," wrote Jill Porter, a Philadelphia *Daily News* columnist. Although she has written against Abu-Jamal's conviction being reversed, she says, "Defense attorneys barely get to voice their objections to testimony before Sabo overrules them with a snarl and threatens to throw them out if they continue to object."

Leonard Weinglass, a nationally-respected attorney who became Abu-Jamal's chief counsel in 1995, argues in a 182-page memorandum of law there were 19 critical Constitutional violations during the original trial.

The Rev. Jesse Jackson called the original trial "a charade, prejudicially carried out by the state for the pursuit of vengeance in the name of justice."

Amnesty International argued that "adverse inferences to [his] past political beliefs and affiliations was . . . used by the prosecution to persuade the jury to impose the death penalty." Citing human rights violations and the myriad inconsistencies of evidence, several countries, churches, organizations, and thousands of individuals have formally petitioned first Gov. Robert Casey and now Gov. Tom Ridge to commute Abu-Jamal's sentence. Among the petitioners are South African president Nelson Mandela, the Southern Christian Leadership Conference, the United Church of Christ, the National Association of Black Journalists, and the National Association of Black Police Officers; former U.S. attorney general Ramsey Clark; former New York City mayor David Dinkins; writers Maya Angelou, E. L. Doctorow, Roger Ebert, Molly Ivans, Maya Lin, Gloria Steinem, William Styron, Alice Walker, and John Edgar Wideman; and actors Ed Asner, Alec Baldwin, Ossie Davis, Mike Farrell, Danny Glover, Whoopie Goldberg, Paul Newman, Tim Robbins, Susan Sarandon, Peter Sellars, and Joanne Woodward. The response of the Fraternal Order of Police was to recommend a boycott against films starring Asner, Farrell, and Goldberg.

Both the state's appellate and supreme courts have rejected Abu-Jamal's appeals. Of the four justices who accepted the lower court rulings, even with their inconsistencies, was one justice who had earlier had a personal confrontation with Abu-Jamal, but didn't excuse himself from the proceedings. Two other justices refused to participate in the decision.

Because of innumerable trial inconsistencies, the Supreme Court's "Keystone Kops" reputation that kept it in headlines on numerous other cases before one justice was eventually impeached, and evidence that Abu-Jamal may have been framed by police who wanted to avenge the death of a comrade by blaming a Black militant who spoke out against police abuse, thousands of Americans have rallied to Abu-Jamal's support.

During his 15 years in prison, Abu-Jamal has continued to write newspaper columns, radio commentaries, and books, usually while being intimidated and harassed by prison officials. The courts have ruled that prisons may discipline disruptive inmates, but they have also ruled that Abu-Jamal was not disruptive, and most restrictions placed upon him were the result of him speaking out about a variety of social issues unrelated to his own case.

In May 1994, National Public Radio (NPR)—which prior to Abu-Jamal's arrest 13 years earlier had broadcast his news reports and commentaries about police–community relations in Philadelphia—abruptly cancelled his commentaries after succumbing to pressure from Philadelphia's Fraternal Order of Police (FOP), a gaggle of conservative radio talk show hosts, and a handful of conservative congressmen. At the time, NPR claimed it cancelled the commentaries because it had "serious misgivings about the appropriateness of using as a commentator a convicted murderer seeking a new trial, particularly since we had not arranged for other commentaries or coverage on the subject of crime, violence, and punishment that provided context or contrasting points of view."

The day after NPR cancelled the commentaries, Senate majority leader Robert Dole, on the floor of the Senate, said he was "pleased that the program was cancelled," and demanded a "closer oversight by the Congress" of the budget for the Corporation for Public Broadcasting which funds NPR.

NPR, says Abu-Jamal, never told him it cancelled his commentaries. (Fifteen months later, NPR's Scott Simon hosted a 30-minute discussion of the case, with comments by Abu-Jamal and several persons associated with the case, but barely mentioned significant trial discrepancies although there was widespread commentary elsewhere.) Temple's Ingram cites the NPR cancellation as one of the reasons why the university also cancelled Abu-Jamal's commentaries. "If that position [to cancel the commentaries] was good enough for NPR," says Ingram, "it was good enough for me." Pacifica, however, had offered the slain officer's family and the FOP air time for their views. They declined.

In February 1995, prison officials suspended Abu-Jamal's family and social visitation rights for 30 days, and barred all media access to him for 90 days for "engaging in the profession of journalism." A five-page disciplinary report, issued June 6, 1995, four days after "law-and-order" Gov. Tom Ridge signed the death warrant, appeared to be retaliation for Abu-Jamal writing *Live from Death Row,* an eloquent series of essays that condemn the law enforcement, judicial, and prison systems for significant civil rights violations. Many of the essays had been scheduled to be broadcast on NPR a year earlier. Among his conclusions were that Latinos and Blacks were victims in 97 percent of all beatings by police officers, and that 93 percent of all police officers in such incidents were White. The book included an afterward by attorney Leonard Weinglass who pointed out innumerable judicial "outrages" at the original trial. Hours after publication, a plane trailing a banner—"Addison-Wesley Supports Cop Killer," hired by Faulkner's widow—flew over the publisher's Massachusetts offices.

The day after he was disciplined, about two months before he was scheduled to be executed, Abu-Jamal wrote, "They want me to die alone—silently. So much do they fear my words that they want me muzzled as they prepare to garrote me."

In a "friend-of-the-court" brief, six national journalism organizations, led by the Society of Professional Journalists, and including the American Society of Newspaper Editors, argued, "Despite incarceration, inmates maintain many of the constitutional rights afforded law abiding citizens including the First Amendment right of freedom of expression." The organizations took no stand on Abu-Jamal's guilt or innocence. In September 1996, a U.S. district judge, after reviewing a recommendation by a federal magistrate, ruled that prison officials violated not only Abu-Jamal's First Amendment rights but his civil rights as well when they opened, photocopied, and widely distributed mail sent to him by his attorneys.

In October 1996, and with the assistance of the Prison Radio Project, Abu-Jamal—shackled and forced to read his scripts that were posted on the other side of a thick plexiglass window—recorded 13 three to five minute segments on a wide range of topics, including Mad Cow Disease, rap music, corporate influence upon the media, the use of tobacco as a drug, racism, and prison reform, but never discussed his own case. Less than two weeks later, the state's Department of Corrections created new rules that forbid journalists from bringing cameras and audio and video equipment into the interview, required them to register as part of a prisoner's 40-person maximum "social list," (not as journalists), and forbid them from being on more than one prisoner's social list. Further, if a journalist wished to talk with a prisoner, the prisoner's allotted time with family and friends was reduced.

David Mendoza, executive director of the National Campaign for Freedom of Expression, says the ban "clearly is intended to silence Abu-Jamal." Six other states have also severely limited prisoner access to the media. California's Department of Corrections in 1996 issued rules that forbid all face-to-face interviews with prisoners, and excluded reporters from bringing even pencils and notepads into the prison. However, the state's Office of Administrative Law has preliminarily disapproved the rules and is awaiting a new submission from the Department of Corrections.

The Supreme Court of the United States, affirming First Amendment freedoms, has ruled that "reasonable and effective means of communication [from and to inmates must] remain open, and no discrimination in terms of content be involved." Pennsylvania's Department of Corrections appears to have violated that Supreme Court ruling.

"We went ahead with the commentaries," says Dan Coughlin, "Democracy Now" producer, "because we wanted to take a stand against growing restrictions on media access to prisoners, and to affirm the right of prisoners to talk with the media and to the public." But there was a third reason—"they were just good commentaries."

Although Temple cancelled an alternative view, apparently listeners of the 24 stations that didn't cancel the programs— including those in New York, Los Angeles, and Washington, D.C.— had no problem with the commentaries. Coughlin says the response has been "8 to 1" in favor of the commentaries.

The PEN American Center, an organization of writers and editors, argued that Abu-Jamal's work "and that of other inmates like him . . . has had enormous value, both in its own right as literature, and insofar as it has alerted audiences to conditions prevailing in our country's jails. Were this means of communication to be broken, prisons would become even more than they are already[,] an opaque and forgotten part of our society, a place where living conditions would deteriorate still further without provoking any public concern."

Reflecting the views of Thomas Jefferson, author of the Declaration of Independence, and James Madison, principal author of the Constitution, SPJ president Steve Geimann argues, "In our American democracy, broadcasters and news organizations seek to offer numerous points of view. Our democracy is strong because we protect everyone's right of free speech, even those whose views we may find objectionable or discomforting."

At Temple University, the departments of journalism, broadcasting, history, philosophy, political science, and religion all teach about the First Amendment and the necessity for all views, even controversial ones spoken by controversial individuals, to be heard. Students learn that denying freedom of speech to others often means we are afraid to face the truth. The university administration has demonstrated to its students, and to the world, that it is uncomfortable with the philosophy that shaped our democracy.

An Obscene Story

Throughout the country, people are creating barriers to what they believe is obscene, trying to ban everything from rap records and music videos to works of literature, newspaper columns, and museum art. Even the courts have become involved, changing definitions as quickly as chorus girls change costumes. Nevertheless, the recent upsurge in obscenity legislation and prosecution had to begin somewhere.

By the time it ended, Sidney Thornacre, a mild-mannered stock clerk from Driven Snow, Pennsylvania, was elected President of the United States without opposition and on a 1-0 vote. It was 1-0 in the popular vote and 1-0 in the electoral college, the first time that anyone was elected president unanimously. How President Thornacre was elected is an inspiration to all people throughout the world.

It all began when the Driven Snow city council decided there had to be laws against obscenity. But the Supreme Court had long ago determined that for laws to be fair, they had to be spelled out—in painstakingly exact detail. According to the Supreme Court, it wasn't good enough just to say that obscenity was bad, the laws had to specify just what was bad.

So, the City Council read the appropriate books and magazines, watched the appropriate television shows and movies, looked into the Internet, and spelled out a series of ordinances so explicit they even made Hugh Hefner blush.

Naturally, the laws themselves were obscene and all members

of the city council were sent to jail for having written them. Afterall, whoever is a part of obscenity must be punished. And that's how the district attorney and his entire staff, who had to first read the ordinances to determine what it was they were prosecuting, were prosecuted and sent to jail.

One after another, the prosecutors became the prosecuted. Although many recognized what would ultimately happen, they had a duty to perform. After prosecuting the guilty for reading the obscenity statutes, they and the jurors willingly accepted their own prosecution. America's sense of family values had to be preserved. Soon, the entire population of Driven Snow was in jail, victims of rampant obscenity.

From Driven Snow, it spread throughout the rest of the country, every village, every state. And then it happened—something everyone feared but no one expected. The president of the United States, hoping to stop the problem, read the ordinance, admitted guilt, then resigned, leaving the country without a president or government—the Congress had been among the first ones to read the ordinance.

And that's how Sidney Thornacre, the only person in the country who hadn't read the ordinance, applied for the Presidency. On that fateful day, he alone went to his precinct polling place—where he was precinct captain, judge, poll watcher, and election counter—and cast his lone vote. Then, he made that vote official by going to the nation's capital. As the country's only member of the electoral college, he cast a unanimous vote for himself for president.

On a wall in the Oval Office, Sidney Thornacre—president of the United States, commander in chief of the Armed Forces, secretary and staff of all the cabinet departments, chief justice of the United States, lone member of Congress and House janitor—has a framed copy of the antiobscenity ordinance—with appropriate sections blacked out.

Of Matrons and Movies

Three middle-aged women, inhibited but longing to find out what the new morality was all about, snuck out of their homes early one afternoon and went to a movie.

The movie was shot in Sweden, but the subtitles were in English. Not many in the audience, other than the three ladies and a small group of cinema students, really cared what the subtitles said.

"They didn't tell us it was a foreign film," protested the first lady.

"I think they're talking Danish. You know how the Danes are," explained the second lady.

The third lady just giggled.

The movie was about a young girl who believed she was frigid. A rather frightening experience for a 14-year-old. So, she went to a psychologist for help. Soon, the psychologist and the girl were in bed together.

"Horrible!" cried out the first woman.

"Disgusting!" protested the second woman.

The third woman just giggled.

The girl, "searching to find herself," traveled to Germany where she met a young student. The two of them did a lot of studying together.

"It's the Supreme Court and its radical rules!" declared the first woman.

"It should have been banned!" declared the second woman. The third woman didn't declare anything. She was too busy watching the action on the screen.

However, this was a well-filmed movie with good color and adequate acting. By Supreme Court standards, it was "socially redeeming."

In Italy, the young girl met a fisherman and in Spain, she met a poet and a prostitute.

"I won't let my family see this!" huffed the first woman loud enough to disturb the other 18 movie watchers.

"Totally shameful," huffed the second woman.

The third woman huffed nothing. It's hard to huff when you're giggling.

After Spain came France. By now, the young girl had an armful of books she had collected throughout the Continent. She had collected the works of Heine, the *Story of Raphael,* and a libretto from *Faust.*

"See! She's adding to her collection of dirty books," snickered the first woman.

In France, there was a vulgar show in a respectable-looking nightclub. The young girl became ill when two women wrestlers began rolling around in the mud. But when the young girl left, she accidentally ran into the city's most notorious district. Frightened, she ran until she bumped into a well-dressed, respectable looking, well-mannered gentleman who offered to take her away from the sordid life. They left in his Rolls-Royce. "He'll save her!" joyfully proclaimed the first woman.

"He's so respectable. Maybe that's the message," happily proclaimed the second woman.

The third woman was having trouble controlling her laughter. The man was a sadomasochist. Looks are deceiving.

"Shocking!" cried out the first woman.

"Disgusting!" cried out the second woman.

The third woman just—yeah—giggled, but it may have had nothing to do with the film and everything to do with her companions.

But the first woman who said "Shocking!" and the second woman who said "Disgusting!" and the third woman who giggled, stayed until the end of the film.

Later, the woman who giggled her way through the girl's European adventures led a citizen's protest against what she thought were pornographic videos at a local store.

Playing the University Grantsmanship Game

You're probably not going to believe this, but a scientific foundation once awarded a $5,000 research grant to a behavioral scientist to study the television viewing habits of cats. The reasoning behind the grant, said the society's spokesman with not even a chuckle, is that animals, especially cats, react to voice and picture patterns on the television screen, although they don't comprehend what is taking place. The spokesman even went so far as to suggest that cats prefer to watch only good television programs and shun the poor ones.

While the officers of the society aren't going to have many

problems—all they have to do is wait patiently for the report and try to act serious about the whole thing—the poor media researcher, eager for tenure and promotion, is likely to be burdened with uncountable problems.

The researcher, a portable laptop computer loaded with statistical programs strapped around his shoulder, timidly approaches the cat.

"Hey, man, what are you doing in my sandbox?"

"Sorry. I'm your average ordinary university media behavioral research scientist, and I've come to interview you about what television programs you watch."

"You feeling all right? Humidity not too high?"

"No, honest now, cat, I've really come to find out what you like on Television. I bet you watch cartoons. Felix the Cat, Krazy Kat, and Fritz the Cat!" The cat yawned, so the researcher tried another direction. "You scout the opposition! Lassie? Rin-Tin-Tin?"

By now, the cat was convinced the researcher was a few numbers short of a full equation, but the researcher was persistent. "How about comedies? Everyone loves sitcoms!"

"Cats aren't everyone."

"It's adventure you like!" beamed the professor. "Maybe a jungle show with lions?"

"Only if the diet is media researchers."

"Drama? Science fiction? Star Trek is all over the tube. Surely, you've seen at least one episode!"

"You're spaced out," said the cat, unsheathing his claws.

"I know!" shouted the professor, "you're a socially-aware cat. You watch, '60 Minutes,' '20/20,' and 'Nightline!'"

"You're loony," the cat replied, waiting for a chance to dial 911 to ask the Media Researcher Unit at the state hospital to make a house call. "I don't watch TV."

"But you've just got to watch television. It's the American way!"

"Look, man, like I've been trying to tell you, none of us cats watch television!"

"*None* of you?" came the startled reply of the media researcher, his Ph.D. dripping with an unused grant. "Then what's the TV doing by the couch?"

"Oh, *that*," grinned the cat, "I like to sharpen my nails; that's the only good piece of wood I can find. It's about all that it's good for."

"Look, cat," the researcher pleaded, "I've got this really neat $5,000 grant to find out what cats watch on television. I can get a publication credit and . . ." The researcher didn't even finish his sentence before the cat's bright green eyes flickered.

"You mean some nuts gave an even bigger nut 5,000 bucks to interview cats to find out what we watch on the scratching post?" And then, the cat began to think. "Let's see, now. He gets $5,000 to interview cats. And, after all, I *am* the most important part of the study." He decided it was only right for him to help. "Look, Prof, like I said, none of us cats watch television. But, I'll tell you what I'll do. You keep asking questions. I keep denying them. You're bound to miss at least one or two shows. If I can't deny I don't watch what you don't ask me, who'll be the wiser?"

The media researcher didn't have any idea what the cat said, but it sounded like a plan to him and just as understandable as what media researchers write. So, once again this media researcher was happy. His career wasn't ruined. There would be a publication credit. There would be tenure and promotion.

In an exclusive section of some American city, there walks a very happy professor . . . and a cat with a $5,000 bankroll.

Cellular Research

People who drive and use cellular phones at the same time have a greater risk of running red lights, stop signs, and getting into accidents than do people who concentrate on their driving, according to a professor at the Rochester Institute of Technology. His research reveals that drivers with a cell phone run a 34 percent higher risk of being in an accident. If they use the phone, light a cigarette, and read the morning paper on the way to work along Pennsylvania state highways, they—well, actually, along state roads they'd probably fall into a pothole before running into another car.

In rebuttal to the professor, the Cellular Telecommunications Industry Association (CTIA)—which for all I know is a clandestine branch of government—claimed that not only was the study flawed, but that fully-charged cell phones don't cause accidents, people cause accidents.

I began to wonder what else is out there we might not know if grant-governed researchers didn't uncover the facts of life. For instance . . .

During the past three decades, psychologists, sociologists, psychiatrists, educators, and "mass communicologists" have secured about $100 million in funding to conduct more than 1,000 studies to determine the effects of violence on children.

The results seem to indicate that violent children who watch violent cartoons tend to become violent, whereas nonviolent children who watch nonviolent cartoons tend to fall asleep a lot. Possibly the latest research might prove that violent criminals who get V-chips implanted within their brains by second year medical residents tend to have more headaches than those who take aspirin.

Two researchers at the University of Wisconsin, armed with a grant, determined that telephones are used to get gossip and news, as well as for relaxation and entertainment. That, of course, is a step beyond the "media behavioral" research scientist who got a grant to watch the television viewing habits of cats.

Somewhere at this very moment, a team of "mass communicologists" is probably conducting a content analysis of the newspapers of western Montana between 1931 and 1935. From three tons of statistical analysis, they'll conclude that there is a correlation between the number of ads in a newspaper and the number of pages. Their 25-page article will be immediately accepted by *Journalism and Mass Communications Quarterly*, the industry's Bible of useless information.

Now, since honesty is its own punishment, I must admit that it's true I have also done some research in the past few years. Among my startling conclusions have been the following . . .

Smoking is bad for your health, especially among middle-age women who shove lighted filter-tip cigarettes into their ears. Smoking, however, is good for the magazine and TV ad departments.

Most people who wear glasses don't have 20/20 vision. Neither do most Washington beltway columnists who not only think they can see into our lives and tell us what we're thinking, but can predict who we'll vote for.

People who listen to Rush Limbaugh have a higher proportion of radios than homes in which the entire family is deaf. However, the deaf people are happier with not being able to hear people tell them about Rush.

People who watch Ricki Lake and Jenny Jones also watch "The Wizard of Oz" and cheer for the scarecrow who's searching for a brain.

And speaking of people with no brains . . . Preliminary research indicates that the only case of a Chief Executive Officer (CEO), getting fired for incompetence was one who told the stockholders they would have to take a smaller profit next year since he was increasing worker salaries and benefits, then hiring more workers to improve the quality of the product. Come to think of it, this may be the only case of finding a CEO *with* a brain.

Most politicians proclaim they're for the working class. Then, after the TV cameras are gone, they go to their country club and agree with their CEO dinner companions that the biggest problem in America is the demands from the working class.

Finally, I haven't done any research in this area, but it would be worth looking into. Remember all those accidents with cell phones? If insurance companies force higher rates on certain classes of people, including men, unmarried drivers, drivers under the age of 25, and those who live in "high accident areas," whether they're safe drivers, shouldn't the companies raise the rates for people who have cell phones? Or, would that cause the cell-for-brains insurance industry to pay more for their own insurance?

A Nation of Polls and Predictions

It was an ugly spring day, but there was hope. Little suns dotted the TV weather map for the next three days, and we were to expect picnic weather.

It could have been true—if the picnic were held inside a heated firehall. Some stations give us seven-day forecasts, as if they think we actually place any credibility in a seven-day forecast when the twelve-hour forecast isn't accurate.

Several months earlier, the weather forecasters traced the history of snow, then brightly informed us that our region was only at the fringe of the upcoming blizzard. The next day, we shoveled 18 inches of white fringe.

A couple of weeks after the Great Blizzard of January 1996, we were told to prepare for anywhere from four to ten inches of snow. The next day, a few lonely snowflakes drifted aimlessly, then evaporated.

We expect weather people to be wrong. They can't help it. In weather school, their professors give them a 60 percent chance of getting an "A," and they end up with a "C," accompanied by a discussion of the history of the highs and lows for that grading period.

Most sportswriters, however, seem to be happy if they guess right half the time. We are subjected to thumbnail pictures of the newspaper's sportswriters, a couple of community residents and 15 column inches of their predictions for several of the weekend high school, college, and pro games.

It's even worse on television. The sportscasters think they should tell us not only their predictions, but also the Las Vegas odds. The reality, however, is they even bungle the scores after the game is played.

We have become a nation of polls and predictions. During the past decade, the news media have changed their role of presenting, analyzing, and interpreting information to predicting what may or may not happen. Reporters who will soon vote in only their second general election now write detailed analyses and predictions of the upcoming elections. We no longer have a need to vote because the media tell us who will win.

Polls now dominate news coverage, and politicians read them as religiously as churches have bingo games, afraid to make decisions without being told what to think. The news no longer is what the candidates are doing, but what other people think of the candidates and the candidates' reactions to the polls. Naturally, our follow-the-sheep nation supports those ahead in the polls. In a convoluted Mobius strip of logic, the media then spend more of their news coverage devoted to people who are ahead in the polls. Unless you're billionaires Ross Perot and Steve Forbes, if you have a brilliant and workable plan for the future of America but are a "third party" candidate or an independent, you get minimal coverage. After all, the polls and predictions proved you don't have a chance of winning, so why should the media waste time and space?

The media also have their own "secret" polls, designed just for election night. In a race for ratings, the media, especially the TV networks, once tried to be the first to predict a winner, based on what they believed was "scientific" analysis of the vote—"With 3 percent of the vote counted, WAFU-TV predicts . . . " When voters, politicians, and advertisers said the early predictions weren't fair—people might change their votes to match the predictions—the networks decided to wait until the polls closed in the East before predicting winners, leaving only about 100 million Americans disenfranchised in national races.

But, the "scientific" predictions aren't necessarily right. In 1948, the *Chicago Tribune* declared Thomas Dewey the winner; Harry Truman had to wait until all the votes were counted until he could continue his presidency. Late election night, November 4, 1996, the Associated Press finally predicted the winners of the races for Pennsylvania attorney general and auditor general. The next morning, the two AP "winners" were losers.

Newspaper editors with nothing better to do with their lives send out a reporter and photographer to do "Person on the Street" interviews. The question of the day to a half dozen people who can't even name their own congressman is "Do you think President Clinton is guilty in Watergate?" As any sophomore math major knows, these polls are unscientific and useless. But, circulation increases another dozen or so that day as relatives buy an extra copy of the paper.

TV polls are even more insidious. For a buck—split between the phone company and the station—you call a 900 number during the 6 o'clock newscast, answer a yes or no question, and hear the results at 11. However, we don't know how many fools wasted a buck, if most of them were rich dowagers with the time and money to call in a dozen times, friends or enemies of a particular candidate or issue, or 13-year-old pubescents who thought by calling the 900 number they'd hear a TV anchor talk dirty to them.

Maybe, it's time the rest of us talk dirty to some of the media.

Withdrawing From an O.J. Overdose

The abrupt end of "Days of Our O.J." in October 1995 caught Americans by surprise, leaving them confused, unable to function, and whining that three hours were long enough for a football game but not acceptable for a jury's deliberation.

Also in withdrawal are the media. More than 1,000 reporters, cramped into the parking lot known as Camp O.J., were credentialed to cover the trial. Thousands more had some part in O.J. coverage; CNN alone devoted more than 600 hours, and 425 reporters and commentators, to the trial. The other networks devoted more time to the case than any other story, including the Oklahoma bombing, floods in the Southeast, and the ethnic slaughter in Bosnia.

Unable to quit cold turkey, the media desperately milked the story of The Juice. Within minutes of the verdict, it seemed as if every reporter in L.A. bought ladders, just so they could peer into O.J.'s Brentwood yard and continue to give the people their daily dose of O.J. in the form of all the gossip that's fit to be smeared.

Newspaper editors, who have been blaming the "newsprint

crisis" for increased subscription costs and fewer newspaper pages, continued to lay off reporters, but always made sure there was sufficient room in the paper for O.J. coverage. After the verdict, they published summaries of every hour of testimony, and what the reporters on ladders really saw in Brentwood, with interminable sidebar opinions of everyone who ever watched a football game or drove a rental car and, therefore, absolutely knew whether O.J. was guilty.

But the most tragic consequence of the ending of the trial is that most of the nation's lawyers are now unemployed. If they weren't working for the prosecution or the defense, they were commentators for the TV networks.

Whenever TV devotes more than 90 seconds to any story, it hires "expert" commentators. During the Gulf War, the networks provided full employment to retired colonels and generals. This time, it was lawyers. The commentators, like most TV anchors, were White, college educated, TV-quality clean-shaven handsome and makeup beautiful, and upper middle class or upper class. Thus, a typical day's news coverage included lengthy snippets from the trial, reporters' comments, reporters talking to each other for their reactions, and reporters talking to lawyers who believed it was their sacred duty to uncover every mole on the face of the trial, yet missed the greater body of criminal justice issues.

The media's failure to recognize and hire others who would have knowledge about crime in America is symptomatic of the media's fetish with what they believe are the "experts." It's no different when two people come into a news room—a well-groomed Suit with a press release about some owner's nephew getting a promotion, and a bag lady with information about police abuse of the elderly. Does anyone doubt which one the reporters will talk to first—assuming Security hasn't thrown the bag lady out already?

Also missing while the media were covering the "trial of the century" was coverage of thousands of murders that happened, and that prosecutors often plea-bargained justice in order to clear the overburdened court calendars, while failing to even acknowledge the victim's families. Also overlooked is that most defendants can't afford "dream team" representation, and receive public defenders who are only a few years out of law school and whose budgets barely cover legal pads. Would it have been too much of a burden for the media to devote a few hours to probing the quality of justice in America when the defendant isn't a millionaire celebrity?

Should the media decide to spend time covering the greater social issues instead of trying to justify themselves by coming up with 100 reasons why the O.J. trial changed civilization, it might look into doing extended coverage of the issues of spousal abuse, the homeless, the health care crisis, street crime, the burgeoning right-wing survivalist and militia movements, teenage alcohol and drug abuse, the economy, America's political process, and the consequences of catastrophic fires, floods, and hurricanes.

The media also overlook society's achievements. It might be nice if the media give as much coverage to the lives of volunteers for the nation's social service agencies as they did for the exploits of $400-an-hour lawyers.

In response, the media titans say they are giving the people what they want, that they are merely feeding the public's frenzy for the sensational. But by devoting the top five minutes of the 6:30 p.m. newscast to O.J., and only 90 seconds to floods in the Florida panhandle, or giving O.J. a six-column newspaper banner and the Bosnian holocaust a two-column headline beneath the fold, the media have told us what they think is important—or what they think the public thinks is important—and we somehow believe them because it's easier for them, and us, to ignore the greater issues. Since the people aren't complaining, the media assume that's what the people want.

When the media increase their coverage of all society instead of one aberration, then maybe they can devote a few minutes or column inches to the celebrity crime scene.

Oh, Joy—O.J. Every Day

Ratings the night the TV networks juggled coverage of the president's State of the Union address and the civil trial verdict against O.J. Simpson, and how newspapers played the two stories the next morning, proved Americans preferred hearing about a "preponderance of guilt" double murderer who was found to be "not guilty but liable" than what the president said that affects 260 million Americans and much of the world.

In a parallel universe that same day, Martha Stewart—owned by Time Warner and once named by a fawning *TIME* magazine as one of America's 25 most influential people—bought out much of Time Warner's stock in Martha Stewart Enterprises, valued about $200 million.

Faced by having to pay a $33.5 million judgment, O.J. Simpson needs to raise money. To guarantee her investment in herself, Martha Stewart needs a jolt of electricity. It seems so simple—bring on the Juice who could give her that shock, then appoint him vice president of the newly-created Fabrication Division.

The cornerstone of Martha's one-subject media empire is the print media. Her column appears in 200 newspapers. With O.J. as a co-writer, she'd easily get the other 1,300 newspapers to print her column. They have already printed enough about O.J. to papier mâché Mt. Rushmore.

The *Martha Stewart Living* magazine goes to 1.5 million subscribers; O.J.'s contribution to the empire could be a monthly magazine, *O.J. Living but Two Others Aren't*.

Martha writes books. O.J. earned $1 million for his first book, a brilliant work of fiction written while in jail. Since then, prosecutors, defense lawyers, detectives, relatives of the deceased, friends, ex-girlfriends, wanna-be journalists, and sun-bleached hangers-on whose prose fit literature as badly as the glove fit at the first trial, have all become millionaires. O.J.'s sequel could pay off not only the civil trial judgment, but also a chunk of the national debt.

Martha is also entrenched in the TV media. Americans would give her "Today" segments a 100 percent share of the morning ratings to watch O.J. cut out then decoupage blonde-hair, blue-eyed paper dolls. Martha might even copyright the O.J. name and image, then launch the O.J. Network—"all O.J., all the time."

Martha plans to do more TV specials. Who else could be her co-star but O.J.? Among O.J.'s previous action-adventure films have been *Killer Force* and *A Killing Affair*. With his acting skills having improved significantly over the past three years, it's time for him to finish that TV deal to star as a Navy Seal who moonlights as an interior decorator. He could even save the producers costs by providing his own black cap and commando knife.

O.J. owns a fully-mortgaged house in Brentwood. What's another house to Martha who owns two houses, a six-acre farm in an affluent part of Connecticut, and a Manhattan condo? She buys the Rockingham house, then sets up tours. Both are expert redecorators—she for the 10,000 Americans who can afford her ideas, he for juries who might wish a rest break. Like the hospitable Democrats who tried to sell the White House, O.J. could charge $50,000 for people to have coffee with him. For $100,000, they get a sleep-over, complete with Martha Stewart seminars on everything from how to cover up blood spots to how to wear clothes that fit.

Martha's hobby is late-night flashlight gardening. O.J. used a flashlight to walk through his garden one night. It's a perfect fit—a package of gloves, flashlights, and seeds of evidence, sold through the Martha by Mail division.

Martha advises people to take a Polaroid shot of every pair of shoes they own, then paste that picture onto the shoe box for easy identification. Had O.J. listened to her advice, he'd have remembered if he owned any "ugly-ass" pair of shoes. Perhaps, an O.J. Photo Service could be added to Martha Stewart Enterprises.

O.J. says a picture of a bruised and battered Nicole was just a case of he and his wife experimenting with Halloween makeup. Martha is on the board of directors of Revlon which could make millions with the Battered Woman Makeup Kit.

Martha gives advice about traveling—"for that nice weekend vacation, try climbing Mt. Kilimanjaro." O.J. could present his slant to travel by discussing ways to navigate urban freeways, and how to lighten luggage while waiting in an airport.

Just about the only medium Martha hasn't tapped are compact disks (CDs). She believes CDs "are dead" because they are "too expensive and transitional." But, an O.J. CD could bring millions. Among his haunting ballads could be "Stranglers in the Night," "Slicing Up Is Hard to Do," and that ever-popular, "Mack the Knife." Martha could even arrange and cater a worldwide "O.J. Means Juice" tour, cosponsored by the nation's electric companies, Sunkist, and Bowie Knives, guaranteed to neatly slice any orange. When O.J.'s singing fame dies as quickly as an innocent bystander on a dark street, he could squeeze a few more million by doing late night TV infomercials.

Finally, Americans love horror and thrillers, whether books, movies, or amusement parks. What could be more frightening than a chain of Martha and O.J. tastefully decorated haunted houses?

Reel Violence

It was yet another stop on the book promotion trail, this time in Philadelphia on a "big time" talk show with a "big name" star. The host was friendly, and discussed my background and the book, a history of animated cartoons, although like most hosts she hadn't read any of it.

"Let's get started by finding out what your favorite cartoon show is," she asked. Five years later, I might have added "Pinky and the Brain," "Freakazoid," "Earthworm Jim," and the "Animaniacs" series, excellent cartoons which had helped bring an end of the spiral into mediocrity. But, at the time she asked the question, most TV cartoons were as creative as cold toast.

"I'm partial to the Roadrunner and Coyote series," I said, then briefly explained how the cartoons, with brilliant writing by Mike Maltese and directing by Chuck Jones, were classic throw-backs to some of the best silent physical comedies of the 1910s and 1920s. I expected an equally soft follow-up question. It came loaded with an explosive not even the Acme Co., the Coyote's supplier, could produce.

"There really is too much violence in cartoons, isn't there?" she rhetorically stated, then spent two minutes explaining her views.

"Actually," I said when she finally had to breathe, "the physical violence in cartoons is completely different from what you see in live action or even in cartoons with human subjects." I got a couple of more sentences in when she came back, expounding the belief that cartoon violence directly leads to violence in real life, and that the studios and networks needed to be more responsible. Perhaps the Industry should establish a commission to review films and cartoons, she suggested.

Keeping my composure, I politely explained that the basis of all literature is conflict, and that most three-year-olds know the difference between cartoon violence and real violence, and if they don't, then parents should learn how to change the channels.

Later, I was able to sneak in my opinion that it was absurd when network television, scared by lobbyists, had temporarily pulled Bugs Bunny cartoons from the air because they didn't think Elmer Fudd should be blasting rabbits and ducks. She came right back at me by pretentiously quoting a research study to support her views, took a triumphant breath, and awaited what she thought would be my feeble response.

Fifteen minutes into what I thought was a mugging—I had wanted to talk about bunnies and tweety birds—I fired back. "I'm well aware of that study," I said, then began to cite other studies that revealed either a slightly negative correlation or no correlation at all between cartoon violence and human action.

"Let's go to the phones," she said. For the most part, the audience asked interesting questions, with the host usually spending more time in presenting her views than I did in answering audience questions. Then, abruptly, she mellowed. "You certainly have a wealth of knowledge," she cooed. "I was wondering, do you have a favorite cartoon show?" Apparently, since I didn't answer correctly the first time, I got another chance.

"Rocky and Bullwinkle," I replied, explaining that Jay Ward's creation probably had the sharpest satire of all television shows. I was going to elaborate when she again explained that the plotting done by Boris and Natasha to the Moose and Squirrel couldn't be very healthy for impressionable minds.

"I believe some studies show that cartoons may affect persons already prone to violence," I said, "but have no effect on persons who are not themselves violent." Commercials saved me from her response.

Back on air, she again introduced me and cited the book I was huckstering. "Let's go to the phones," she said again, and again the audience was more interested in the origin of cartoons and how they're made. Five minutes before the hour, it was time to close it up, but not before one more question.

"By the way, one other thing before you leave," she asked, "what's your favorite cartoon show?"

"This time I was determined to get it right. "Beany and Cecil?" I asked hesitantly. When she said nothing, I briefly discussed the 1950s cartoon show created by Bob Clampett who had been one of the Warner Bros. pioneer directors. "I just loved all the puns and double entendres," I said, awaiting her response that cartoons were responsible for the moral breakdown of the American family, and that the world was at risk because of the conflict between Dishonest John and his targets Beany Boy and Cecil the Seasick Sea Serpent. But, she didn't. All she said was, "That's nice," thanked me for showing up, again mentioned the book, and went to another set of commercials.

I left the studio convinced I was yet another batch of chum for talk-show sharks—and wondering if I would ever get my favorite cartoon show right.

Escalating an American Paranoia

Worried that a gang of thieves will break into your house, and that your dinky 9 mm. won't have enough firepower to stop them from taking your family's jewels? What if an alien nation launched an invasion, and your .357 Magnum liquified in your hands? How about those tank-sized rats in the basement who frightened your pet lion—or the moles who are building a city in your back yard and are planning to vote you out of office?

Fortunately, there's a solution. Get Rhino-Ammo, the "defensive" hyper-destructive hollow-nose bullets that fragment into hundreds of razor-like pieces within the body. "The beauty behind it is that it makes an incredible wound," David Keen, owner of the Florida-based Signature Products, told the media the last week of 1994. "They're going to die," he said. "There's no way to stop the bleeding. I don't care where it hits. They're going down for good." The package for Rhino-Ammo proclaims, "the wound channel is catastrophic. . . . Death is nearly instantaneous."

A second bullet, the Black Rhino, even more destructive, was designed to penetrate body armor, the kind police officers and some criminals wear. To allay Americans' fears, Keen promised that the Black Rhino would be sold "only to the right people," the 400,000 law enforcement officers and the 275,000 federally-licensed gun dealers. If the wrong people get the bullets, it's only because the "right" people gave it to them, Keen said.

In a nation in which 1.1 million violent crimes were committed with a gun the year Rhino bullets were developed, and there were only 80,000 instances of the use of guns for self-defense, according to the Department of Justice, it's reassuring that only the "good guys" will get the bullets.

Federal laws prohibit the manufacture of "cop killer bullets," made of special metals, plastics, or coated with teflon. However, these bullets don't fall under these regulations because Keen claims they're not made of the prohibited materials.

The story of the Black Rhino began when Keen first fed it to his hometown newspaper, the *Huntsville Times*. After several other publications, including the *National Enquirer,* turned it down, Keen sent samples and test data to *Newsweek* when it expressed an interest in the story. The news brief in the December

19, 1994, issue opened with a description of what the bullets were likely to do, based on Keen's claims on the package, then quoted an unnamed federal narcotics agent—"they'll be used against the good guys."

The Associated Press quickly picked up the story, leading its December 27 coverage with an ominous message—"Two bullets more deadly than those used in the Long Island Rail Road massacre last year are about to be sold, despite fierce opposition from gun control advocates and police."

Within hours, most of the news media reported the latest "advance" in firepower, causing panic among the public, angry charges against Keen by the nation's police forces, and proposed federal legislation to ban "cop-killer" bullets, all reported by the national media.

The next day, Keen went on NBC-TV's "Today" show to declare he was temporarily suspending production of the Black Rhino, but was continuing with plans to distribute the "less deadly" Rhino ammo.

And then ABC's "Nightline" checked out Keen's claims, and determined that the Rhinos it tested were no more devastating than an average hollow-nose bullet, devastating enough but not "catastrophic." As for the Black Rhino, "Nightline" said it couldn't confirm that such an armor-piercing bullet even existed.

The news media now turned to claim the bullets were really a hoax. Keen's response was that the bullet "Nightline" had was a "work-up" load Rhino, and not the actual bullets.

In its February 1995 issue, the *American Journalism Review* reported that Keen was "shooting blanks," and that the bullets were "too bad to be true." Keen says the *AJR* review was based solely on other articles and not on an analysis of the facts. "They slammed us," he says, bitterly claiming, "Nobody [in the media] lied to us more than *AJR*" in getting the story.

But, Keen faced attacks from an even deadlier foe. The National Rifle Association (NRA), knowing the public was irritable at widespread violence in America, had claimed, almost from the day of the Rhino's nationwide disclosure, that the bullets were a hoax, certainly no more devastating than anything else on the market. Furthermore, the NRA also put the word out that Keen himself was a member—or at least a plant—of Handgun Control, Inc., whose purpose was meant to stir public fears about guns so they would support handgun registration.

"The only friendship I'm going to have is the NRA," Keen said, "and I've made an enemy that's very dangerous." Keen also claimed, "I am more frightened by the NRA than the death threats I have received." Three months after the controversy began, Keen simply said, "It's been a very bizarre three months in my life." But it wasn't yet over.

That spring, *Handgun* magazine conducted tests revealing that the .45 Rhino, now renamed the Razor, left a wound channel 5 inches wide and $7\frac{1}{2}$ inches long in a test against ordnance jelly. Jan Libourel, editor of the 180,000-circulation magazine, says the bullets, although not as catastrophic as what Keen claimed, were nevertheless more deadly than almost all other bullets on the market. However, critics point out that ordnance jelly, while often used to simulate humans, still is not human, and that not only was the magazine the "lapdog of the manufacturers," the magazine's "political agenda" was suspect.

Then in August, eight months after its first report of the catastrophic effect of the Rhinos, the AP distributed an article that tended to confirm the *Handgun* report. The AP had contracted with the H.P. White Laboratory to test the Razor against three other high-tech 9 mm. bullets. Both the Razor and Glaser bullets, each of them composed of lead pellets within a plastic-filled shell, left almost identical wounds when fired into ordnance jelly. All four bullets—Razor, Glaser, MagSafe, and Federal—were deadlier than whatever else was available to civilians, but none could penetrate body armor. However, the laboratory cautioned that because the Razor and Glaser bullets require high gun pressures, the risk "is that it could damage your gun or cause it to blow up."

In order to get a story, says Keen, the media "pit one group against the other," with the controversy partially stirred by "information merchants eager for sensational headlines," but who didn't check out the truth.

Maybe Keen's original claims were all hype by a company that was trying to switch in a post–Cold War era from making protective coatings for the Stealth aircraft to a consumer-based industry. Maybe Keen really does have a secret bullet—that Black Rhino he took out of production at the end of 1994—that is more devastating than anything else on the market. Whatever the truth is, the Rhino stirred America's fears, and the media were right there to tell us the bullet existed—or didn't exist—or that it may exist. Either way, the story played well in headlines and the evening news for about two weeks, then died while other claims or hoaxes moved to the media's short attention span.

Labels of Violence

On a hot, muggy summer day, with my brain waves set on pause, I decided it was time to check out the low prices at the nearby air-conditioned discount department store.

Among Barbie dolls and Mutant Ninja Turtles were two aisles of fake guns, everything from 98 cent plastic water pistols to a Super Soaker 100 "for the serious water gun enthusiast."

Cap pistols are as popular today as when they were first invented in the late 19th century. For $1.97, any kid can own a black 12-shot ring cap gun; extra caps are only 87 cents. If that model doesn't appeal to everyone, there's a dozen more that might, and none cost more than five bucks.

For those who want to play "cops 'n' robbers," for under four bucks each are copies of 9-mm. auto-power chargers pistols, an assortment of .22 short-barrel Saturday night specials, a clip-loaded dart gun, and a silver-plated die-cast metal repeater pistol that the package proclaims is "recommended for ages 4 and over." Of course, just to make sure the "good guys" always have the edge, there's an assortment of handcuffs, police batons, tin police badges, and Dick Tracy wrist radios.

For the Old West historians among the bubble gum set, there are bow-and-arrow sets and replicas of the Colt .45, advertised in newly-packaged die-cast metal as the "widow maker," and several "Old West" supershot rifles that white men thought Indians called "sticks that pour fire," but which the Indians knew were the weapons of their own genocide.

Future GI Joes, inundated by nonstop Saturday morning TV watching, can pick from an assortment of almost every weapon of war except for full-scale Cruise missiles, and even these might be on some kindly old Gepetto's work bench almost ready for Christmas delivery.

For those with more immediate needs, there's water balloon grenades, X-1 recoil blasters, X-2 Nitro Blasters "with a thunderous sound," Whistle Missile Skybolts, machine lasers, and a pulsating Fazer II with a vibrating handle and a box that begs children to "try me."

Especially popular among cookie crumblers are the high-tech "safe" Nerf guns, among them a Nerf slingshot, a "high powered, fast action," Nerf bow 'n' arrow, Nerf Missile Blaster, and the Nerf Missile Storm that can rapid fire four foam missiles. For the more affluent, there's the Nerf Hydro Bazooka with double punch on sale for just $14.83 and the Nerf Arrow Storm Gatling unit rapid fire system for a mere $22.96, the package larger than the three-year-old who's looking it over.

Just 50 feet away in the sporting goods section, among Bowie knives and an assortment of .22 single-shot rifles and 12-gauge and 20-gauge shotguns, are "fast shooting, accurate," BB pistols and rifles "with constant firepower," all for under $50 each.

Want even more firepower? Just go about a quarter-mile away to another store where a new Smith & Wesson .357 magnum is only $269.95. Can't afford that much? Pawn shops in any larger city have .22s for under $100 or, for under $500, semi-automatic military assault rifles that can easily be converted into illegal 900-shot-per-minute automatic weapons.

Last year, there were more than 60,000 deaths, about 2,000 of them accidental, from firearms. Another 90,000 were injured. Among high school students, gunshot wounds are the second leading cause of death. Of the 200 million firearms in the country, 60 million are handguns. Only the National Rifle Association believes it's a constitutional right for individuals to bear arms because even the courts have repeatedly ruled the Second Amendment applies to militias, not individuals.

And now the television networks have figured out if they didn't do anything about violence on the public airwaves, then Congress would. So, the geniuses who gave us "Cop Rock" and numerous variations of the Amy Fisher story, cancelling the critically acclaimed "I'll Fly Away" and "Brooklyn Bridge," decided labels will help parents select just the right programs and, thus, reduce violence in American society.

These same six-figure blow-dried TV geniuses—whose window-darkened limousines pick them up from fenced-in suburban estates and drive them to work in circuitous patterns to avoid seeing the city—are now trying to make us believe that labels, similar to the movies' rating system, are going to make our children less prone to imitate what they watch. And they sound like they actually care about God, mother, apple pie, and the right of all citizens to bear arms and still be free from violence.

Of course, we are carefully assured by the networks—whose cash crop on Saturday mornings are the companies which make the toys of violence—that they care about us and our advertising dollars. Exempt are sports and TV news which, reflecting American society, are probably the most violent hours on the air.

Nevertheless, we have labels. Just like the labels that Tipper Gore got record producers to put on albums, and that teenagers now scavenge record stores to find. Just like the labels that tell 13-year-olds that "R"-rated movies are the ones with the gratuitous sex scenes, filthy language, and excessive violence. The same labels that are supposed to keep mothers from taking their seven-year-old daughters to see "Jurassic Park" which has a PG-13 label. Labels don't work for record albums; they don't work for the movies. And until we reduce violence in society, there's no way they're going to work for television.

An American Triangle: Violence, the Media, and Individual Responsibility

① In Ohio, a five-year-old boy watches moronic TV cartoon characters Beavis and Butthead, imitates their reckless use of matches, burns down the family trailer, and kills his two-year-old sister. The fire department, most of the community, and the mother who had left the children alone, blame the cartoon. MTV eliminates pyromania scenes from cartoons.

② In Pennsylvania, Texas, New Jersey, and New York, five teenagers, imitating a scene from "The Program," a film about excessive football conditioning, lie down on the median lines of highways. Three are killed; two are critically injured. The communities blame the film, and Touchstone Films responds by deleting the scene from all prints.

③ In California, a 18-year-old boy murders a friend's father, then pours salt into the knife wounds. "I just seen it on TV," he confesses.

④ In Florida, a 15-year-old boy murders a neighbor. In Rhode Island, a boy hangs himself after watching a magician perform a similar stunt. The parents of both boys sue the TV networks for negligence.

In Washington, D.C., a media-rich city with one of the nation's highest crime rates, Congress held hearings in 1993 on TV violence, and U.S. Attorney General Janet Reno threatened the TV networks to either reduce the levels of on-air violence or face government intervention. She has a large base of support.

During the past four decades, there have been about 8,000

media-and-violence studies. No one disputes the fact that in the four decades that television has become a major form of recreation, society has become more violent. The National Coalition on Television Violence claims about one-fourth of all prime-time TV shows are violent. The average child watches 27 hours of television a week, with the TV baby sitting in the average inner-city urban home about 70 hours a week. By high school graduation, the average child, according to some estimates, will have been exposed to about 12,000 TV murders and about 200,000 acts of violence on television.

Even if we eliminate the preposterous assertion by some groups that the Roadrunner–Coyote cartoons are among the most violent shows on the air, the reality is that there has been a significant increase of on-air violence. A Times-Mirror poll in 1993 revealed that 72 percent of all Americans think TV entertainment shows contain too much violence. But, what people say—and what they watch—aren't comparable since the only statistics the nonprint media notice are the box office receipts on films or advertising revenue and ratings for television shows.

Since the media do not lead society, and usually pander to society's worst tastes, it's only logical to assume that American society has not only allowed but—by their viewing patterns—encouraged the increased levels of on-air violence. Without question, it seems as if some TV shows and many films are produced solely to package the most creative acts of violence to manipulate people into spending a couple of hours of escapist fun watching the conflict between good guys and bad guys kicking, biting, stomping, maiming, zapping, knifing, shooting, chopping, and crashing into each other.

Nevertheless, using the same data from the 3,000 studies, isn't it possible to conclude there is only a minimal cause–effect relationship? Isn't it possible that persons who normally have aggressive behavior patterns or who live in homes where such patterns are present may be more inclined to increase their own aggressive behaviors? And, isn't it possible that those without such personality traits or environmental exposure would not commit acts of violence even if every TV show had excessive levels? Certainly, it's a leap of faith to believe that Quakers, if shown enough television violence, would buy guns and mug Baptists.

If we eliminated all media violence, as demanded by the shrill cries from our moral protectors, then we will be forced to eliminate most Nintendo and Genesis games, ban TV reruns of the "Three Stooges" and "M*A*S*H," pull the plug on MTV, smash tapes and CDs, stop singing "The Battle Hymn of the Republic," shelve the four-star four-hour film productions of *Gone With the Wind, Gettysburg,* and *Schindler's List,* stop the reprint publications of *Moby Dick, The Red Badge of Courage,* and *Uncle Tom's Cabin,* block publication of *Hansel and Gretel, Snow White,* and most of Grimm's fairy tales, rewrite virtually all of Shakespeare's plays, forbid the telling of Aesop's fables, prohibit TV news from appealing to our sense of the morbid by leading newscasts with auto crashes and wars, and order a complete rewrite of the *Bible,* which has more violent acts per page than even a *Dirty Harry* movie.

But, the Federal government says it has no plans to curtail anything but the broadcast media. Besides, the government says it has the authority of the Communications Act of 1934 which declared that because of the limited number of airwaves, the government has the right to regulate radio and television to meet "the public interest, convenience and necessity." And, thus, we have a double standard. But, since 1984, we have developed newer technology that has created an unlimited information superhighway to allow the average TV set owner to receive more than 50 different signals. By 2000, home TV sets may be receiving more than 500 signals. If we continue to regulate content in one medium, no matter for whatever reason, and if we put even more fear into already greedy TV executives who will do whatever the government says as long as it doesn't pull their lucrative station licenses, then government will intrude on all other media. Even if *all* TV shows become "violence-free," there will still be violence in American society, more than in any other civilized nation.

If the Federal government truly wants to reduce violence in society, it might try looking at broader causes other than the media. It might face up to the National Rifle Association lobby and severely restrict access to assault rifles and handguns. It might work to develop programs to reduce racism, poverty, war, worker exploitation, and unemployment. And for those persons who truly are violent, perhaps there needs to be tougher laws, better prisons, and more responsible rehabilitation programs.

Even more important, maybe we can start taking responsibility for our own actions and stop blaming the media, no matter how irresponsible, inept, or manipulative we think they may be.

America's Ding-a-Lings

America's telephone companies—they're the ones with the ding-a-lings—have been wallpapering the country with notices of how cost efficient they are. I have a friend who switches long distance phone companies every two or three months, staying just long enough to take advantage of the inducements to switch. She's long past the $25 free usage credit, and is now working on getting a two-week vacation in the Bahamas.

Switching long distance phone companies is relatively easy. Getting a phone in the first place isn't so simple, as I found out after moving. A few of the details are hazy, but I'm sure this is what happened.

"I'd like a phone," I said to the friendly smile.

"Ours or theirs."

"Ours or their what?"

"Ours or their telephone. For only $5.95 a month, you can rent a nice, beautiful, well cared for, always faithful telephone from us, or you can go to one of those cheap back alley stores that sell molded plastic they claim is a telephone, but is really nothing more than a fusion of leftover chemicals from Chernobyl."

I chose theirs. She asked me to pick a color. I asked for black. She told me candy apple red, tangerine, sunny yellow, lemonade, autumn gold, avocado, tropic green, white, cream, ivory, espresso brown, and 258 other colors no one but phone designers ever heard of, but no black. I chose blue.

"Would that be electric blue, robins-egg blue, porcelain blue, or midnight blue?"

I told her to surprise me. She did. "Would you like to be able to call someone?"

"Doesn't my phone allow that to happen?" I naively asked.

"Oh, no, sir," she pleasantly informed me. "You need to call another phone company."

"But aren't you the same people?" I asked.

"WHAT!?" she screamed offended. "We're not the same people. We're different! We're our own monolithic monopoly!"

So, I called another monopoly, a "Baby Bell" that gave me even more options and add-ons than come with a new car. The first option I was given was to not have my name in the phone directory for which I had to pay the phone company a monthly charge not to do anything. During the next 11 hours, I also made decisions between rotary or pulse; chime, buzz, or gong; and call waiting, call forwarding, and call block, all of them leaving me call-pletely confused. But, at least I was assured of continuous uninterrupted service.

"If something goes wrong with my phone," I rhetorically stated, "I just call you."

"After figuring out where the problem is and how to fix it."

"If I knew what was wrong, why would I have to call you?"

"Because you have to know who to call. If it's in your telephone, you must call whoever sold you the phone. But, if it's in the inside wiring or any other problem, we'll come by and charge you 40 or 50 bucks plus labor and maintenance."

"But, it'll be fixed, right?"

"Unless it's in your outside wiring. If that happens, you just call AT&T or some other long distance service provider, and they'll charge you another 40 or 50 bucks plus labor and maintenance." She took a quick breath, then continued. "Now, would you like our Reach Out Plan?" I wanted to reach out, but restrained myself, eventually learning that for a flat fee I could make an hour's worth of long distance calls anywhere in the country, except for long distance calls in something I was told was a local long-distance area, which I doubt anyone understands.

It was finally time to add up the charges. She primed her computer, then began running the calculations—$4.75 for a dial-tone, $3.50 for the federal line charge, $5.30 for local calling, $5.95 for the first phone rental, $11.90 for the other rentals, $3 for the colors, $1 for the first push button and $11 for the other buttons, a few bucks for product and service charges, a few more bucks for accessories, the state's relay surcharge, state and federal taxes, something for the 911 line, the $100 deposit—"Did I also mention the installation charge? If we have to come out there, it'll cost you big-time, but if all we have to do is to throw a switch in our office, it's only $40. By the way, are you making a whole lot more since you moved?"

"What if I decide I don't want a phone?" I wearily asked.

"No problem," she said sweetly. "That'll only cost you ten bucks a month, and you'll still get an 18-page bill you won't understand."

The Beeper Cacophony

It might have been an enjoyable party, but I didn't experience much of it since beepers and phone chimes were going off all evening, and all I heard were excuses of why used car salesmen, real estate agents, and grocery store clerks had to either find a telephone or unsheath a 0.7 watt cell phone from their hips.

"So, what's your sign?" asked a striking brunette who was beeped and never heard from again, at least by me. Apparently her sign was AT&T.

The knock-out redhead and I talked for five minutes before her beeper alerted her to call her service which relayed a call from her boss who wanted to know what color dress she was wearing to work the next day so he'd be able to color coordinate his staff. At least that's what I think she said, but I wasn't sure because she was beeped again.

The swaggering high school English teacher was beeped, checked his message, pulled a cell phone from inside his jacket pocket, and called what I assumed was someone's pager service.

While waiting for a movie usher and waitress who simultaneously excused themselves to answer their pages, I overheard three people by the bar ask each other what our hostess must have been thinking to have actually invited someone so low on the prestige scale that he didn't have a beeper and car phone.

"Could be a diversity thing," said one politically correct matron. "You know, we invite a black and a beeperless columnist to our party."

Feeling alone and needing a drink, I asked the bartender for a virgin Piña Collada, but before he could crush the ice, he received an emergency fax from Starbutt across the room who needed two whiskey sours with a twist of lemon.

After almost an hour of microwave bombardment, I noticed another soul all by himself.

"Party seems to be dragging," I said, opening the conversation.

"Yeah," he mumbled. "I just hope I get some action tonight."

"Since everyone's telephoning everyone else," I said, "I doubt there's much action anyway, especially when everyone seems to have blurred the lines between business and personal lives."

"It's now been 93 minutes, and no one has paged me," he said dejectedly. "It's so humiliating."

Not having done my good deed for the day, I sighed, and shuffled off to a telephone in the foyer. His pager beeped, and he rushed to a phone about 15 feet away to chat with me about the price of kumquats. He was most thankful, especially when I didn't try to talk to him again so he could carry on simultaneous conversations with the striking brunette, the knock-out redhead, and some guy who was selling life insurance.

About the time I was ready to leave, the hostess told me I had a telephone call. It was Marshbaum wanting to know if I needed him to come in early the next day.

"How'd you find me here?" I asked.

"I was driving along Route 11 finding dumb things for you to write about when I thought I should check in. So I called Horsehide who paged Littany who beeped Bullnose who said you were at some muck-a-muck's party, so I called."

"You have a car phone?!" I asked.

"Had to, Boss. Also a pager, CB unit, fax, laptop computer, modem, and portable satellite dish. Gotta be on top of things in case you need a dumb idea at a moment's notice."

"When's the last time I needed you moments from deadline?" I asked.

"Makes no difference," he said. "Sometime you may, and you'll be happy you could get to me."

"But I don't have any of those communications devices."

"Check your office in the morning, Boss. Got some nice units for you, too. It's only costing you a thousand or so a month to be popular."

"Marshbaum!" I shouted, "I don't have an extra thousand a month."

"No problem, Boss. It's all tax deductible."

The Impersonal Society

Some of my favorite people are the five ladies at the Bloomsburg, Pennsylvania, branch of the Philadelphia Federal Credit Union. Over the past decade or so, they have put up with a lot from me, with hardly an audible sigh, although I am sure there was a lot of cheering when my wife took over balancing the checkbook a few months ago.

The Credit Union ladies know my account numbers and status

better than I do, have bailed me out of numerous problems, and have even gotten used to the reality that I know my accounts not as numbers but by colors. ("Could you please check my balance on Red savings, then transfer 50 bucks into Red checking, 30 into Blue checking, and 95 to pay Blue loan?")

Even when they've had a long and tiring day, the ladies smile, joke, and ask questions about how my family and I are doing. The only thing they get from my "small potatoes" accounts is the occasional box of candy or a green plant and the satisfaction they're doing a good job, which doesn't even begin to add up to the personal attention they provide to keep my financial affairs in order.

But, during the past few years, because of a conspiracy by the grand poobahs of the urban corporate office who are into things like "time management studies," the ladies have been slyly trying to convince me to use the push-button telephone to call an 800 number of a central computer where a digitized voice will tell me the status on my accounts, and allow me to electronically transfer funds from one account to another, and even pay bills. My human tellers even sweetly point out that it's easy to do telephone-to-computer transactions which are efficient and save me the $2 fee for almost every transaction a human teller has to do. I, of course, have just as sweetly explained that I have no ability to comprehend laborious written instructions that require me to push 132 different buttons just to hear a disembodied voice tell me my account is overdrawn.

With MAC drive-ups, direct deposit, and the phone, I don't ever need to talk to a human again. The reality is that I am willing to pay a penalty just so I can talk to a friendly voice in a rapidly increasing technologically imperfect impersonal society.

At one time, all telephone calls had to be made through a local operator who knew as much about you, your family, and the community as you did. Then, technology let us bypass a human, and do our own calling.

Call the average business and you now are greeted by a digitized voice giving you a menu. Listen to all the choices, push another button, and hear another menu. Some companies have four or five levels of menus, all so you can finally push a series of buttons and hear, "I'm sorry, I won't be in for the next six months. If you wish to leave a message, press 1; if you wish . . . "

We don't go to seamstresses anymore because we can now order by menu-driven telephones from the mail order department the same clothes everyone else is wearing. From vending machines, we can now buy not only candy bars and soft drinks, but insurance, VCR tapes, and even aspirin and condoms—and never have to talk to anyone. We speak into a clown squawkbox to order fast-food which we eat in the car on the way to an aerobics class that treats us to a recorded cadence.

Although most clerks at supermarkets and department stores, who are usually paid minimum wage and receive no benefits, make at least an attempt to be friendly, an increasing number barely make eye contact while they languidly pass items past an electronic scanner.

With the computerization of America, you can now have your computer talk to other computers and make airline and hotel reservations, order furniture, hire a nanny, and get information from data bases instead of from librarians, all without ever talking to a human.

On newspapers, we have replaced the wise older proofreaders and typesetters with dispassionate computers that have a passing knowledge of grammar and no knowledge of the community. Reporters are already researching and writing stories by calling up data bases, transmitting the finished product electronically to editors who send it electronically to the press—and no one has to talk with anyone else.

Even the supercilious lines that sound as if we care about each other—"I know where you're coming from," "I understand your pain," and "Thank you for sharing that," among dozens of others—are nothing but warm fuzzy codes so we can pretend we are communicating while we plan our next sentence.

In California, neighbors stand next to each other before their fire-torn houses. For many, it's the first time they have talked to each other in weeks.

It seems the only other time we talk with each other is when we unite at sports events to shout "kill the umpire!" Most other communication seems to be flipping fingers and calling lawyers. Indeed, the Age of Communication has now become the Age of Uncommunication.

Scanning an American Life

I'm so excited!

I've just been accepted as a member of Sam's Club.

Because there are only 435 clubs in the country, I had to drive 45 minutes to the closest one, then sweat 20 minutes in line, wondering whether the Wal-Mart board of directors would accept me. Unlike country clubs, whose membership criteria is based upon social status and the ability to pay outrageous dues, Sam's Club has numerous restrictions.

For example, you can't become a member unless you work for local, county, state or Federal governments; a school or college; a hospital or financial institution; an insurance, transportation, or utility company; or are a real estate agent, nurse, or other professional; or are either on active duty or retired from the military. Persons who hold membership in the 32 million member American Association of Retired Persons are also eligible.

Others accepted into the club include Wal-Mart and Sam's Club vendors and associates, persons who own or manage a business or who have purchasing authority for businesses, and anyone who is self-employed. Finally, Sam's will accept any of the 34.6 million persons who have a Discover Card, or are part of what Sam calls an "affiliated" group, defined as "a selected credit union or association, company, or customer of selected financial institution 'Depositor Clubs.'" There's also a category for "additional qualifying group." The only ones deliberately excluded appear to be members of the press, unless they can meet the rigid requirements of being at least 50 years old, owning a Discover Card, or finding a bank that will cash their paltry paychecks.

At the membership counter, a semicheerful associate asked me to fill out an application, pay $25 for one year's exclusive membership, and step to a floor-painted triangle to be photographed. Armed with a photo-laminated bar-coded blue card, I was ready to wheel my oversized shopping cart through the 120,000-square-foot warehouse in search of five gallon drums of pickles, 10 pound cans of corn, and a skid of soft drinks.

Checkout time.

At most supermarkets and discount stores, pimply-faced high school students earning not much more than minimum wage so they can afford CDs, designer jeans, and monthly car payments scan $50,000 to 60,000 of merchandise a day. Somewhere, management then praises themselves for lowering labor costs while a mainframe computer system records and analyzes inventory.

It's not much different at Sam's. However, at Sam's, the pimply-faced all-of-the-above clerk first scans the ID card, then records each purchase. At its best, it may mean special coupons from manufacturers. At its worst, it means Sam's eventually sells the data to a health insurance company that raises my rates because it determines I bought too many bags of junk food.

Legally, anyone can obtain voluminous data about anyone who has ever registered to vote, owned property, sued, been sued, or arrested, served in the military, been married or divorced, licensed by any government agency, or even attended a public school.

The *illegal* trade in information gathering and surveillance— does anyone think it's impossible to learn how much money you have in your savings account or the latest reason why you had to go to the hospital?—is a multi-billion dollar a year business.

In his last year in the Senate, Alan Simpson (R-Wyoming) proposed a national photo ID card, not unlike the one that Sam's issues, for $25 a year. With multilayered paperwork in a bureaucratic hierarchy, figure at least $10 billion to implement this scheme. The intent may have been to assure us no illegal immigrants are allowed to buy bulk food at Sam's. But, the reality is that it's another way for the government to track its citizens, somewhat similar to the universal IDs issued by the Soviet Union, the Republic of South Africa, and almost all dictatorships.

We already have nearly universal driver's licenses and state-issued photo ID cards, as well as universal red-white-and-blue cards of patriotic social security numbers issued to babies. The intent six decades ago was simply to record every working individual for social security purposes; almost every other use is illegal. However, almost every agency and business from the IRS to colleges to the local video store now track taxpayers, students, potential employees, and customers by social security numbers.

What we don't need is another way for government or private business to track our lives.

Windows Not of the Mind

I just wanted to buy a portable typewriter. A portable *manual* typewriter. The kind I could throw into the van, and take anywhere.

I didn't need a portable with a screen, hard disk drive, and a $2,000 price tag. I didn't want to add a $600 printer, nor a $500 word processing program that would allow me to create multicolored Christmas cards. I just wanted something that didn't run out of battery power every four hours.

I went to three discount stores and one of the larger chain stationery stores where salespeople gleefully showed me a choice of electronic typewriters, dedicated word processors, and a dozen models of computers, all discounted for the holiday season. But no typewriters.

Smith Corona, the last American company to manufacture typewriters, had learned it could exploit Mexicans as easily as Americans, and took its business out of the country in 1992. Two years later, it stopped making typewriters.

I first learned to type when I was 11 years old. I had broken my right wrist, lamely tried to write with my left hand, and figured out I could put words onto paper by using the fingers of my left hand to punch out keys of a stand-alone upright Royal manual typewriter. My handwriting never improved; my typing did. Using a two-finger hunt-and-strike system, I surf the keyboard at 60 to 65 words per minute. I am not as fast as my father who typed 80 words a minute, but he had to use all ten fingers.

All through college and my first newspaper jobs, I used manual typewriters, ripping, cutting, and pasting together sentences and paragraphs into comprehensive 600-word stories. It wasn't until after I completed doctoral studies in the mid-1970s that I finally bought an electric typewriter.

So I wouldn't be swallowed by the impending technological revolution, in 1982 I bought a "state-of-the-art" computer with two disk drives and 16K of memory, quickly produced "perfect" copy, and wondered how I could ever have written anything that couldn't be inserted or deleted by a couple of keystrokes.

During the next decade, I progressed through two other computers, then to a Pentium, with 3,000 times the memory of my first computer and 50 times the hard drive storage capacity of my second one. My new computer has two floppy disk drives, a CD-ROM that holds three disks, and a speaker system that rivals anything high school kids put into their Camaros. Reluctantly, I gave up MS-DOS, and installed Windows 95, the deified omnipotent operating system that does everything from answering the phone to finding a cure for cancer.

However, I refuse to upgrade my word processing software. With each "improvement," the company increased the size of the program, making it possible to create complex graphic-laden newsletters. But in doing so, it had lost sight that the one thing a word processing program should do is to efficiently process words.

A few years ago, the university where I teach cancelled its courses in Typewriting (I, II, III, and Workshop), apparently sensitive to giving college credit for something that probably should never have been college courses in the first place. But, like matter, nothing is ever lost in an academic universe. So, the College of Business added Keyboarding. It was a more rigorous course. Not only did students have to learn how to "keyboard," they also had to master the 200 or so commands that would allow them to flawlessly print out their resumes, then breathlessly wait for corporate America to throw contracts at their feet. But, just in case anyone thought "word processing" was too simple and the future wouldn't be paved with clauses of comfort for its graduates, the college created oh-so-'90s upper division courses, Electronic Document Preparation and Business Document Generation.

Both the College of Business and the College of Education now teach their students desktop publishing, and one of our graduate programs teaches students in a dozen courses to produce interactive videos and instructional CDs. However, none teach the writing and editing skills necessary to wrap up the pretty packages within 64 megs of RAM.

In our journalism classes, 19-year-olds quickly learn that computerized spell checks, grammar checks, thesauruses, and style books can reduce their stress levels. Aided by programs that lay out templates and don't require them to know how to figure ratios and conversions, they soon design full-color pages that almost rival anything *USA Today* produces. Sadly, if they master computerized graphics and page design, they will earn at least $5,000 a year more in the media than their fellow students who master writing and editing. It probably doesn't matter.

Editors now spend less time editing than they did a decade

ago, forced to do not only their own jobs but those of the back-shop composing staff who were laid off or fired when publishers upgraded their plants' technology.

Today, first graders in my local school district are being taught to use computers. During their 12 years of basic education, they'll learn most of their skills from software programs loaded into machines that resemble TV sets.

Some day, in our technologically perfect society, the power will go out and we'll be forced to confront our own illiteracy.

Curbing the Paperless Explosion

It seemed like such a good idea at the time. A computer program that not only lets you fill in crossword puzzles, but also gives you hints, scores your results, and even lets you create your own puzzles. It was the perfect gift for my wife who lets several cups of coffee and the morning newspaper awaken her, then spends 10 or 15 minutes filling out the crossword as dessert.

But, a week after I gave her the super puzzles disk, she still hadn't installed it in the computer. Finally, she admitted that doing crosswords on a computer screen just wouldn't be the same as relaxing at the dining room table.

For most of us, newspapers, which have been around in one form or another for most of recorded history, just "feel" right. We can read them all at once or let them lie around, reading an article now and then whenever we have time. Unlike radio, TV, or the movies which manipulate the audience into a predetermined time frame, the print media allow audiences to read at their own pace, and on their own schedule.

We can cut out a picture, an article, or column, stick it on the Fridge or put a Post-It note on it and send to a friend. We can tear out an ad or coupon and use it later in the week. We can make printer's hats for our children, or take the day's news to the beach. When we're through reading it, we can put the newspaper over our faces to block out the sun. It's possible to take a portable computer to the beach, but when you put it over your face, you get real bad tan lines, and an even worse headache.

But, the Generation X-cess electronic whizzes and "mass communicologists"—who profoundly state that newspapers aren't even good enough to wrap fish or line bird cages anymore—

claim the future is in the computer. They believe all knowledge can be encapsulated, then dished out at the user's preference.

The alarms have already been sounded. Newspaper circulation will decline by 14 percent by 2001, declares Forrester Research of Cambridge, Massachusetts. On-line news and special interest computer programs will spell the decline of not only newspapers, but also all television and print media as 53 to 60 percent of all homes will have PCs by 2001, the 20th year after the development of PCs, say the forecasters. About one-third of all newspaper executives said that the Internet is the "top reason" why the print media won't be as strong in five years, according to a survey by the Hearst corporation.

Interested only in the latest news about your favorite heavy metal band? Just type it in, then let the computer do the searching. Want only information about gardening? Bring up the right menu, spend another five minutes to select the appropriate submenu, then scroll through a list of titles until you find something interesting. Everything is available, and no self-serving gatekeeping editor is there to filter out 95 percent of the day's news. But editors help reduce the information overload that leaves most of us unable or unwilling to sort through piles of gigabytes to find what's important and what's fluff. Even newspapers and magazines have begun going on-line with stories and videos, figuring it'd be easier to make a buck off people who just want to read about the latest O.J. development than to understand all the news.

Actually, since large masses of the nonreading public seem to buy Sunday newspapers for the coupons anyway, it may be more logical to computerize everything. That way, readers can search for the right coupon—avoiding local, state, and international news—send an electronic signal to their grocery store, then pick up their discounted food whenever it is convenient.

With the local print newspaper, we see many things at once, subconsciously noting the size of headlines and the placement of stories; we get a "feel" for what is important, and how stories relate to each other. Even if we flip through each section to get to the horoscope and comics, we absorb some news along the way.

But, America's Chip-for-Brains have a response. With "pagination," they claim they can turn a screen into a miniature newspaper, complete with heads, pictures, and graphics. All we have to do is try to read that full page on screen that's the same dimensions as a junk mail letter, move our mouses over what looks interesting, magnify the story, then scroll through it a few lines at a time until we need new glasses. Most of us can't even program a VCR, and these geniuses with their soft floppies really believe we'll become technologically sophisticated enough to nimbly wander through a maze of electronics and menus and actually "find" all the news that's fit to scroll.

Embedded within the computer age, the "futurologists" further argue that the death of print media is predetermined in an environmentally-friendly paperless world. At first, it seems as if the 25,000 60-foot trees we need to kill to produce *The Sunday New York Times* could be better used. But, almost all newsprint is now recyclable, and the Newspaper Association of America points out that forests are being grown specifically for newsprint production, significantly reducing the erosion of our existing forests and timberlands—and possibly stabilizing the rising cost of newsprint.

The reality is that newspapers will be around as long as advertisers determine it's profitable for them to continue to buy space on a piece of pulp paper 15 inches by $22\frac{1}{2}$ inches. When they get better results from handing out flyers in mails or running 30-second spots on "Gilligan's Island" reruns, then newspapers in print will no longer exist. Hopefully, advertisers will continue to recognize the reality of why newspapers are important. We may complain about the local paper, but we still read it, each in our own way.

So, whenever someone tells me that newspapers are dying, that in a decade or two they'll join the other dinosaurs of history, I tell them about my wife, her coffee, her voracious appetite to learn a little more about our world, her ad-clipping scissors—and her daily newspaper puzzles.

The $6 Million Journalist

Journalists are confined by having to report reality. But, often we wish we could report stories that don't exist, but should—such as . . .

Pop vamp Madonna today announced she plans to wear clothes on her next world tour. The Material Girl's "Justify My Blonde Ambition Garment Tour" begins April 15 at L.A.'s Salvation Army Value Store and concludes two months later at London's Carnaby Street. Representatives of the mass media decry Madonna's plans to be clothed as "another cheap publicity gimmick," and vow to picket her shows.

After two days of heated discussion, members of the Association of American Publishers voted to "significantly reduce "the number of ghost-written movie star books and to increase publication of books that focus on important social issues. The Association has also voted to limit publication of the number of purple-prosed romance books, mostly inaccurate weight-loss and personality-make-over books, and all books with the name O.J. anywhere in the text.

In the spirit of the book publishers, NBC surprised its affiliates with its early morning announcement that it will bring back "I'll Fly Away," the critically-acclaimed TV series that focused on the nation's civil rights struggle during the early 1960s. In its last year, the series finished 86th of 93 prime-time series. "While it's true that only six million households a week saw the series when it originally aired," said network VP Seymour Schlock, "we have a responsibility to enlighten the masses to help them better understand their nation's heritage."

Central High School says that it has reached "an all-time high" in graduating students who are literate. "We hit 75 percent this year," said principal Ed Cashion. Unfortunately, one-third of the faculty are being required to attend summer school to take remedial courses in the three R's since they spent more time in college taking education courses in how to teach than in learning what to teach.

KFAD-TV, impressed by the work done at Central High, fired news anchorbabe Susie Sweetwater. "Although she was gorgeous, smiled better than any other person on the air, and didn't do too bad with one- and two-syllable words," said news director Barry Cheeseball, "Susie just wasn't a journalist, and we have exceedingly high standards for reporters in the local market."

The *Wattabago Tribune* signed award-winning investigative reporter David Bergman to a three-year $6.4 million contract. Bergman, who had been the clean-up hitter with the *Daily News* the past four years, was granted free agency status in January. "We believe in the American philosophy of paying employees what they're worth," said *Tribune* publisher Arthur M. Greeley.

In a related story, Philadelphia Phillies pitcher Harry Horsehide became the highest paid person in sports when he signed a three-year contract for $96,000 a year.

And, finally, Avarice K. Toadstool, president of Amalgamated Conglomerate Media Industries, having finally bought up all book publishing, newspaper, and magazine companies in the country, says he finally understands why his employees need better working conditions. From his company headquarters in Bermuda, Toadstool says his company won't fight the effort by his 25,000 Third World employees to unionize. "They deserve representation," says the CEO, "and I encourage my loyal employees to avail themselves of the better benefits, working conditions, and grievance procedures the union can provide."

Patriotic Unemployment

I had gone into the unemployment office to pick up a copy of the monthly fiction from the Bureau of Labor Statistics when Robinson came out, smiling and holding what appeared to be an unemployment check. Robinson? The same Robinson who had worked more than 30 years in one job? Never late to work, never sick. Never promoted or demoted. Never stole; never argued; never complained. Loyal as a puppy. "Robinson?" I asked cautiously.

"Hey, man, good to see you. You still working?"

"Of course I'm still working. There's news to gather, stories to—"

I didn't have a chance to finish. He grabbed my arm, looked around, then dragged me into a corner away from traffic and peering eyes. I figured he had a choice piece of whistle-blowing.

"Don't say anything," he cautioned. "I'll get you out of this."

"Out of *what*?" I asked nervously.

"Out of employment. Quit now before they get you."

"*Who'll* get me?"

"The Feds."

"The *FBI* is after me?" I asked, frightened at the thought of being chased by an agency whose first director smoked cigars and wore dresses.

"FBI. CIA. VFW. Save yourself. Quit now and turn yourself in for unemployment compensation."

"You're a nut!" I proclaimed.

"Patriot!" he proudly corrected me. "I'm defending God, mother, apple pie, and the flag. If it weren't for me, the country would collapse."

"Being unemployed is patriotic?" I asked suspiciously.

"Ever since corporate America claimed that a higher employment rate led to inflation, and that continued employment could lead to the collapse of the money market."

Robinson cautiously checked for Feds, then cautiously explained corporate America's version of voodoo economics. When employment is high, the Federal government doesn't lower interest rates, something business depends on. As important, the longer a worker stays on the job, the higher the salary is; the higher salary forces the employer to raise rates and prices to the consumers who then demand more wages from their own employers. Conversely, a higher unemployment rate leads to lower wages since employers can pick and choose who they want; this results in lower prices on consumer goods. Further, by downsizing the work force, corporations last year gained enormous profits, allowing the boards of directors to reward their CEOs with an average 23 percent pay raise. It's the American Way!

"You're a journalist!" Robinson proclaimed. "You're already suspect as being unpatriotic. Save yourself. Quit now."

"But, Robinson, I *like* my job."

"Think you'd like a few years in Leavenworth? Treason isn't taken lightly in this country."

"But I'm still earning a salary, and you're unemployed."

"And a *patriot*!" he reminded me.

"That may be true," I agreed, "but you're still only earning unemployment—"

"—welfare, food stamps, and AFDC!"

"AFDC?! Your wife left you six years ago. Both your children are out of college. How did you get Aid to Families with Dependent Children?"

"I adopted two orphans from Rwanda. It was a patriotic responsibility. Did I ever tell you about Vocational Rehabilitation? They pay me to learn a new job. All I have to do is go to school a couple of hours a day and collect a paycheck."

I figured since there were mounting shortages of welders, nurses, and plumbers, he'd be enrolled in one of those programs. "Journalism," he said matter-of-factly.

"Journalism?" I asked incredulously. "A University of Michigan study showed that of all college-educated professionals entering the work force, the pay of journalists is at the bottom. While the average profit for newspapers is above 20 percent, a fifth of all reporter salaries are below the nation's poverty level. Even with poor pay and benefits, thousands are trying to get into the field, but there aren't openings!"

"Exactly!" said Robinson, smiling. "Exactly."

Traded for Two Rookies, an Editorial Clerk, and a Future Draft Choice

Finstermeister was furious. He stomped up to the desk of the city editor and shoved the afternoon edition of the newspaper in his face.

"How dare you!" Finstermeister demanded, his rage filling the news room.

The city editor peered over his stack of press releases, and with embarrassed compassion in his voice said, "Sorry."

"Sorry? Is that all you have to say!?"

"You know how reporters are," said the city editor. "They're a zealous bunch, and sometimes there's no stopping them when they sniff out a story. I was hoping to tell you before it hit the street edition, but . . . well, with all these press releases, I just didn't have time."

"You had time to trade me!" thundered Finstermeister, upset that after 15 years on the *Daily Tribune*, he was being traded to the *Morning Bugle* for two rookie reporters, an editorial clerk, and a future draft choice.

"It was in the best interests of journalism," said the city editor.

"The contract requires that with that much seniority, I must be allowed to approve the trade," Finstermeister said smugly. "And, I don't like Maine!"

"Don't you remember," the city editor reminded him, "you waived that right three years ago in order to get only a six-day week? It was just after your third child was born and your wife had two cops drag you home so you could also meet your first two children."

"But, Boss, I'm a darned good reporter."

The city editor shook his head sadly. "We don't need an environmental reporter any more. The readers want gossip about the stars. Fashion stories. More about investments and jobs and where to find good meals. Important things like that. We'll just add an occasional assignment to Smogbound's beat."

"But Smogbound covers business, and he's on every freebie list ever minted."

"Business. Environment. It's all reporting."

"I can do more than just cover the environment," Finstermeister begged. "My rookie year I led the league in rewrites, obits written under deadline pressure, fire alarms, and garden club parties.

Five years later, I was a Pulitzer finalist for that series on hazardous waste dumping!"

"I admit you had some good years with us," said the city editor, "but you're not as young and as aggressive as you once were."

"Two years ago," shouted Finstermeister, "I took the Pulitzer for the series on design flaws and construction blunders on the Bellevane Nuke." Finstermeister was now inches from the city editor's face. "Oil! I did that series that proved Magnum Oil was price-fixing. I wrote about acid rain, the utilities' rate-gouging schemes, sewer run-offs, cloud seeding—"

The city editor cut him off. "Don't you understand? No one cares about the environment anymore."

"I'll learn to make charts and graphs!" Finstermeister cried out. He paused a moment, then desperately suggested, "I'll go back to editing the home improvement tabloids."

"You're a star, Fin, and we need to get rid of you while you still have some value. Those 16-hour days are breaking you down."

"Was it my salary? I'll take a cut. I don't need $11,000 a year. That's too much for a reporter anyhow."

"That's generous, Fin, but for your salary, we can get two cub reporters and have pocket change left over. Besides, you fit the *Bugle*'s needs, and the people they're sending us fit ours."

"I was president of the Society of Professional Journalists!" Finstermeister blurted out. "Didn't that bring a lot of prestige to the paper?"

"It's the system, Fin. You knew it when you came here."

Finstermeister looked around the newsroom, searching for understanding faces, but all the other eyes were buried in newspapers, hiding from reality. There would be no help from his colleagues today. "What about the readers?" asked Finstermeister. "A lot of people bought the paper because of my reporting."

"A month from now," said the city editor matter-of-factly, "they'll forget your name. They'll find other heroes." Suddenly, the city editor became menacing. "And don't try retiring early, or jumping the team once you're at the *Bugle*. The commissioner frowns on things like that."

Sadly, Finstermeister shuffled his feet, resigned to his fate. "When do I report?"

"Take a vacation first and report in three days. The *Bugle* likes its reporters fresh." He paused a moment. "One other thing, turn in your style manual before you leave."

Downsizing Baseball's Problems

Dozens of major league baseball owners say player payroll has become excessive the past few years, with some players now being paid as much as $7 million a year. Their solution is to create a salary cap, a maximum payroll that would level the playing field so all teams could be equal, thus giving the Colorado Rockies the opportunity to win a World Series and sell overpriced T-shirts and mugs with pictures of blizzards on them.

The players claim the salary cap is a sham since the wealthier teams have won no more games than the less affluent, and the owners are already making excessive profits. In rebuttal, the owners say that only a few of them are making excessive profits, while the rest are only making outrageous profits.

The players rightfully point out that baseball operates as the nation's only legal monopoly, and that because of the failure of government to impose antitrust sanctions, as it would against another benevolent megamaniacal-conglomerate, the government encourages the owners to treat players as chattel, to be bought and sold at will. The owners complain that free agency is a Communist conspiracy, and that the players are nothing but million-dollar crybabies who are better protected under slavery than freedom. They say if the major leaguers don't like playing for one owner, not only are there 27 others who won't let them work either, but that thousands of minor leaguers are just salivating for the chance to chew and spit in major league parks.

Because owners, players, and even federal labor mediators have been unable to solve the problems, it's finally time to turn to the source of all great wisdom—newspaper columnists. Fortunately, I have a solution.

Using private industry as a model, I propose there be layoffs, known among corporations as "downsizing." The owners could eliminate one player and his million buck salary. That would allow a larger pool of money for the players, while also allowing owners to keep their profits. The downsizing allows worker exploitation to continue without fear of the industry closing down and the end of baseball caps worn backward as a national fashion statement.

Analyzing the playing field, it's apparent that every player except one has a place to be. There's bags for first, second, and third, a home plate for the catcher, mound for the pitcher, and billboards on the fence to designate the three outfield positions. The only player who doesn't have a designated spot is the shortstop.

The fans probably won't object to one less player since they don't complain when airlines lay off mechanics, and hospitals lay off nurses. And they certainly don't complain when newspaper publishers and broadcast station managers order "downsizing" of the reporting staff in order to increase corporate profits.

To compensate for the smaller work force, we could move the third baseman a few yards closer to second base, bring in the leftfielder a few yards to help cover the hole at third, and require the centerfielder and rightfielder to cover more territory. Although the layoff would increase the workload, it would maintain owners' earnings-to-profits ratio, and continue to provide them with the income sufficient to be able to afford German-made luxury cars, overpriced country club memberships, and rent on apartments for their mistresses.

Equally important, it would preserve the inherent right of owners to continue to make idiotic statements to a fawning press corps, and would assure the continuation of the responsibility of all Americans to take out a second mortgage to afford stadium parking, admission, and the right to eat three buck overdone hot dogs, drink a four buck cup of warm beer, and say how wonderful America's pasttime is.

Laying Off Marshbaum

It was late Friday when I somberly called Marshbaum into my office. There was no way to break it to him gently, so I laid it on the line.

"Marshbaum," I said, "I'm going to have to lay you off."

"What'd I do wrong, Boss?" he asked, wounded.

"It wasn't anything you did," I said reassuringly. "It's what you are."

"I'm your foil," he said. "When you need someone to come up with dumb ideas that have an edge of truth, I'm it."

"That's true, but you're also a white male, and I've used you too much."

"That's my job!" said Marshbaum. "I'm the one who makes you look good."

"You're the one who's going to cause me problems with diversity committees," I replied.

"You telling me that because I'm a white male you have to lay me off?"

"I have no choice," I said showing him a study commissioned by the Screen Actors Guild and the American Federation of Television and Radio Artists, and conducted by a research team at the University of Pennsylvania. According to the research, of more than 19,000 speaking roles in almost 1,400 shows over 10 seasons, women comprised less than one-third of all speaking parts. The study also said Latinos, Native Americans, the elderly, and the disabled are almost invisible on TV, and lower class persons were represented in only 1.3 percent of major characters in prime time although there are ten times that many in the general population. Even more incriminating, the study reported that almost two-thirds of all on-air TV journalists are men, and that four-fifths of both those cited as authorities and those whom the networks consider news makers, are men.

"But that's TV," said Marshbaum haughtily. "We're print."

"Makes no difference," I replied. "If they can target TV, they'll find us next."

"Even if the networks believe the report, they won't do anything about it."

"And what makes you think that?"

"Because TV's never done anything socially responsible," said Marshbaum smugly.

"I still have to lay you off," I again told him.

"Sure," Marshbaum said cynically, "then you'll up and move the column to Mexico and take advantage of lax labor laws. You'll hire cheaper minorities, and not give them any benefits."

"That may be true," I admitted, "but that's only because you're a white male who has been with the column a long time, so all new hires will be done at entry level salaries and minimal benefits. That's the American way! Besides, it'll only be just long enough to get women and other minorities as foils into my column, then I'll lay them off."

"What woman is going to be as big a schlemiel as I am?" a tearful Marshbaum asked. "I'm the best there is! No one can act dumber than me!"

I acknowledged it would be exceedingly difficult to find anyone like him. "You'll be able to get unemployment," I said. "Maybe even food stamps."

"I want a job," he protested. "The one I've held for years. Every time you were stumped for ideas, I did something stupid. Made you look like a genius. Stupidity is my life!"

"Marshbaum," I said, "don't you understand? If I use you much more, I'll probably be caught in some poll that academics conduct when they have nothing better to do with their time."

"But you use women," he said, his voice straining. "What about Susie Sweetwater, your shmuck of a TV news reader? What about Art Buchwald? He's not going to give his foils their notice just because they're white men?"

"I believe they were grandfathered in," I said.

"Breslin!" Marshbaum thundered. "No one's telling Jimmy Breslin to get rid of Fat Thomas and Marvin the Torch!"

"Marshbaum," I said, "it'll only be a few weeks. A decade or two at the outside." Reluctantly, he packed up his things and shuffled out the office. The last time I saw Marshbaum, he was reading a Spanish language book about transsexual surgery.

An Unequal Competition

And so there they were. The two of them. Locked into a professional struggle that neither of them knew about. He was a journalist. She was a young college graduate. Both wished to become teachers.

But she had one thing he didn't have—a state credential. She had taken almost two years of education courses. He hadn't.

Normally, he would have been one of the first to be weeded out, but somehow the clerks didn't notice he lacked the state credential. So there he sat. Facing the deputy superintendent of instruction, a man who had state credentials. An administrator who told him that without a general secondary credential the district wouldn't hire him.

"You need several courses. History of education. The philosophy of education. Educational methods. About 15 in all, plus student teaching," he said.

"But I want to teach writing, not education," he replied, noting that he had thought hard about changing careers.

"I understand that," said the deputy superintendent, "but we require that every teacher have a mastery of the concepts of education."

"I have a master's in journalism and professional experience," said the applicant, pointing out in one long breath-drenched sentence that in addition to having written for newspapers and magazines, he had a number of awards. "Isn't that enough?"

"I'm sorry, it really isn't."

He explained he had taught creative writing part time at a state university for three years, then pulled his relatively-high student evaluations from a folder. The deputy superintendent quickly scanned them, then put them aside.

"That doesn't eliminate the requirements. You can't teach in public schools until you learn how to teach."

"But I taught!" the writer argued.

"But you haven't taken education courses," said a most petulant deputy superintendent.

"I took two courses," said the writer, "and didn't see anything challenging in either of them." This insolence, of course, upset the deputy superintendent whose mission now was just to get rid of this pest.

"I would like to hire you, but—"

"But I don't have a credential! What about the other applicants? Do they have my experience? My writing ability? Or, do they only have your license?"

"The state requires," said the deputy superintendent, his attitude bound by a set of conventional regulations, "that a person have a number of courses in education. As I mentioned earlier, it's important to know how to work with students of this age group."

"Doesn't knowledge count?" the writer demanded. But before the deputy superintendent could answer, the writer continued, "In one of your district schools, a guy with a psych degree and no media experience is advising the school newspaper."

The deputy superintendent coughed, then answered, "In that situation I believe he was already on the faculty, but because of a reduction in enrollment in psychology courses, the district either had to lay him off or find him another position."

"So you threw him into journalism."

"We didn't throw him anywhere!" snapped the deputy superintendent. "His credentials include teaching English, and he expressed an interest in teaching journalism."

"I have an interest in nuclear physics," the writer said sarcastically. "Of course, I don't know anything about it, but I'm interested in teaching it. I'll even take courses in education so I'll know nuclear physics better. And judging from what I've seen of your students, I could probably teach nuclear physics better than some of your English teachers are teaching writing!"

There was nothing anyone could have done. And so the young lady, with a degree in English who took all the education courses and completed student teaching but whose only published work were two poems in a college literary magazine, earned a position teaching creative writing and advising the school newspaper and literary magazine.

Occasionally, she mentioned something she learned from a class she took in college. But she never knew that the competition for her job had been her former teacher.

An Hour a Day

It's dark and lonely at 3 a.m. on the 51 miles of roads between Bloomsburg and McAdoo in rural northeastern Pennsylvania. But, Bloomsburg is home, and McAdoo is where the Consolidated Cigar Corp. is, and that's where Jack W. Smith works. From 8:45 a.m. to 3:45 p.m. Almost every day, Mondays through Fridays, and occasionally Saturdays.

He says he'd move closer to his job, but he's hoping he won't have to work there much longer. He would like something better, but it's a job, and in this economy it's the only thing he can get. The job calls for him to take 300-pound rolls of paper and slit them into sizes to wrap tobacco. It was tough at first. His back and arms ached, and he suffered innumerable cuts. It's not easy when you're 54 years old and have never worked so hard in your life at physical labor.

"I'm one of the hardest working people they have," Smith proudly says, pauses a moment, then says, with equal pride, he's "just so happy to have a job."

For most his adult life, he was employed. For four years, he was a cook in the Navy's submarine service. After that, he spent a year selling men's clothing. Then, in 1960, he got a job as a reporter with his hometown newspaper, the *Berwick* (Pa.) *Enterprise*, an 11,000 circulation afternoon daily that would eventually be merged into a sister publication in the early 1980s.

Jack Smith had never taken a journalism course, hadn't even gone to college, but the editor was willing to try an enthusiastic cub who said he learned quickly and could "find all the news."

During the next 12 years, he proved his words, covering everything from PTA meetings to the police beat, digging out stories that reporters with years of experience and two college degrees couldn't find. And when his editor retired, Jack Smith was the natural replacement, a job he held for six years.

But, after 18 years as a journalist, he was 40 years old, not making a lot of money and had minimal benefits. He also had a wife and three sons. It was time for a new job, one that gave him the freedom he never had.

Taking a second mortgage on his house and everything in savings, he and his wife, Gail, opened a gift store in 1979. In the next few years, they made the business one of the more successful ones in nearby Bloomsburg. So, he did what many businessmen did—he expanded, opening stores in Berwick, about 10 miles away, and in Williamsport, about 40 miles away. It was 1987, the end of the prosperity phase of the Reagan–Bush era and the beginning of the recession. In 1989, he was forced to declare bankruptcy. He lost his house, most of his possessions and, more important, his self-respect. He was 52 years old.

He says he begged his former publisher for a job, but was curtly told there wasn't anything available. Not as a copyboy; not even as a janitor. He took state civil service tests, scoring in the 90s, but was never hired, even for entry-level public information jobs, something even 21-year-olds with a fraction of Smith's knowledge and experience could do. He was the highest scorer in a five-county area for a state social service job, but was never hired. He applied for other jobs, but says in most cases he "never got past the receptionists."

Maybe one of his poker buddies could help him out, he thought. After all, they had been friends for several years. But the one who was an executive at a lingerie factory and the one who was partial owner of a carpet mill said there wasn't anything. And the longer Smith was unemployed, the farther they strayed from friendship, and Smith never knew why.

He had no job, his savings was gone, and he had no health insurance. Not many unemployed people can afford almost $5,000 a year for health insurance.

For a few months in 1990, he worked for the Census Bureau, eventually becoming a field supervisor in a five-county area. He got the Bureau's highest evaluations, but the job ended, and he was again unemployed. He was even desperate enough to consider several minimum wage jobs, knowing that an income of $8,840 a year wasn't enough to support one person, let alone a family. Alas, he didn't even get the minimum wage jobs.

Once, he even applied for a job cleaning wards in the VA Hospital in Wilkes-Barre, but never even got an interview. But that's how he got the job at the cigar factory. The owner of the plant, a friend who thought it would be demeaning to offer a job as a laborer to someone who had been a Navy vet, newspaper editor, and successful businessman, told Smith's wife, "If he's going to wash walls, have him come see me."

So, Jack Smith became the oldest slitter in a cigar company. In six months, he lost 30 pounds as his body wearied under the physical demands of his new job. Yet, he stayed with it, taking all the overtime he could. "When I don't take the overtime," he says, "my check doesn't stretch as it should."

It stretches even less now since his rent was increased 30 percent. "The landlord said she had trouble meeting expenses," Smith says.

The month the rent went up, he began repaying a college loan. He had begun taking college classes, one or two at a time, shortly before his business failed. He had earned 47 credits when he ran out of money.

Gail has taken part-time jobs and stood by him, although she cries a lot. "My biggest joy is my family," says Smith, himself shedding a small tear when he says "we've become more cohesive the past few years. We're hanging tough together."

It's been almost two years now since Jack Smith was first hired as a slitter. It's been four years since his business failed, and society remembers his failure, not his success. He keeps applying for jobs. He keeps getting rejected. He's optimistic about the job he's doing, about his own life, but has lost some of his faith in the country that says it values opportunity, age, experience, and ability. It is something he thinks about five mornings a week as he drives an hour in the dark to get to work as a laborer.

[In 1994, Jack Smith began working as a bartender in a Berwick restaurant. Almost two years later, he and Gail opened a small co-op crafts store in a converted church.]

'We're Management; We Don't Have to Tell You Anything'

Shirley Collins sat in a nondescript office, facing the editor of the *Globe-Times* of Bethlehem, Pennsylvania. Nearby sat an outside consultant and an attorney from Chicago. We're restructuring the newspaper, said the editor, reading from a prepared script; your work is unsatisfactory, he claimed. You're being terminated, he emphasized.

In the seven years she had been at the newspaper as feature news editor, Shirley Collins had never received a formal evaluation from any of her supervisors, although she did receive several awards, the most recent being second place for lifestyle sections in the annual Keystone awards contest of the Pennsylvania Newspaper Publishers Association.

But, the well-rehearsed script the company provided its participants April 5, 1988, didn't allow the editor to give individual evaluations the day of her firing. Nor was it likely they would.

On the day she was fired, Shirley Collins sat there, and listened to an editor claim that her work was "unsatisfactory." We have an agreement, the editor read, explaining that if she signed the eight-page agreement and resigned rather than be fired, she would receive "extra benefits," including about one week of severance pay for each year worked, continuation of health and life insurance benefits for a limited time and, if eligible, be able to collect all pension benefits due.

Of course, there were a few "tradeoffs" in order for Collins to receive all these "extra benefits"—she would have to agree to give up many of her rights. For one year, she would be forbidden, without *Globe-Times* consent, to associate in any way with any newspaper or magazine publishing company or any radio or television station that broadcast news programs within 25 miles of the *Globe-Times*; for two years, she would not be allowed to associate with the Times Mirror Co., publisher of the competing Allentown *Morning Call*, or Thomson Newspapers, Inc., publisher of the nearby *Easton Express*. Not only couldn't she work for those organizations, she couldn't even deliver newspapers for them or rent an apartment if the owner was one of the forbidden companies.

Among other rights she would have lost had she signed the

agreement, she would have had to agree to never disclose the contents of the termination agreement, except to immediate family and her attorney; "cooperate with and assist the *Globe-Times* in any investigations, proceedings, or actions" relating to her employment or "to any matter in which I was involved or of which I had knowledge of while an employee of, or a consultant for, the *Globe-Times*"; and pay all costs and expenses incurred by the company should it bring any charges against her for violation of the agreement, or should she bring any charges against the company "relative [to] any such action, proceeding, claim or charge."

And then there was Paragraph 6 which deleted her statutory and Constitutional rights, including the right to bring charges against the company for violations of Title VII of the Civil Rights Act, the Age Discrimination in Employment Act of 1967, the Fair Labor Standards Act, the National Labor Relations Act, and the Pennsylvania Human Relations Act.

Shirley Collins refused to sign the agreement. She was again urged to consider the many "extra benefits" she would get from signing, and was told that Management was sorry that she chose not to take advantage of those fine benefits. She didn't know why she was being fired. She was a 55-year-old woman, with a master's degree in library science, and another master's degree in journalism from Columbia University, which she had earned shortly before she was hired at the *Globe-Times*—and she was unemployed.

By the end of the day, more than two dozen employees would be fired, including more than 40 percent of the editorial staff. By the end of the year, there would be several resignations, and more than 50 would have been fired; about two-thirds of the editorial staff would have been fired or left voluntarily as Management shuffled personnel, trying to find what it believed was the right combination to bring the newspaper out of a financial tailspin brought about when circulation plummeted from 39,572 in March 1981 to 21,702 in March 1988.

In an industry of one-newspaper towns, the *Globe-Times*, at one point one of the nation's better smaller newspapers, should have had its own comfortable monopoly. But in the 1980s, like most newspapers, it hadn't effectively planned how to compete with a regional daily, alternative sources of advertising, a recession, a population shift to morning newspapers, a reduction in the reading habits of most Americans, and a demographic time bomb that exploded when the advertising industry increased its emphasis on quality numbers rather than mere quantity.

The *Globe-Times* solution was a massive restructuring, focusing on image and a misguided effort to promote what it thought was "community journalism" at the expense of the hard news stories readers needed. Two months before the purge, the newspaper fired Mary Wagner, a 21-year employee who was one of the better police reporters in America. Management later claimed she was fired because she was a poor writer who committed errors and wasn't a "team player," charges completely unsubstantiated. When the staff, shaken by her firing, asked the editor why Wagner was fired, he coldly replied to two of their representatives, "We're management. We don't have to tell you anything." Later, Management admitted it fired Wagner because she spoke out against what she, and most of the editorial staff, saw as a deterioration in quality, and because Wagner had begun to figure out what Management was planning.

But the problems Wagner pointed out, and typical of what was happening to newspapers during the past decade, became apparent with the one-day purge. Many of those fired were in their 40s and 50s, had worked at the newspaper two or more decades, and were arguably among the better workers in the industry. The purge left the newsroom decimated, stories uncovered, "happy news" filling the front page, and the readers wondering why they should even subscribe anymore.

Most of the staff who remained were uncertain of the direction the newspaper was taking—or even if they would have jobs the next week. By the end of 1989, even the editor who had fired Mary Wagner, Shirley Collins, and more than a dozen other reporters was gone.

Less than two years later, on November 4, 1991, the *Globe-Times*—its circulation below 19,000, its credibility shot—was merged into the competing *Easton Express*.

Pennsylvania law, like that of most states, gives private-sector employers in nonunion operations the right to hire and fire "at will." The "employment at will doctrine," with very few exceptions, essentially states that private sector nonunionized employees are at the mercy of the employer. The concept is that the management may fire an employee "for good cause, for no cause, or even for cause morally wrong . . . " *[Payne* v. *Western & Atlantic RR],* Tennessee, 1884.*]* The United States is the only major industrial democracy that does not have federal legislation prohibiting unfair discharge. About 22 million Americans work under collective bargaining agreements; 60 million do not.

Most employees believe employers have a right to hire and fire "at will," not knowing that employment in much of the public sector and on unionized newspapers, magazines, radio, or television stations and networks gives the worker innumerable benefits and rights, including the right to be fired only for "just cause."

If the story of the *Globe-Times* had applied only to one newspaper, it could easily be dismissed as unique in American journalism. Journalists and the public could look over the events, argue about them, perhaps sympathize with the workers who were fired or with Management that says it needed to make changes to regain financial stability. Perhaps many might even think that some of the employees deserved to be fired; perhaps some would think that management was morally and ethically wrong in how and why it fired many of the staff.

However, the issues aren't of personalities or events, or even in management's decisions that led to the crisis or its efforts to recover. The issues are universal in American labor and in the newspaper industry, but more so when members of the editorial staff must carry the burden of loyalty to their profession and the community against loyalty to the corporation that pays their salaries, knowing they could be reprimanded, demoted, or fired at any time for any reason.

Had there been a union at the *Globe-Times*, the employees would have been able to take advantage of well-established multi-step grievance procedures detailed in the collective bargaining agreement, including the right to go to binding arbitration in the case of termination or arbitrary job changes. In the United States, about one half the union-protected workers whose cases go to binding arbitration are restored to their jobs, often with back pay. The collective bargaining agreement would also have detailed specific agreements with respect to promotion, termination, restructuring, or a layoff. Further, the employees would have been protected by state and federal labor codes.

Without union representation, the workers had yielded equity, for management has the money and resources to bring in consultants and attorneys to keep former employees, most of whom can't afford $150 to $200 an hour lawyer fees, from mounting a significant legal challenge.

But there is still a "stigma" within the journalism profession about being a union member. "It's OK for blue-collar workers," goes the refrain, "but we're professionals." Perhaps one day, the professionals will realize that in the United States, the division by traditional class—lower, middle, upper—is no longer viable, and there truly has been a division along lines of the underclass, the workers, and the management; journalists must again recognize that they have far more in common with the coal miner than they have with the CEO.

The tragedy that is partially shared by the *Globe-Times* is not only the failure of newspapers to understand their audiences and the principles of journalism, but also of society to adequately protect all its workers.

INTERMISSION

Selling Out America by the Yard

With the arrival of Spring, it's time once again to go through the house to find white elephants. Not the Caucasian males who are running Congress, but attic stuffers that can be cleaned up and sold at a yard sale. Here's a list of some of the better items, available at bargain basement prices.

The first thing I'm getting rid of is my entire shelf of computer books. Maybe when the software companies figure out that clear, concise writing is the motherboard of effective communication, I may again buy some books. In the meantime, perhaps some needy family that can't afford dumbbells might stop by and purchase my collection.

One of my favorite books is *The Rights of the Worker*. But, in the present anti-labor mood of the country, this book is now categorized under fiction. It'll be available at a low take-it-away scab price.

Other items on the bargain table include:

Two dozen diet books. The only thing I lost on this was a lot of time and money.

Two dozen dog obedience books. Kashatten, one of the world's smartest German Shepherds, and I, whose intelligence remains in question, flunked out of not one but two dog obedience courses. But at least she's been able to get me to sit, heel, and roll over on her command.

A sheet of apostrophes. This one should go quite fast since ads, flyers, and newspaper articles prove there's a desperate need for apostrophes.

A case of White-Out. This also should go fast because ads, flyers, and newspaper articles also prove that when apostrophes are used, they're used incorrectly.

Here's a 2-for-1 special. I once bought several dozen bumper stickers, "You've Got a Friend in Pennsylvania," hoping that by keeping the stickers off car bumpers, we might not give any neighboring states the impression that the Commonwealth doesn't know grammar. But then, Pennsylvania came out with an equally ridiculous slogan, "America Starts Here," and I just gave up.

A well-worn TV set, suitable for decoration or to hold plants. The set had survived 6,245 different talk-show hosts, the O.J. marathon, and "Thirtysomething." But, with deregulation by the Federal Communications Commission, the set imploded.

A 1,000 piece jigsaw puzzle of the Statue of Liberty. It once was assembled, but is now mostly in pieces. But, I'm sure someone out there, possibly a recent immigrant "yearning to breathe free," might wish to restore Lady Liberty before Congress deports him.

A tattered copy of the Constitution, with part of the First Amendment missing. With the new Congress, I probably won't have any need for the rest of the Constitution anyhow.

The one thing I am saving is a copy of a piece of paper that says, "Governments are instituted among men, deriving their just powers from the consent of the governed. That whenever any form of government becomes destructive of these ends, it is the right of the people to alter or to abolish it, and to institute new government."

The Communist Manifesto? No, the Declaration of Independence.

Confusions

I'm confused about a lot of things in the media that don't seem to make any sense. For instance . . .

• <u>Howard Kurtz</u>, media reporter/editor for the *Washington Post* said on CNN's "Reliable Sources" that the reason he sent two reporters home from the floods in North Dakota in May

1997 was because "after a week of flood coverage, people get tired." He said "they need to go home to their families." Barbara Cochran, president of the Radio and Television News Directors Association, chimed in that with television, "you're making a decision about dozens of people. It's very expensive to keep the satellite trucks and the edit packs and the camera crews and everyone out there and they get tired. . . . So there is a reason to pull them out."

Am I missing something here, or weren't there about 12,000 reporters and crews accredited to cover the three weeks of the 1996 Olympics? And didn't about 4,000 reporters and crews camp out next to the courthouse for the first marathon O.J. trial. . . . And didn't the TV networks run 30-minute, one-hour, and all-evening "specials" on top of nightly news stories about O.J.? But, then again, a celebrity accused of murdering two people is probably more important to Americans than a flood that forces about 100,000 people to be evacuated and causes over $1.5 billion in damage, including wiping out a major farm industry.

• In the month of the floods, Chicago's WMAQ-TV, owned by NBC, brought in TV talk show host Jerry Springer to do commentary on the 10 p.m. evening news. Calling Springer "the poster child for the worst television has to offer," and infuriated over what she believes is a deterioration of TV news integrity, Carol Marin resigned after an 18-year career at the station, the last 12 as co-anchor of the evening news. Springer said what he thought about the subsequent controversy over his hiring and Marin's resignation—"It's only reading a teleprompter," he said about TV anchors. "I mean, they make it seem like journalism."

Marin is right; there has been a deterioration of TV news, much of it brought on by insipid infomercials designed as news, an obsession with police and fire stories, and a hyperactive quest for ratings. Springer is right; there is little resemblance between TV news and journalism. However, Springer—who has done graduate work in government, was mayor of Cincinnati, and spent several years as an award-winning field reporter and anchor of a Cincinnati TV station—seems to be an ideal commentator, even if the station hired him not for his mind but because he could bring in ratings. Certainly, Springer doesn't confuse the entertainment and acting he does on his tabloid TV show with journalism; just as most viewers probably don't confuse the scripted acting on TV newscasts with journalism.

If newspaper reporters resigned because they didn't want to

work for a medium that publishes sleazy advice columns, the horoscope, and pablum features about new shopping carts at the local supermarket, there wouldn't be any newspapers left in America. Alas, after just two commentaries, Springer resigned, having been blasted by the nation's journalists, almost all of whom piously proclaimed how bad TV journalism has become.

• The Food and Drug Administration (FDA) and the tobacco industry are negotiating a $300 billion "settlement." In exchange for an immunity against being sued for wrongful deaths because of tobacco addiction, catastrophic illness, or death, the tobacco industry will agree to severe restrictions on advertising. Among the restrictions will be bans on outdoor advertising, the placement of ads in several thousand publications that "could" be directed to youth, all logo-oriented promotional items sent in exchange for coupons, and campaigns using symbolic humans, such as the Marlboro Man. Although the federal government has every legal and Constitutional right to protect the health of the people, doesn't it seem odd that the tobacco industry is willing to give up many of its Constitutional First Amendment rights? And, doesn't it seem that this universal squeezing of advertising will benefit not only the larger companies, already well-positioned in the market, but also magazines with a substantial "adult" audience?

• I'm a little confused on this next one. Millions of parents who preach the gospel not to trust Big Government now admit they are too stupid to determine what TV shows to watch. Their solution is to give the federal government the authority to order the creation of labels for record albums, movies, and now TV. These same parents, preaching "family values," also want government to ban liquor ads on TV, create an anti-abortion Constitutional amendment, and for all I know determine how many children each couple should legally have.

• Finally, digital television, scheduled to be in all our homes by 2003, is designed to guarantee better video and audio quality. I assume this means that when the cable goes out, we'll get crystal clear pictures of snow.

PERSUASION

A Medal for the Army

More than four million medals were awarded to Americans who participated in the Gulf War. A high-ranking Army officer, trying to justify the cost for what might have been a bad case of medal inflation, said that the awarding of the medals was not only good for morale, but also good public relations for an Army that had severe morale problems following the Vietnam War. For most of the military in the Gulf, it was not only their first taste of combat, but also their first medals.

Once soldiers lose their combat virginity and realize that promotion is based on how colorful their chests are, they're going to want to continue to invade countries and humiliate peacocks. The Pentagon is only happy to oblige, as this semiofficial not-so-secret transcript of a recent Pentagon meeting reveals.

"Col. Klunk, as our top PR advisor, I believe you have some ideas on how to get more medals."

"Thank you, Gen. Kuhster. The Gulf was a PR coup for us, so we need to intensify our existing positive behaviors by reversing counter indicative negative behavioral attitudinal objectives."

"In English, Colonel."

"We follow it up with the same thing. After all, in PR, imitation is the sincerest form of guaranteeing you won't have to have an original idea."

"You want us to invade Iraq again?"

"No, sir! In PR, duplication is bad; imitation is good. We invade Saudi Arabia. Same weapons and tactics. Different country. Wipe them sheiks clear into democracy and force them to grant equality to all their citizens!"

"But, Colonel," said the chairman of the Joint Chiefs of Staff, "if Saudi Arabia becomes a true democracy, it would have to allow women and gays to serve in combat units."

Col. Klunk immediately saw the problems of a democratic invasion, but was undeterred. "Bosnia and Rwanda! It's a two-fer! Why, them poor SOBs facing ethnic annihilation need all the help they can get. We'll call it a global humanitarian mission. Those weeping sister knee-jerk liberals on the Eastern papers would fall for that in a drop of a politician's morals."

"Not good," said the general. "Our ambassador from Exxon doesn't think Bosnia or Rwanda have any resources worth protecting."

"We'll find another country in Africa. Makes no difference which one. None of the media give much coverage to Africa anyhow."

"Africa's out," said Gen Kuhster, reminding Col. Klunk that even the Army needs probable cause to launch an invasion.

"Puerto Rico!"

"Two problems. First, Puerto Rico is an American commonwealth. Second, most are in America anyhow."

"Let's run this one up the flag pole and see who salutes it," said the military flack. "We launch a Defcon 1 invasion of Colombia, neutralize the opium dens, and make the world safe for lite beer. More than anyone else, the media will love us for that!"

"Can't do that either, Colonel. Half the White House staff would turn their noses up at even the slightest suggestion that we curtail the coke trade."

"We invade France. I never did like those snooty snaileaters."

Gen. Kuhster again shook his head, explaining that no matter how arrogant the French are, they're still allies.

"Some allies!" whined Col. Klunk, "They don't even let us invade their country so we can boost morale."

"Now, Colonel," said the chairman soothingly, "the Pentagon isn't opposed to sending combat troops all over the world, we just don't like the countries you've suggested."

"I know where you're coming from," said the flack, "and I appreciate your input into this, but let me share this possibility with you. We develop a series of attitudinal objectives, take a proactive stance, and target our selected publics."

"In English!"

"We find out what people Americans don't mind wiping off the face of the earth, then invade them!"

"You may be right," said the chairman of the Joint Chiefs. "We need to find the most worthless piece of real estate on earth where nothing useful happens, where double-talking greedy little toads are running the show and are too tied down by scandal to even mount an opposition. We do that, and we'll have good PR—and more medals."

And that's why, on a humid summer morning, a crack team of Navy Seals, a ranger company, Delta Force, and two divisions of combat-trained ribbon-bedecked soldiers were seen marching down Pennsylvania Avenue on their way to the Capitol.

Chicken Advertising

A recent study indicated that the U.S. Army spent about $100 million last year for advertising, about twice what Kentucky Fried Chicken spent. No matter how it's figured, the chickens get better cluck for their buck.

So, one day the secretary of the Army, several of his top aides, a few assorted generals, a marketing specialist, a communication consultant, and a gold-chained advertising account executive met in a top secret session.

The marketing specialist, with 20 feet of computer paper spread across two tables, babbled endlessly about chi-squares, gamma coefficients, multivariant analyses, and focus groups. He thanked the generals for their time, dropped a four-figure bill in their laps, then abruptly left for another meeting, probably with the Navy to keep them from falling further behind the Marineland budget.

The communication consultant suggested that sergeants should do a better job of "bonding" with their recruits. Moments later, he was recalled to active duty and sent to Alaska. It was now the adman's turn.

"Larger billboards?" the adman weakly suggested, hoping not to be sent to his former assignment in Yugoslavia where he handled both the Bosnian and Serb accounts.

"What do the Chicken people have that we don't have?" asked the Secretary.

"Their Colonel?" he lamely suggested.

"Their *Colonel*?" thundered the Secretary. "We have colonels of our own. And generals! All those generals running around here are a menace!"

"I don't think you understand," explained the adman. "Their colonel is a nice grandfatherly type that people can relate to."

"What about our uncle?" scowled the Secretary.

"He was cool when we had the draft," said the adman, "but now that we have a volunteer army, I don't think Uncle Sam is the appropriate image. After all, he's got that beard and funky hat and—"

"Do we have any admen in Iraq, yet?" the Secretary asked an aide.

"No problem," said the adman wiping his brow. "How about increasing the choices a soldier has?" After the laughter died, the Secretary explained that soldiers don't have choices. "Chickens have choices," said the adman. "There's also regular and crispy."

"Think!" the Secretary commanded. It wasn't something admen usually do, but if it would keep him from exchanging silk Gucci shorts for olive drab, he'd try thinking.

"Family plans?" the adman meekly suggested. When no one said anything, he brazenly continued. "We develop a real family plan. Mother. Father. Two kids. All in the Army. Remember, the family that shoots together is the family that dies for their country together."

"I'm not sure it'll fly," said the Secretary. "After all, Congress is still trying to cut us back."

"It flies for the Chickens," said the adman. "Their family buckets are very popular."

"If we wanted to be popular, we'd have kept the communications guy," said the Secretary. "We're spending too much and getting too little. We're in a slump."

"When the Chicken has a slump," said the adman, "it has a sale. How about a 2-for-1 sale? Maybe two guns for the price of one. Two pairs of combat boots or whatever."

"Sometimes one adman is twice what we need," moaned the Secretary who began signing travel orders.

"No biggie," said the adman. "I'll get a line on something. Lines! That's it! Soldiers are always complaining about lines. We claim that the Army doesn't have lines. No lines. Faster service."

"I'm sorry," said the Secretary, closing his note pad, "but lines are what makes this Army great. Fortunately, with the budget cuts there will be even longer lines."

"Sir," said the adman ominously, "don't you want parity with the Chickens? It could force Congress to stop your cuts and increase your budget."

"Parity" was apparently the magic word. The Secretary stood up, looked at all his aides and generals, and boldly announced that the misnamed Army Intelligence Corps will immediately begin surveillance on the Chicken Place. "And as far as this advertising account executive is concerned," said the Secretary, "give him the best suite in the Pentagon. He could very well be our secret weapon in this war of image."

Missing in Atlanta

It wasn't at opening ceremonies. It isn't being seen very much around the athletes. And it certainly won't be in the closing ceremonies.

Whatizit, the sneaker-wearing starry-eyed blue blob mascot of the 1996 Summer Olympics, is more of a Whereizit.

The Atlanta Committee for the Olympic Games (ACOG) says there is no place for a Whatizit in the ceremonies because the mascot is more for children than for the pageantry and sophisticated "ooh/ahhs" the Committee expects from 75,000 stadium fans and a couple of billion TV viewers.

Whatizit was first revealed at the 1992 summer games in Barcelona—following a closing ceremony performance by Opera tenors Jose Carreras, Placido Domingo, and Luciano Pavarotti. It was the first computer-generated tech-age mascot, described by some as a scrawny mutant of a giant blue raisin and an overstuffed tick, a protozoan in red Keds, or even a giant sperm in sneakers. Many even dubbed him "Bubba the Blue Slug." But, the president of the International Olympic Committee liked him, and so he stayed.

During the four years since Barcelona, the ACOG, based upon innumerable interviews with children, redesigned him to be more cuddly. Several thousand children submitted names, and a committee of children in Atlanta decided Whatizit would be the species name for the blue blobs, and Izzy would be the user-friendly name for the Olympic's "official character."

The Ogilvy & Mather advertising agency created the official Izzy story, determining he is "a mischievous teenager who lives with friends, family, and athletes—all called Whatizits—in a fantastic world inside the Olympic torch." Inside of that world, Izzy dreams of being the first Whatizit to compete in the Games.

ACOG paraded the redesigned Izzy before the world in myriad promotions leading up to the Olympics. Children love it; adults think of it as a blue Barney.

Robert Hollander, ACOG's director of marketing, told the media "We felt we had a chance, through a mascot, to bring messages that were everything from geography, history, cultures of the different countries, sports, language, in a medium that kids really understand, which is video."

At electronic kiosks in Atlanta, an animated Izzy answers questions—punch the button about equestrians, for example, and watch Izzy ride a horse and answer basic questions, including how to purchase tickets. On video games, Izzy led children through a quest for five Olympic rings. On QVC, a home shopping cable channel, 1,000 Izzy games sold out in 12 seconds. Izzy animated cartoons and plush toys bring the Olympic message to millions of preteens.

In print, Izzy is ubiquitous. On T-shirts, caps, water bottles, and even Hallmark cards, Izzy lives, giving a face to a $1.7 billion show of pageantry and athletics.

Although the ACOG doesn't want Izzy mingling in its celebration, it doesn't object to collecting licensing fees for companies to use Izzy's image to bring the Olympic message to most of the world's five billion people. Izzy's picture on official merchandise should account for 20 to 30 percent of the $2 billion in licensed Olympic merchandise, says Hollander.

Izzy is just one of a couple of dozen Olympic characters, most of whom were treated better by their sponsors at the actual games. The first Olympic mascot was a dog for the 1932 Olympics in Los Angeles. However, the next mascot didn't show up until 1968; the Winter Games in Grenoble featured Schuss, a skiier; the Summer Games in Mexico City featured an unnamed jaguar. Subsequent mascots were Waldi, a dachshund at the 1972 Summer Games in Munich; Olympiamandl, a snowman at the Innsbruck Winter Games; Avrik the Beaver for the Montreal Summer Games; Roni Raccoon, (1980, Summer, Lake Placid), Misha the Bear (1980, Moscow, Summer); Sam, Walt Disney's eagle, for the 1984 L.A. summer Olympics; Vucko the wolf at the Sarajevo Winter Olympics that year; Hodori, a bowler-wearing cute tiger at the 1988 summer Olympics in Japan; Howdy and Hidy polar bears for the

Winter Olympics in Calgary; Cobi, a strange-looking dog with sunglasses for the 1992 Barcelona Summer Olympics; Magique, a mountain fairy that looked like a puffed balloon star and half-normal human for the Winter Olympics; and 13th century Norwegian twins Haakon and Kristin for the Lillehammer Winter Olympics in 1994. All of them had official roles. Even Cobi who was universally disliked when first unveiled four years earlier, was soon was accepted by the Olympics and fans.

Mascots, more than any one athlete, help identify and promote a team, event, or company, giving what the owners and promoters hope are "warm fuzzy feelings" that lead to the purchase of tickets and merchandize. Almost all sports teams have mascots, whether the more popular ones from the cat and dog families or the more unique furry green "phanatic" of the Philadelphia Phillies and the funky chicken of the San Diego Padres.

Several companies also have official mascots. There's Ronald McDonald for the world's biggest fast-food burger chain, and Charlie the Tuna who is never caught by Starkist.

States have official animals—whether it's California's grizzly or Texas' armadillo—as well as official flowers, birds, and insects, all of them representative of the state, and suitable for inclusion on innumerable marketing opportunities.

Mascots also identify the major political parties—Democrats have the donkey, although it once had the rooster; Republicans have the elephant. Uncle Sam is America's "official character," the dragon is China's, and a bulldog is England's. Even stamp conventions have mascots. China plans to have an official mascot for the 1999 World Philately Exhibition.

The Olympics likes to proclaim that in its own way it's a metaphor of the human spirit. When the sugary hype is stripped away, it may be true. But, also true is that how the Olympics used Izzy to bring recognition and income to itself, then abandoned him for the run of the Olympics when his immediate usefulness was over may be a more accurate representation of the "human spirit."

Advertising in Media pushes a product: Sex, Jeans

Jeanetics and the Cool 'Wannabe'

It's the end of summer, and time to fork over what's left of my salary to buy a few pairs of new blue jeans for my sons. Not just any pair, but ones that are faded and torn in the manufacturing process. It's some kind of a "fashion statement."

More than 28.5 million teenagers spend about $18 billion a year, half of it in August, for clothes. Parents and relatives spend another bazillion or so dollars. I usually wait until the last week, hoping there will have been a massive switch in advertising strategies, and jeans won't be the one item that identifies everyone who wants to appear to be young, cool, and "with it."

Just about everyone is wearing jeans. Students and teachers. Patients and doctors. Lawyers, cops, and criminals. In upscale Manhattan, the Yuppie crowd wear jeans with a blue blazer. In middle America, reporters wear jeans with inexpensive shirts and ties. Wannabe rappers wear baggy jeans, and wannabe sex kittens wear low-cut form-fitting jeans with strategically placed designer holes cut in places that only the size 3 models the companies hire as shills would be happy with their placement.

Cowboy President Ronald Reagan wore jeans on his Santa Barbara ranch while taking one of about 10,000 vacations from his demanding eight-hour a day work schedule in Washington. Nuclear engineer and former president Jimmy Carter wears jeans since he was a peanut farmer and later became active in the Habitat for Humanity program of building houses for low-income families. During their cross-country campaign of 1992, Bill Clinton and Al Gore, those affable Ivy League lawyers, wore jeans.

On labels wide as barn doors, to be displayed on bodies nearly as wide, are free advertising for Calvin Klein, Gloria Vanderbilt, Liz Claiborne, Ralph Lauren, Sergio Valente, Vidal Sasson, and Guess? (no, I don't know Miss Guess's first name!). Even Georgio Armani, manufacturer of astronomically-priced upscale suits, ties, and shirts, is manufacturing astronomically-priced jeans.

About 450 million pairs of jeans, made from about 9,000 tons of denim, were sold world-wide last year, accounting for about $9 billion in sales. The leader is Levi Strauss Co. which in more than a century has sold more than 2.5 billion pairs of jeans, and currently has a 20 percent share of the market, ahead of Lee and

Wrangler, both VF Corp. divisions. The annual advertising budget solely for rivets-on-the-pockets, buttons-on-the-fly Levi 501s, the tight-fitting straight-legged, narrow-ankle, rump-enhancing best-selling jeans in the world, is about $20 million a year.

When Levi Strauss made his first pair of jeans in 1853 during the California Gold Rush, he didn't worry if *GQ* or *Vogue* gave it their seals of approval. The pants, first known as waist overalls, were strong and durable. Miners and farmers liked them. The poor, who couldn't afford expensive wool slacks, liked them.

In the early 1860s, Strauss changed the original brown canvas overalls to an indigo-dyed denim fabric. Later, he added suspender buttons instead of belt loops. In 1872, almost two decades after Levi's were first made, Jacob Davis, a tailor, added rivets to pockets so they'd be stronger. Other innovations included stitched patterns on the back pockets the following year, and a fourth pocket (the watch or coin pocket) in 1890. A fifth pocket (a second one in the back) was added 15 years later; belt loops were added in 1922, and the red tab in 1930. Even with all these inventions, for more than a century the rest of America never wore jeans, lest others believe they were miners, farmers, or poor.

Then, in 1957, Elvis wore a pair of black denims in *Jailhouse Rock,* and the rock and roll generation began demanding jeans. A decade later, the hippies started wearing bell-bottom jeans; a decade after that, John Travolta wore jeans in the hit movie smash *Urban Cowboy,* and Americans rushed out to buy 600 million pairs of jeans.

The year of the pseudo-cowboy was the year Calvin Klein merged sex and denim, and the stock in jeans companies went higher than a novice bull rider at the local rodeo. It was in 1980 that 15-year-old starlet Brooke Shields seductively asked, "You know what comes between me and my Calvins?" She then cooed "Nothing," and jeans became the aphrodisiac all America wanted. Soon, it seemed as if every clothing manufacturer was rounding up the denim supply and painting it onto their come-hither emaciated models. Women who could pour themselves into a pair of designer jeans with nothing hanging over were soon admired in our society; they apparently mastered the art of self-restraint to be thin enough to be uncomfortable. Size 14 women were trying to merge into size 8s, believing they'd look sexy being strangled in denim.

Sex continued to pour out of America's clothes in the 1980s as stone-washed and faded ripped and torn jeans, which exposed flesh while deceiving America into believing the appearance of an active life complete with peek-a-boo sex was better than the real thing, became America's fashion statement.

However, just to make sure they don't miss any of the market, several companies began making roomier jeans, with VF's Lee division coming up with a series of ads for Easy Riders, targeted to the 25–44-year-old market, that showed women struggling to get into the tight-fitting jeans.

"If you really want to relax," suggested a Lee print ad, "maybe it's your jeans that should loosen up." Another ad asked, "Need a little more room in your jeans? Try Easy Riders from Lee. The brand that fits."

Wrangler targeted readers of *Cosmopolitan*, *Glamour*, and *People* with its campaign—"Our philosophy on fit: Jeans should take his breath away, not yours." Wrangler, a rugged wear line targeted to the country music market, is sold to the theme of "Most country stars wear Wranglers." For one of its major campaigns, Wrangler hired country singer George Strait to model the Wrangler brand, and told the public, "A western original wears a western original."

The company advertises heavily on The Nashville Network, and spends almost $1 million of its $10 million advertising budget to sponsor the Professional Rodeo Cowboys Association, placing its print ads on almost every available space, including barrels in barrel races. Other advertising is placed in *Horse Illustrated*, *Western Horseman*, and *Quarter Horse Journal*, as well as *Field & Stream*, *Sports Illustrated*, *Rolling Stone*, and *People*.

Although continuing to emphasize the poured-into-denim look for both men and women, Levi's countered with the looser fitting 560s. But, to hold the market on the "original jeans," Levi's increased its promotion for the 501s on FOX, MTV, and Nickelodeon, with the "got to be real" campaign to make sure the consumer knew that the jeans with the "button fly" was the original, not some baggy imitation.

During the 1990s, Calvin Klein, leading the fashion industry with sexual-oriented advertising, continuing to sell sex and jeans, posing pliable and emaciated nude women draped over brawny men wearing nothing but—what else?—their Calvin Kleins. In 1991, Calvin Klein spent $1 million just on advertising space to run an erotic 116-page photo spread of naked men and women, jeans, Harleys, and tattoos in 250,000 copies of *Vanity Fair*'s normal 850,000 circulation run. The section, Klein told *TIME* magazine, "is a fantasy about a rock concert. You see the band on stage, backstage, after the show. The wild and crazy groupies. The people living in the motorcycle world. It's about excitement. Hot and sweaty rock 'n' rollers who wear nothing but jeans and skin. It's about denim. People love it." That year, Calvin Klein spent $10 million on advertising, most of it mixing jeans and sex. The following year, Calvin Klein dropped jeans entirely in one of its ads, posing rapper Marky Mark on posters wearing nothing but an alluring smile and a pair of undershorts. In the summer of 1995, Calvin Klein shocked America once again by running an ad campaign featuring panels of sexually-provocative pubescent boys and girls. He never revealed their ages, but dropped the campaign a couple of months later against strong public outrage.

In the fall of 1996, Levi Strauss introduced the wide-leg SilverTab jeans. Targeting the 18–24-year-old market—and designing the legs to be 18- to 24-inches wide, as opposed to the narrower 14-inch 501s—the company's ad agency created ads around twin themes of sex and humor, and poured much of the $50 million ad campaign into TV sitcoms "Friends," "Seinfeld," and "The Single Guy," and onto MTV and VH1 cable channels. Within months, several other jeans manufacturers began making the wide legs, and targeting similar audiences.

The next fashion statement probably won't be denim underwear, although consumers can complement their jeans with denim vests and jackets, or make an alternative lifestyle statement with denim skirts, jumpers, or coveralls.

And that's why I'm again saying goodbye to my paycheck, resigned that for another season jeans are, apparently, what everyone else wants whose mind has been fashioned by multi-million dollar advertising campaigns that survey the market then tell us not only what we want, but what we need.

Sex and the Single Beer Can

The First Commandment of successful advertising is as simple as some of the campaigns—Sex Sells.

Car manufacturers paint two-door convertibles fire-hot red. Jeans manufacturers fleece the public to believe there's nothing sexier than someone in tight jeans. And beer companies have spawned bikini-clad lithe spirits to con cigar-chomping overweight never-hunks in grease-stained sloppy T-shirts to swill one or two six-packs every Sunday afternoon in front of a football-filled television set and believe they're the sex machines all America is looking for.

Throughout the country, we're exposed to Blondes in Bikinis. For variety, there's Blondes in Tank Tops, Blondes in Halters, Blondes in Unbuttoned Short Shorts, Blondes in Cowboy Hats, and Blondes in Paint-Them-on-My-Body Jeans. When the beer companies decided they should show a little more "multi-culturalism" in their advertising, they added brunettes and redheads—and put them into bikinis, tank tops, halters, unbuttoned short shorts, cowboy hats, and jeans. Three decades after the beginning of the civil rights era, the breweries finally found white-looking size 5 black women to promote beer—and gave them the opportunity to stretch out on white sand and lure customers into an idyllic setting of sun, surf, sex, and beer.

During the holidays, the models wear clinging dresses with hems somewhere about waist level—red and white for Valentine's Day; red, white, and blue for Independence Day; orange for Halloween; furry red and white for Christmas; and green for St. Patrick's Day. Michael Shea's places a blonde in a slinky green dress cut above mid-thigh, a shamrock, and a beer bottle to entice the public to try "a naturally pure golden lager." Miller Lite, the nation's third best-selling brand behind Budweiser and Bud Lite, places three women in short green dresses and asks America's sex machines to "triple your Irish."

On billboards, posters, and banners, the message is clear—drink beer and achieve great athletic and sexual satisfaction. Lured by the advertising, Americans are going to parties and bars to deliberately get drunk, apparently believing they can do things drunk they can't do sober—like vomit all over their dates.

Upon such dreams, Anheuser-Busch, Miller, and Coors, all of which connect sex and the consumer, accounted for 79.4 percent of the 189.4 million barrels of all beer produced in America, more than 80 percent of the $51.6 billion spent for beer in 1995, and about 89 percent of the $705.9 million spent on advertising, about 85 percent of it on TV advertising, according to *Beverage-World*, which tracks the industry.

Although the major beer companies effectively use humor, athletes, celebrities, and race car drivers—somehow tying together "responsible driving" and drinking—their print advertising is more sex-driven. Miller, with 22.8 percent of the domestic beer market, is the second largest brewery, behind Anheuser-Busch (46.8 percent of the market) and ahead of Coors (10.7 percent). One of Miller's more popular campaigns was to promote its genuine draft product by showing a dress and shirt on a clothesline. In case the consumers missed the subtlety, it also has posters of models in skin-tight swim suits, one of whom caresses a Miller Genuine Draft beneath a waterfall.

Waterfalls or showers are the setting for almost every brand in the Anheuser-Busch, Miller, and Coors lines. Coors, with an annual advertising budget of about $120 million, extols cool, clear water—and string bikinis, cleavage, and beer. Its slender D-cup women are often seductively stretched out on beaches, purring about "real beer satisfaction."

For a few years, Coors used slinky and campy Elvira to promote its beer, especially at Halloween. However, in 1996 it dumped the "Mistress of the Night" and poured pseudo-actress Pamela Anderson Lee into a shrunken dress, figuring more beer drinkers prefer Lee, who pretends she's a lifeguard on "Baywatch," than Elvira who has no pretensions.

In case a few rugged he-men aren't into beaches, there's macho-man motorcycles. One Coors poster shows a lady in short shorts, a halter top, and a leather jacket standing next to a Harley-Davidson. For the sophisticated beer guzzler, there's a poster of a model in black heels and a short black cocktail dress about to straddle a Harley Softail. Her fuel of choice? Coors Extra Gold. Possibly unwilling to pay a six-digit licensing fee to Harley-Davidson—or having already spent its budget on $10,000 a day models—Michelob Dry, an Anheuser-Busch product, has a model in black heels and a black cocktail dress merely caressing a beer bottle. For "variety," Budweiser, also an Anheuser-Busch product, has a brunette in a short red dress sitting seductively on steps.

Nevertheless, most of the nation's major breweries have copied each others' "sophisticated" look to promote their "premium" beers, hawking their not-so-subliminal attempts to make people believe that beer and "class" are synonymous.

Not so sophisticated is Colt .45 from G. Heilman, which once promoted its product by having a seductive woman in a short silky blue dress down on her hands and knees, her cleavage and come-hither look telling men, "Everytime." Keystone State, a Coors product, uses blue-and-white striped one-piece swimsuits on its models to promote the brand's label color. Killian's, another Coors brand, uses red. Its model is a tall redhead in a white bikini who exalts salivating men to "try a tall cool red one." Evoking an Irish theme, Mickey's features a large-busted model in a body-hugging green swim suit; between her spread legs is an obviously-phallic Mickey's wide-mouth bottle.

Missing from beer advertising is "beefcake," male models in muscle shirts and Speedos. Although the average per capita consumption of beer is 56 gallons a year for men who drink beer, according to *Impact Magazine*, women are now about 35 percent of all beer drinkers, almost half of all lite drinkers, and consume an average of about 14 gallons a year. When the breweries and their ad agencies figure out that women respond to beefcake, they'll supply it. But, for now, women apparently are lured to beer for other reasons.

For more than 50 years, the liquor industry kept ads off television, promoting their products mostly in magazines, targeting a "more sophisticated audience." Then, in 1996, the industry decided that it will consider TV advertising. The TV networks, Congress, the Federal Communications Commission, and President Clinton were appalled at this blatant violation of a "gentleman's agreement." Most TV stations say they will still ban alcohol ads, not because they're good citizens trying to keep their audiences from buying liquor, but because they're afraid other advertisers might pull out or that the government will issue sanctions. None seem worried there is a First Amendment violation somewhere in all this. Ironically, most liquor companies and TV stations say one of the reasons they hadn't aired liquor advertising is because they feared backlash from newspapers.

KRIS-TV (Corpus Christi, Texas), an NBC affiliate, became the first TV station in the country to air liquor advertising, placing them in the late-night hours. The station was immediately subjected to a massive letter-writing campaign orchestrated by something called the Corpus Christi Business Alliance.

Beer ads, of course, have saturated TV sports coverage. Nevertheless, the nation's largest breweries all talk about "responsible advertising," and how they deliberately avoid targeting the younger generation. Part of that is because the Federal Trade Commission doesn't allow it.

In December 1996, the FTC cited Stroh Brewing Co. for a TV ad that ran on MTV's "My So-Called Life." Stroh's says it didn't even know the ad was accidentally placed by MTV on a "kid's" program until contacted by the FTC. For its part, MTV acknowledged that the ad was placed accidentally during a "last-minute programming change." About one-third of the MTV audience is under 18.

Alerted by what the FTC did to Stroh's, Budweiser decided to pull its $2 million a year from MTV and send it to VH1 which skews to an older audience.

With gross sales of about $9 billion a year, and 46.8 percent of the domestic beer market, Anheuser-Busch is well ahead of the field. Its Budweiser brand, with 39.4 million barrels brewed a year and 20.9 percent of the domestic beer market; and Bud Lite, with 18.2 million barrels and 9.7 percent of the market, are the two best-selling brands in the country. About 90 percent of its $280 million a year advertising budget goes into television. However, unlike other major companies, Anheuser-Busch doesn't advertise on MTV because, says the company, "MTV skews too young."

The nation's breweries also say their advertising isn't sexist, something the FTC and FCC haven't sanctioned. However, breweries have been using women as lures in beer advertising since the late 1800s. The first ads featured pictures of the breweries and their logos, cartoony bartenders, or families enjoying beer. However, by the early 20th century, the companies began using women in their advertising. Most ads featured merely the face, heavily made up. The more adventurous featured women from the waist up. Most of the women had long flowing hair, possibly a subliminal message that the models had "let their hair down" for the male beer drinkers. Images were lithographed onto beer trays, coasters, and posters, and etched into newspapers and magazine advertising. Often, the breweries combined women, beer, and the latest autos, especially during the first two decades of mass production.

For several decades before Prohibition, Budweiser had featured the angelic-appearing "Budweiser Girls" on trays and related advertising media. Marathon featured a "bobby-soxer" in a tight sweater and short skirt suggestively posed next to a bowling alley, with the slogan, "Strikes You Right." Rheingold brought national attention to its product with the annual Miss Rheingold contest from 1940 to 1965. Rieger & Gretz Brewing Co. of Philadelphia, like many other breweries, combined the "angelic" with the sexual, featuring women in translucent gowns for annual calendars.

With the "sex revolution" of the 1960s, and increased competition, the major breweries lost whatever was left of their ages of innocence, and combined suggestive slogans and nearly-naked women with the "come hither" look.

Stroh's, the nation's fourth largest brewery, tweaked the public in 1991 with a campaign for its Old Milwaukee Brand that featured the Swedish Bikini Team, four platinum-blonde women who parachuted into a camp of men. The campaign was supposed to be a parody of the sex-based campaigns of the other breweries, but was killed after one season when several Stroh's employees protested the use of sexism to parody sexism.

Disregarding Stroh's experience, Coors unleashed the Artic Angels in 1993, three blonde women in thigh-high black boots and body-tight black body suits to promote Artic Ice. However, Janet Rowe, Coors manager of corporate communications, claims her company hasn't used sexist advertising "for some time." Not even the Artic Angels? That's a "local promotion discretion," says Rowe. Almost in the same breath, she admits the company "has not developed any formal new policy on women in bathing suits."

Nevertheless, although Coors' TV advertising is using more humor and less sexism, the bathing beauty posters are still prevalent in beer stores. Even against such formidable competition, Stroh's stuck by its earlier decision to reduce sexism in its ads, although one poster shows a model wearing a Chicago Bears jersey and biker shorts.

"Our whole campaign now," says Burke Cueny, Stroh's marketing director, is "more taste, more character. We're interested in featuring our beer in everyday situations as opposed to a fantasy-setting agenda."

Although Anheuser-Busch still fuses women, sexual suggestion, and beer, the print ads tend to be less "racy" than those of the other companies, although they still feature women in short and tight dresses or modest bathing suits. The company began cutting back on the bikini crowd in the late 1980s. "There are other ways to convey the message," says one of the conglomerate's spokesmen.

Genesee, distributed primarily in New York and Pennsylvania, doesn't connect sex with beer. With production of 1.9 million barrels a year, and annual gross sales of $200 million and a $2 million ad budget, Genesee is the seventh largest brewery in the country. Hugh Crossin, Genesee's director of advertising, says even with a healthy advertising budget, the company has no plans to succumb to lust. With only a 1 percent market share, Genesee, says Crossin, "can't compete with the giants, so we must establish our own identity."

Yuengling, the nation's 13th largest brewery, with gross sales of about $200 million a year, sells about 90 percent of its 275,000 barrel annual production in eastern Pennsylvania. Like Genesee, Yuengling also avoids sexist advertising. "We haven't had to resort to those tactics," says Dave Casinelli, vice president of sales and marketing for the nation's oldest brewery. He says Yuengling sells "on the basis of consistent qualities. We just can't compete with the majors."

Competing with the top three companies would be economic disaster for most of the other breweries. The cost to produce one poster for distribution to beer stores and customers could be $100,000. With few exceptions, almost all of the $7.4 million advertising budget for breweries not in the Top 10 is directed less on image, and more on product and substance.

"We don't need sex to sell our beer," says Dan Straub, president of Straub Brewing, St. Marys, Pennsylvania, which promotes its all-natural beer on the basis of taste, quality, and being "honestly fresh." Word-of-mouth, posters, and "a lot of community service" make Straub known in western Pennsylvania.

However, if Straub would stop worrying about quality, slash a few hundred thousand from research and development funds, cut back on the quality of his ingredients, then triple his $100,000 a year ad campaigns, he could hire a couple of models with IQs the size of their busts and put them into G-strings to coo to the public, possibly at a community service wet T-shirt contest, "I like to be Straubbed." Maybe then the nation's 46th largest brewery could sell more beer.

The Stupid Season

With less than a month before high school graduation, it's time for the annual Stupid Season.

It begins with a senior "skip day," as if the seniors haven't skipped enough times already. So, most of the seniors skip off to party somewhere, while the smarter seniors skip classes *and* the party.

At least one fifth of the nation's 13 million 13 to 15 year olds will attend proms, that ubiquitous cap to a 12-year flirtation with education and future unemployment, and for which hundreds of newspapers and magazines will tell them what to do and how to do it. Boys once wore sports suits, and girls wore dresses to the prom. But, with the schools still hung over from the "Affluent '80s," it's now a rented tux and mirror-shine shoes for about $100, or a new $150–$500 prom gown which will soon hang in the closet as moth food. About 98 percent of the girls buy a new dress, averaging $200, according to *Your Prom* magazine.

Haircuts are about $10 for guys; perms are $25–$100 for the girls. Add in another $100 for nail polish and fake nails, lipstick, mascara, perfume, and new hose. For that special splash of color, you need a $5 carnation boutonniere for the guy, and a $20 orchid corsage for the girl—or, maybe a $60 bouquet of a dozen roses.

Some boys rent new cars; almost half, says *Your Prom* will arrive in a $200–$250 a night limousine in vain attempts to impress whoever it is they believe they must impress. The rest apparently wash, wax, and vacuum their own cars, relatively recent pretend high performance red or black models which they park over four intersecting spaces so no one can hit their turtle-wax shine. To support the turtle, they work 20 to 30 hours a week at a minimum wage dead-end job. When anyone asks why they don't just quit and spend the time studying, or getting involved with extracurricular activities, they say they need the job to support their car and stereo.

A long time ago, the boy's extended family worked on a special meal for the prom couple. For some, circumstances allowed a nice dinner at an inexpensive restaurant. Now there's often only one parent in the house, and dinner is about $20 to $25 each.

Juniors once decorated the gym for the prom. Now, it's held at the country club or the "Sweet Magnolia Room" of the high-rise hotel. Add tickets for $20–$35 per couple, and prom pictures for about $25.

There once were live bands. Now, it's usually a DJ stuffing CDs and tapes into a 125-watt super system. It makes no difference since most of the seniors haven't a clue of what music is anyhow. (After all, they didn't have time to join the band or chorus since they had to work that dead-end job to pay for that turtle-wax car.)

Sometime during the evening, in a country which says it doesn't believe in royalty, a king and queen are announced and, like the monarchy in England, no one seems to know what it is they're supposed to do.

Many schools have figured out ways to make the prom night extra special by extending it until morning. They take the students' car keys, bring in a lot of donated food, and hold hourly raffles of everything from CDs to a car. But, for most, the prom is over by 11. It means another $10 for after-prom dessert and drinks, or a $5 contribution at a back-woods keg party. For some, it means another fifty or so bucks for the after-prom motel room. (Somewhere in all this is the second mortgage most families take out so their sons and daughters don't feel emotionally deprived.)

Let's move on to the graduation itself. The Supreme Court has ruled that prayers at graduation violate the Constitutional provisions of church–state separation. However, many school administrators apparently don't believe the Constitution applies to them. Tossing out excuses that would embarrass even an obtuse 10th grade civics student, the educational leaders claim that the Supreme Court ruling "isn't really final," that it "violates our freedom," or that "we've always done it, and we're not going to change now." Of course, their arguments sound strangely like ones many school officials said after the Supreme Court ruled segregation unconstitutional. At the same time they're making plans to defy the Constitution and the Supreme Court, the administrators are throwing thousands of students into detention for daring to defy even the most insignificant rule imposed by the schools themselves.

After prayers, the graduation speakers talk about how good the graduates' education has been, what glorious futures they have, and how they are the movers and shakers of tomorrow. Few point out the world they are about to move and shake has yet to reduce wars, poverty, crime, the health care mess, racism, sexism, and all the other -isms. No one says the SAT scores have been dropping for the past two decades, that 10 percent of the 2.5 million graduating seniors are functional illiterates, that the economy is in a sinkhole, and that exploitation of the work force is a reality far more ominous than losing the basketball championship. Sadly, until the graduates get their wake-up calls, they will continue to polish their cars and overspend their allowances on self-indulgent frills.

Tanness, Anyone?

Between a carpet of knee-deep snow and a nimbostratus ceiling, one of my friends is still sporting her summer tan. I know it's phony—and she knows that I know it's phony—but I have long ago stopped teasing her about it.

In her never-ending quest to appear to be beautiful and healthy, she has slathered skin tanning lotion into every pore of her body, laid out on roofs and beaches to catch whatever ray was passing by, and goes to a tanning salon twice a week. I'm not sure she's ever stepped into the surf.

For decades, I have endured the scorn of these fake-skin friends, their hair bleached to fireball yellow, their skin tanned to the color and consistency of obsidian, as they sweat their lives away, ruled by the nation's mass media which give them myriad examples of what editors think are the "beautiful" people. If the advertisers would just get skin cancer and shut up, the world might be a better place.

Nevertheless, I have always been content to know I had more genetic pigment than all of them, and don't need to cremate myself on a roof top to be healthy. A "natural 7," I reason, is far better than crapping out with a "phony 10."

Once, women desperately wanted to look pale. Ashen was to be admired. Pallid was wonderful! The lighter the skin, the healthier they believed they were, even if it meant hiding in a basement and fighting any attempt by Vitamin C to force its way into their lives. These women would read *Macbeth* and admire the ghost. Any darkness of the skin reflected that they weren't women of leisure, but (horrors!) *working* women—the kind who go outside and have to (shudder!) *do* things.

It changed in the early 1920s, not long after fashion designer Coco Channel took a yachting vacation and came back tanned. The newspapers and magazines reported how beautiful and healthy she looked. Women, who longed for, but could not afford Coco Channel creations, now decided they could try to become as tan as their favorite designer. Not just a little suntanned, but an I'm-darker-than-Bill-Cosby-tan as they soak up those ultraviolets!

During the next few decades, when America couldn't find enough sun to char their skin and fry their brains, they bought sunlamps, reflectors, and gallons of "fake tan" lotion, guaranteed to make their friends believe they had just returned from a decade in Bermuda—or Nigeria.

By the 1960s, physicians were declaring suntans to be unhealthy. Have you ever seen what a couple of hours a day in the sun can do to an unprotected body over a few years? If you don't have to chase away knife-wielding scouts from the Tandy Leather Co. from trying to skin you, then you have a chance to live until a ripe old age of at least 40. And if Tandy doesn't get you, there's a pile of melanoma waiting. Ever see what cancer of the eye or ear looks like? Ever see a jellyfish on a rotting log? Cancer scare? There's still sunblock. Just pick a number. Any low number. You'll "protect" yourself and darken up just like that Ban de Soleil model—and look just as good. After all, would advertising agencies lie?

Advertising from "fake tan" companies guaranteed the world's fair-skinned population they could get all the tan they wanted "without the harmful effects of the sun." The Food and Drug

Administration said the companies weren't telling the truth; the Federal Trade Commission struck down almost all the advertising claims as phony.

Exit fake tan lotions, enter suntanning salons. In the semi-privacy of a casket, people could pay $20 for 15 minutes, slobber even more lotion on themselves, and look even healthier. The owners of the tanning parlors claim the harmful effects from the sun are UVB rays, not the "healthy" UVA rays of the caskets. Not so, say the nation's dermatologists, who are no match for the UltraSun Turbo 20,000 or the mountains of advertising that would fill all the nation's potholes and probably the Grand Canyon.

By the mid-1990s, Americans bought more than $400 million in lotions and blocks, all declaring the best way to avoid melanoma was by slathering goo all over their bodies and getting just the right tan. After all, Coppertone's ads—in newspapers, magazines, and on billboards beginning in the 1950s—showed a playful puppy pulling down the bathing suit of a little tanned girl. Would Coppertone do anything to harm puppies *or* little girls?

Now, while many people desperately want to have dark "healthy" skin, they aren't willing to appear to be "ethnic." So, just in case someone could confuse them with being Black, Hispanic, Jewish, or any other genetically dark-skinned type, they strip their natural hair color, pour one of 100 shades of blonde dye onto whatever is left, and become extras for what's left of the beach blanket surfer craze. Just as they believe the advertising agencies wouldn't deceive them, they believe that blondes have more fun. Didn't that great American philosopher Lady Clairol say it? It must be so. And, of course, there are about 65,000 solutions on the market, each advertised as the greatest miracle since coconut oil, just designed to make you have fun while you lose every follicle in your genetic pattern.

Cramping Up for Health

On bicycle paths and highways, on dirt roads and in parks, in heat, rain, and snow, people are darting in front of cars, chased by dogs and preppy muggers, in a never-ending quest for a faddish youth and the right to believe they match up to all the media models and their plethora of books and exercise videos.

And so it happened that one cool morning while walking in

the park I was caught in the middle of the morning madness. From out of nowhere hundreds jogged past—sweating and straining, air cushions on their soles, earphones on their heads.

I was spun around several times. Dizzy, I tried to regain my composure, only to be hit again, as if the joggers were oblivious to everything else. At first frightened, but now angry, I tried to get up, only to be knocked down by another cluster of runners. Finally, I trapped one. Actually, he tripped over me.

"Confess!" I shouted. "Why do you run? What compels you?"

"Health," he said, panting and wheezing. "Makes your heart beat faster. By beating faster, it exercises it. Becomes stronger. You get a resting rate of 50, maybe 60. Read it in *Cosmo*."

"Why couldn't you just take a pill for it? Lots of pills will make your heart beat all over the place, then stop on command."

"Must experience pain," he wheezed. "Article in *Modern Maturity* said so."

"Do you experience a lot of pain?" I asked.

He took a series of small breaths, then told me that his feet hurt a lot more since he started running. He even blurted out that so did his ankles, thighs, knees, arms, neck, and even stomach. "We have to go through it to make us healthy," he said. "By staying healthy, I can work longer so I can buy more things."

"Like what?" I asked.

"Like these track shoes," he said, pulling one off a swollen foot while massaging a muscle cramp. "These shoes are made specifically for runners. They're completely cushioned, with special arch supports, a reinforced toe, and special color stripes to give it that extra special look of authenticity. They only cost $159.95, too."

"And they last for years," I said admiring the canvas.

"Oh, no! They last three, maybe four months. Even with these custom-made ten buck running sweat socks, all that sweat can really wear out a pair of shoes."

"I notice that you're wearing a floppy hat. Is that a runner's hat?"

"Sure is. Cost only $9.95, and worth every penny."

"The headband and wristbands?"

"Ten bucks."

"The wrist wallet?"

"Only $14.95."

"The suit?"

"If we don't have the proper suit, we'd be humiliated in front of our friends and neighbors. This one cost only $129.95 on sale, but it'll last at least another five, maybe six months. Besides, these are specially made to allow us to perspire more. That way we lose more water. Five, ten pounds at a time."

"That's a lot to lose at one time, isn't it?"

"If it wasn't for the specially-coated salt pills, we'd lose even more."

"How much?"

"A buck a pill. You need two, three pills a day. Then, there's the mandatory stop at Duffy's."

"The tavern on Hydroponic Avenue?" I asked.

"You don't want to lose too much fluid. That isn't healthy. So, after we run, we all stop over at Duffy's to get a few drinks and buy some more pills."

"You drink beer after a healthy run?" I asked suspiciously.

"Beer. Whiskey sours. Carrot juice. Whatever keeps the machine going."

He paused a moment, his breathing down to only 80 puffs a minute, then continued. "I'd sure like to talk with you longer, but I don't want to be too far behind. It's bad for the image. Besides, I've got to get to work. Make more money. Buy more running clothes."

"What do you do?!" I shouted after him.

"Advertising executive," he shouted back. "If you get a chance, stop by Duffy's for a drink. He'll also give you a good buy on track shoes, sweat socks, hats, sweatbands, wrist wallets, and running suits."

Death by Healthy Doses

They buried Bouldergrass today. The cause of death was listed as "media-induced health."

Bouldergrass had begun his health crusade more than a decade ago when he began reading more than the sports pages of his local newspaper, subscribed to his first magazine, and decided TV news could be informative if it didn't mention anything about wars, famines, and poverty.

Based on what he read and saw in the media, Bouldergrass moved from smog-bound Los Angeles to a rural community in scenic green Pennsylvania, gave up alcohol and a two-pack-a-day cigarette habit, and was immediately hospitalized for having too much oxygen in his body. To burn off some of that oxygen, he joined two-thirds of America's "beautiful people" on the jogging paths where he believed he was sweating out all the bad karma. In less than a year, the karma left his body which was now coexisting with leg cramps, fallen arches, and several compressed disks. But at least he was as healthy as the media told him to be.

To make sure he didn't get skin cancer from being in the sun too much, he slathered four pounds of No. 35 sunblock on his body every time he ran, and went to suntan parlors twice a week to get that "healthy glow" advertisers told him he needed. He stopped blocking when he learned that suntan parlors weren't good for your health, and that the ingredients in the lotions could cause cancer. So, he wore a jogging suit that covered more skin than an Arab woman's black chador with veil—and developed a severe case of heat exhaustion.

From ultrathin models and billions of dollars in weight-reducing advertising that told him "thin was in," he began a series of crash diets. When he was down to 107 pounds, advertising claims told him he needed to "bulk up" to be a "real man." So, he began lifting weights and playing racquetball three hours a day. Four groin pulls and seven back injuries later, he had just 2 percent body fat, and a revolving charge account at the office of his local orthopedist.

Several years earlier, Bouldergrass had stopped eating veal as part of a protest of America's inhumane treatment of animals destined for supermarkets. Now, in an "enlightened" age of health, he gave up all meat, not because of mankind's cruelty to animals, but because a TV panel revealed that vascular surgeons owned stock in meat packing companies. Besides, it was the "healthy" thing to do.

For a couple of years, lured by a multi-million dollar ad campaign and innumerable articles in the supermarket tabloids, Bouldergrass ate only oat bran muffins for breakfast and a diet of beta carotenes for lunch, until he found himself spending more time in the bathroom than at work. He eliminated the muffins entirely after reading an article that told him oatmeal, bran, and hood ornaments from Buick Roadsters were bad for your health.

Bouldergrass gave up milk when he learned that acid rain fell onto pastures and was eaten by cows. When he learned that industrial conglomerates had dumped everything from drinking water to radioactive waste into streams and rivers, he stopped eating fish. Then, he gave up pasta after reading about all the creepy crawlers who become fat from dough.

At the movies, he smuggled in packets of oleo to squeeze onto plain popcorn, until he was bombarded by news stories that revealed oleo was as bad as butter, and most theatrical popcorn was worse than an all-day diet of sirloin.

When he learned that coffee and chocolate were unhealthy, he gave up an addiction to getting high from caffeine and sugar, and was now forced to work 12-hour days without any stimulants other than the fear of what his children were doing while he was at work.

Unfortunately, he soon had to give up decaffeinated coffee and sugarless candy with cyclamates since both caused laboratory mice to develop an incurable yen to listen to music from the Grand Funk Railroad.

Left with a diet of fruits and vegetables, he was lean and trim. Until he accidentally stumbled across a protest by an environmental group which complained that the use of pesticides on farm crops was a greater health hazard than the bugs the pesticides were supposed to kill. Even the city's polluted water couldn't clean off all the pesticides. That's also when he stopped taking showers, and merely poured a gallon of distilled water over his head every morning.

For weeks, he survived on buckets of vitamins because all the magazines told him that's what he should do. Then, after reading an article that artificial vitamins shaped like the Flintstones caused dinosaur rot, he also gave them up.

The last time I saw Bouldergrass, he was in a hospital room, claiming to see visions of monster genetic tomatoes squishing their way toward him while mumbling something about cholesterol and high density lipoproteins. Tubes were sticking out of every opening in his emaciated body, as well as a couple of openings that hadn't been there when he first checked in.

Shortly before he died, he pulled me near him, asked that I write his obit, and in a throaty whisper begged, "Make sure you tell them I died healthy."

Mixing a Bitter Pill for America's Drug Companies

The advertising copy for the front of packages of Legatrin and Q-Vel were once similar. The only major difference was that Ciba's Q-Vel uses capitals; and Columbia's Legatrin used upper and lower letters. Beneath their logos, in small type, both companies proclaim the nonprescription drug was a "Muscle Relaxant/Pain Reliever." In bolder white letters, they also proclaimed each "Prevents and Relieves Night Leg Cramps."

Not so, said the U.S. Food and Drug Administration. Not only didn't the drugs prevent and relieve night leg cramps, but the quinine in the drugs could also cause severe medical problems, including visual, auditory, and gastrointestinal symptoms, as well as liver injuries, kidney failure, and severe dermatologic and blood damage. Hospitalization and deaths have occurred from reactions to the quinine, said the FDA which ordered the companies in 1995 to stop manufacturing and shipping over-the-counter medicines containing quinine. Not affected was the use of quinine for treatment of malaria. Because of almost insignificant doses, the FDA order didn't apply to the use of quinine in beverages.

Columbia's Legatrin was the source of $4 million of its $9 million per year income; Ciba sold more than 1.3 billion cartons of Q-Vel between 1986 and its termination.

A century ago, Americans unknowingly took alcohol and opium-laced drugs that were advertised as curing every medical problem from "indiscretions of youth" to syphilis and cancer. The patent medicine quacks were making $100 million per year from drugs that not only didn't cure anyone, but could lead to even more severe medical complications. Of that $100 million income, about $40 million went into bribing legislators to do nothing, and for newspapers and magazine editors to accept the ads and not investigate patent medicine claims.

In the U.S. Department of Agriculture, chemist Harvey Wiley spent 25 years trying to convince Congress that the patent "snake oil" medicines were harmful, only to be persecuted by his superiors. Finally, during the first five years of the 20th century, several national magazines, risking their own financial health, refused to accept patent medicine advertising, and launched major investigations that laid out the facts behind all the "wonder drugs." But, the states' legislatures and the Congress refused to do anything, their allegiances paid for by business, pharmaceutical manufacturers, and by the medical establishment itself.

Taking on the drug lobby, publisher William Randolph Hearst, then at the peak of his power, directed *Good Housekeeping* to establish a laboratory to investigate claims of all Hearst's advertisers, and to issue a "seal of approval" if the product did what it was meant to do without harming the public.

The Progressive administration of Teddy Roosevelt, spurred by the articles of several investigative journalists, had demanded the passage of a pure foods and drug act. But, lobbyists had bottled it up in a congressional committee.

Then, in 1905, journalist Upton Sinclair went undercover in Chicago's meat packing houses to document corruption within the U.S. Department of Agriculture that allowed companies to package diseased meat. After most newspaper and magazine publishers—themselves subject to bribes and lobbying by the meat packing and drug industries—rejected Sinclair's investigation, a socialist company published the first of several articles that eventually led to the book-length publication of *The Jungle*, now regarded as one of the nation's most brutal novels. The novel so inflamed the country—causing Americans to boycott packed meat and foreign countries to refuse shipment of meat packed in America—that Congress had little choice except to pass the Pure Foods and Drug Act first proposed by Dr. Wiley.

Nine decades later, Americans may become upset with the high cost of drugs, but because of the FDA, we no longer worry about the safety of the medicines we buy from the neighborhood pharmacy; and, because of some courageous journalists, we aren't as suspicious of the advertising claims made by the pharmaceutical companies.

INTERMISSION

Dysfunctional Thoughts

Is anyone else tired of hearing people claim they were from a "dysfunctional family" in order to justify their life's problems? Have a bad hair day? It's all because of the gene pool in your dysfunctional family. Greedy and self centered? You're from a dysfunctional family. Nasty to your neighbors and coworkers? Dysfunctional family. Abuse your wife or children? Yep, Dysfunctional Family Syndrome. Rob a bank? Kill a cop? Just chalk it up to having come from a dysfunctional family.

And, speaking of dysfunctional families, does anyone know what the Queen of England does? So far, thanks to television, for the past four decades we now know she dresses well, and can ride a horse and wave at the same time. But, what else does she do? Elizabeth II seems to be a nice lady, but she could easily be the poster queen for what happens when generations of royal families intermarry.

Why do the news media salivate all over their VDTs whenever anyone with a royal moniker does anything more than just wake up in the morning? Are more people than me suspicious of journalistic quality when our daily newspapers put royal sex scandals on the front page and *People* magazine devotes full pages to the "Royal Watch"? I wonder how many stories were spiked by the editors in order for them to splash the news that Fergie and Di sunbathed topless, that there was a major scandal in both Di's and Charles's affairs of state, and that some rich American consort was caught sucking toes? Add in the royal divorces, and two dozen forests had to be leveled to provide the paper for the "exclusives." Schlock romance novelist Barbara Cartland and the editors of the *National Enquirer* not our mainstream media should be the ones worrying about which royal retard is fooling around with which commoner.

Prince Charles who, if he weren't heir designate to the throne would probably be just another tweed-suited geek with a bagload of money, voluntarily pays $1.25 million a year in taxes on income of about $5 million. However, the Queen earns $50-60 million a year, and the State pays for all of her living expenses, including five official residences, the planes, helicopters, and Britannia, a 412-foot yacht that carries a crew about the size of the population of Cleveland. Beginning in 1993, the Queen has now voluntarily agreed to pay taxes on her income. Normally, that would be about $20 million, but the *Magna Charta*, or some such unenforceable document, allows her and the government to figure out an appropriate queen tax. The "appropriate" tax is estimated at $3-5 million a year.

At least there is a way for England to rid itself of its debt. In America, our debt is piling up at the rate of $13,000 a second. Now, to someone making $50 million a year, $13,000 may not be much, but $13,000 a year is about what distinguishes a family of four as being below the poverty level. It'd be boorish for us to ask the Queen for a few bucks, especially since the royals are now quite happy about not having to defend the actions of its former colonies.

However, I have a couple of ideas about how we can rid us of debt.

Illusionist David Copperfield has made a railroad car, an airplane, and the Statue of Liberty disappear. Maybe it would be worth it to pay him a few million to work on the national debt.

If magic doesn't work, and how Congress appropriates its pork can only be described generously as magic, maybe we could package the Royals into an afternoon soap, add a couple of hunks and hunkettes, then sell them all to some American network. My first thought is to drop "Days of All My Royal Romances" onto PBS since the national beg-a-thon network goes into orgasmic veneration over anything British. But, alas, we'd want to make money off the deal. So, we must pitch the other networks.

With the cost to produce a one hour prime time TV show averaging about $2 million an episode, and figuring 22 shows a year, that's at least a $44 million outlay. But, being producers, we do what every other producer does—we skim the profits, and take our rightful $10 million a year. At that rate, and assuming we can keep the debt from increasing more than $13,000 a second, we should be debt free by the time the TV networks get an original idea.

Wonderings of an Idle Mind

A lot passes through a columnist's mind while waiting for those great thoughts to lead to a weekly column. For instance . . .

Why is it that just about everyone believes he or she can become a writer part time and earn goo-gobs of extra money, but when I say that I'm thinking of doing brain surgery part-time for spare cash, they all walk away from me?

We all know that Superman is a journalist—and, of course, most journalists are super men and super women. But, does anyone know how Superman gets all that time off to pursue truth, justice, and the American way? Has anyone ever actually seen Superman attend a city council meeting or even a PTA meeting? When was the last time you actually saw him writing a story against a deadline?

Bruce Wayne, of course, kept his day job as owner of Wayne Industries so he can Batmanize riddlers, jokers, and a few million people into paying eight bucks for movie tickets.

Other multimillionaires have chosen to put their money into more important things than destroying evil. A Saudi prince in 1995 put up $500 million to bail out a near bankrupt EuroDisney. In a couple of years, Europeans will probably be going to Prince Al-Waleed bin Talal bin Abdulaziz al Saud Land.

Does anyone else think it's ironic that the Arabs, who have been taking over British businesses and New York taxis for over a decade now, have been invading French-owned businesses, long after France sent its Foreign Legion into Arab lands?

Almost every country except the United States has a minister of culture. This means either we don't have any culture or that politicians may think culture is what's grown in petri dishes. Either way, the lack of such a department says quite a lot about American values.

And speaking of American values, it seems that every time I turn on a TV set, some actor or actress is pumping the Charity of the Moment. There's perennial favorite Jerry Lewis and Muscular Dystrophy. For the homeless, we have Billie Crystal, Whoopie Goldberg, and Robin Williams. There's outlaw country singer Willie Nelson for Farm Aid, and the squeaky clean Osmonds for the Miracle network. Even Sally Struthers gets into the picture by pumping for some starving foreign children who need our $15 a month so they can take correspondence courses and become brain surgeons. With all the good charities taken up, I wonder if some aspiring actress was denied an audition because her agent couldn't find her a suitable charity.

Why does almost every starlet who's taken three acting lessons believe she has been given innate wisdom to "feel" her character and rewrite the script?

Why do starlets say they'll do nude scenes "only if it's pertinent to the story," expose themselves in five centerfolds and 18 scenes in three movies, become mini-stars, then declare that because they believe in "family values," they won't do nude scenes no matter what the story line?

Why does the average person know who John Wayne Bobbitt, Tonya Harding, Joey Buttafuoco and almost every unclad starlet in Hollywood are, but have never heard of George Gershwin, Medgar Evars, or any of the members of the Supreme Court? And, can we throw some of the blame to the media for pandering to our lowest basic instincts?

Why do TV interviews always have cutaway shots of the reporter pretending to pay attention to what the news source is saying? Do we really need to see the reporter silently emoting three times in a 90 second interview?

Does anyone know why the TV camera focuses on the outfielder watching the homerun ball hit over his head, rather than on the batter who's running the bases? Couldn't those TV geniuses have figured out by now how to do a split screen?

Several years ago, the late night talk shows booked authors for the last segment. Now, Jay, David, and Conan book mounds of noise disguised as alternative rock groups. Does this indicate a change in American culture and values, or only that associate producers no longer can read?

And, while we're discussing TV, does anyone else get upset when newscasters pronounce nuclear as "Noo-kuhlar," February as "Feboo-ary," and library as "Lie-barry"?

Councils on literacy have done a wonderful job of creating flyers and bulletin boards to tell about their programs. But, if you're illiterate, how do you know what number to call?

Isn't anyone else offended that Pennsylvania's government and tourism industries have run a PR campaign to make the world believe, "America Starts Here"? The reality is that a better slogan might be "America Falls Into Potholes Here."

Why does it seem that small companies are trying to make us believe they're really large, with fancy titles for their staffs, while the megaconglomerates shower us with advertising they think will make us believe they're really our hometown neighbor?

Does anyone know why people pay $10 to 15 for T-shirts that advertise company names and slogans? Shouldn't the companies pay *us* to be their walking billboards?

The current fad in advertising is the semipersonalized telemarketers—"Hi, how you doing today?" Naturally, they're not selling anything, they just want to "take a poll" or do something nice that will improve our lives. I wonder if we could take a lesson from corporate America and establish a system that tracks incoming calls and responds the way American business responds to us. Here's an idea. "You have reached the Schmidlapp Residence. If you are a bill collector, please press 1. If you wish to sell us a new and exciting product, please press 2. If you have a credit card you're hawking, please press 3. If you want to protect our credit cards from theft, press 4. If it's an extended warranty, just punch up number 5. For telephone companies that have 45 reasons why we should switch from our current phone service, your number is 6 . . ." We could set up an entire minute of menus, then when that poor fool falls for one, and punches the button, we'll just route him further. "You have pressed 2, telling us you're selling a new and improved product. If you have a product with wheels, press 1 . . ." If the telemarketer survives to the seventh submenu level and thinks he's found the right number, we just let him hear the final message, assuming he hasn't taken a pound of Prozac in the meantime—"You have punched the following numbers: 2, 3, 8, 5, 4, 7, and 9. Now, push No. 86."

When he does, the phone disconnects.

Finally, for the past five decades, millions of Americans have wondered how it was possible for the Holocaust to have occurred. We need look no further than America's reading habits for the answer. In 1993, the worst-selling single issues for *Time* and *Newsweek* were cover stories about the war in Bosnia. For *U.S. News & World Report*, the worst-selling cover story was about the famine and anarchy in Somalia. The best-selling issues? Cover stories about Rush Limbaugh and lesbianism.

ENTERTAINMENT

Three Nights a Week

This is the true story of a better-than-average musician and a slick out-of-town entertainer.

It all began one afternoon when the struggling musician lined up a paying audition at a local nightclub. One hour—$50. If the audience liked what it heard, there would be a contract. Four hours a night; three nights a week; $50 per person per night. Not much, but it was work, and recently the musician's bass was in the pawn shop more than it was on stage.

Hopefully, this gig would last a few weeks, giving him spending money so he could cut back the hours on his day job as a carpenter. He called up a better-than-average drummer who was working at a drive-through car wash, and began searching for a lead singer.

Enter, the slick out-of-town entertainer.

At one time, Slick was an opening act lounge entertainer. For years, he had made the rounds of clubs in Reno, Tahoe, and Vegas. But it had been awhile since Slick was on stage, and now he was broke. The musician knew Slick needed money, and Slick knew that the musician needed him in the trio.

Four hours before the audition, Slick showed up for rehearsal, and almost as soon as he unpacked his guitar began whining. The songs weren't right. The arrangements weren't right. The harmonies weren't right. The only thing right, of course, was Slick.

Later that evening, the trio went to the club, two of them hoping that Slick wouldn't desert them, and Slick planning to desert faster than crowds leaving a free bar when the booze runs out.

For a 50-buck hour, the trio gave the audience what it wanted. When the set was over, the club manager agreed to hire the impromptu trio. Four hours a night; three nights a week; $50 per night per person. If the trio could "bring in a clientele," there would be more nights, more pay. But it wasn't going to happen.

"I'm not going to do it," Slick told a mutual friend of the bass player and expected the friend to tell the musician. "These guys aren't any good," Slick proclaimed.

"They're tired. They had to work day-jobs. They'll get better. A week of rehearsal and—"

"Place is a dive. Look at the crowd. Bunch of drunks. Tell them I'm out."

"You tell them," said the friend curtly.

The following Thursday night, the musician and the drummer, with a replacement lead singer/guitarist, opened at the club to an appreciative audience. They danced; they drank more beer; they left nice tips. Everything seemed to be going well. But two weeks after that, the club manager said he couldn't afford the trio—who were getting $50 per person per night. "I'm sorry," he apologized. "You guys were good, but I just can't afford it." It was just a matter of finances. It happens all the time.

The next week, the trio was replaced by . . . Slick who, the night before the audition almost a month earlier, had left his home phone number with the manager. And, said Slick, he was willing to work three nights a week for a hundred bucks a night—as a solo—thus saving the club about $150 a week.

Goodbye Trio; Hello Slick.

In a couple of weeks, many of the faithful customers, the ones who drank buck-a-mug beer and wanted dance music not ballads and folk music, began to leave, and a lot of new customers, who didn't come to dance, began sitting at the tables, buying three-buck mixed drinks and four-buck sandwiches. They didn't care how Slick got his job, or that he wasn't reporting his wages to the union. Slick was happy; the new audience was happy; the club manager was happy, and even raised the wage another 75 bucks a week.

But, revenues began falling a little, then a little more. Although the audience was buying more expensive drinks, they were nursing them longer, just sitting and talking and not leaving as much for the waitresses as the beer crowd had. Soon, even this audience slowly began to leave. People can dance to the same music night after night, but they can't listen to the same tunes night after night.

Now, Slick is no fool, and sometime in the past month he had asked another club manager to drop by the club one evening, while there were still a lot of customers. Three months after his first set, after Saturday evening's last set, moments after he packed up his guitar and collected his pay, Slick gave notice. Five days later, he was at a new club. The original club no longer had a Slick, and the revenues fell even further as the new faithful crowd went somewhere else, and the old faithful crowd had long ago deserted, and Slick was somewhere else, making money on an endless journey to capture what once might have been.

Sounds of the Concrete City

On Fifth Avenue near Rockefeller Center in the Concrete City, a trio of steel drummers beat out a Jamaican tune. The three Jamaicans, in New York because of the "opportunity" they heard exists, arrive every day at mid-morning; they leave every day in the late afternoon, seldom staying until 5 p.m. Very few people stop at 5 p.m.; they have those damned subways and trains to catch, and there's nothing more important than making your connections and leaving the City, even if it's only to Long Island.

Nearby, each with a predefined space against the walls of commerce on this warm Spring day, are a brass quartet, a saxophonist, and a couple of guitar players forced to endure an acoustic lifestyle to avoid getting disturbing the peace citations.

Pleased to receive random applause and the change dropped into open instrument cases, they blend their melodies into the noise of traffic. Maybe a club owner will one day hear them, and sign them to a six-night-a-week contract. Maybe they'll one day play in Lincoln Center or even Carnegie Hall. Maybe a big-shot music producer one day will stop, offer words of encouragement, or hand them a long-term recording contract. Maybe they will be able to leave their crowded Lower East Side or Queens tenement apartments or row-house existence and move into one of the outrageous rents of "oh-so-tony" Tribeca or the rarefied atmosphere of the Upper West Side. Maybe. . . . There are so many maybes and so few choices.

A few yards away, in counterpoint to the cacophony of the streets, is a flutist, her long black hair tied in the back by a blue and green silk scarf; a peace symbol, conspicuous by its presence in a city that shows little tranquility, caresses her bosom. She sits on the sidewalk, her back against a 21-story spire of steel and glass that blocks out the sun, places an earthenware flute to her lips, and blends haunting Mozartian melodies into an upbeat jazz tempo.

"That's very pretty," I say as she gently lets a coda float off.

She looks up, and her eyes smile, telling me, "Thank you." She continues playing.

"You been here long?" I ask.

She stops, looks at me, tries to figure me out, then quietly answers, "Since the White Rabbit died." A strange answer in a strange town. She puts the flute down across an open case that has 10, maybe 15 dollars, mostly in change. On a good day, street musicians can make more than $100, but this lady probably won't make half of that today. She looks up, questioning. "Why did you stop?"

"Maybe it was the music."

"Maybe it was because you're a reporter." She has me pegged, but before I can ask her how she knows, she answers. "Your eyes are beautiful, but they're always searching."

"Would you mind answering a few questions?" I ask politely.

"No," she says equally polite, "but I'll play you some songs."

"Songs are nice," I counter, "but I write about people, not songs."

"Doing a story on street musicians?" she asks, knowing the answer.

"Maybe. Can I interview you?"

"You don't need to ask me questions. Listen to the music. It's all there. There is no secret."

"Can you at least tell me where you were born? Why you're here in New York? If you're a music teacher; member of an orchestra? . . . Waitress? Secretary? Is this a way for you to make some loose change?"

She smiled, a clever somewhat impish smile. "Does it matter? Listen . . . Just listen to the music." Again she placed the flute to her lips, closed her eyes, and squeezed every emotion from "Where Have All the Flowers Gone?" She looked up. I was still there. Perhaps that surprised her. "Why?" she asked. Just "why?"

"Who knows," I answered flippantly. "Might be a good story." She looked at me, searching for her own answers. "I liked the music,"

I hastily added. "There's something more than the music."

"There's nothing more than the music," she said.

"How much can you earn in a day?" I asked. "Do you mind people running past you? Do the police hassle you?"

She answered with "The Sounds of Silence."

Maybe she once had sung of war and protest; maybe she once was a social activist; maybe she still is; maybe she once was an executive, like the thousands who rush past her every day as they try to claim their place in the "me generation"; maybe . . .

All around is the reality of the city, of people waking early, grabbing trains and subways, rushing to work, expediting the day, worrying about performance ratings and promotions, lost sales and the stock market, mergers, acquisitions, and even bankruptcies, fortified by a lunch of Maalox and martinis. Perhaps one day, before their first heart attack, they may be able to afford one of those overpriced $500,000 mid-town condos where they can plant a potted tree on the veranda or move to a home in the suburbs where there are lawns. Perhaps one day they, too, will stop and listen to the sounds of silence.

Voices of America

In 1974, on the fifth anniversary of the Woodstock Concert, I interviewed several persons who were at Woodstock. During 1970 and 1971, I had interviewed several persons of the Ohio National Guard. Each of the discussions is part of a longer interview. The interesting juxtaposition of their stories—which suggests there wasn't much difference among the American youth, whether soldier or protestor—is a tribute to an age, and to a people.

KENT, Ohio, May 4, 1970—The spirit of last August's Woodstock Nation was murdered early this afternoon in the northern Ohio city of Kent when Ohio National Guard troops opened fire at Kent State University, killing four persons and wounding at least twelve others. The four dead students at Kent State were walking past a 1,000 student demonstration against the war in Vietnam.

"They got their own nation—the Pig Nation. We got ours—the Woodstock Nation. It's where we could liberate our minds from the American bullshit, and just groove on the beautiful vibes.

It was our own celebration of life. But the pigs wouldn't let it be. John Sinclair is looking at 10 years for giving two joints to a nark. I don't fuckin' care what their fuckin' law is, they went after him. They went after him 'cause he was leading the Revolution. And they got Abbie [Hoffman] and Jerry [Rubin]. Abbie got up on stage and tried to tell everyone all about Sinclair, and fuckin' Peter Townsend [of The Who] tried to throw him off the fuckin' stage. They told everyone to listen to their music, but they didn't have no fuckin' feelings about what was happening."

"I was 20 years old. Same age as them. I didn't get to go to college. Parents couldn't afford it, and I don't get no breaks. I'm working at an auto parts store right now. Makin' a few extra bucks on weekends servin' my country. I put most my Guard pay into a separate account. Maybe some day I'll go to college. Maybe I'll just pack it up and move to Colorado. But, shit, them hippies! They don't know how good they got it. Mommy and Daddy payin' all the bills. Parties all week. They get those high-pay jobs when they graduate. This is the best god-damned place they'll ever live in. Ain't no better place anywhere on earth, and all they want to do is tear it down."

"When I heard that the festival was being moved [from Walkill to White Lake, N.Y.] I was going to pack it up and take a week's vacation. Just leave. I'd heard about all those long-haired hippies and what they do to property. All that dirty language and the nudity, and how they want to destroy our country. But my wife and I, we just couldn't afford to take a vacation, so we took a deep breath and just waited. Y'know, it wasn't all that bad. Oh, there were a few that thought they were the Hell's Angels, but most were decent and respectable. A lot of us in town made sandwiches and gave water to them. Didn't charge them anything either. Not like them stores that charged a buck or two for a 29 cent loaf of bread. Things like that. But most just gave them the food. You treat them well, they treat you well. No need to hate. Them and us, we didn't agree on politics. But, now that we seen all that's happened over there [in Vietnam] maybe they were right all along. Maybe they were just tryin' to tell us something, and we just didn't listen."

"They called us on a Saturday afternoon [May 1]. I don't think it began as a war protest. I think that they [the students] were drunk and looking for more excitement when the bars closed. They sure as hell made a mess out of that town! Broke damn near every window; set fires in the streets. Don't know why they sent us in. Students do it every spring. I thought the civil authorities should have handled it, but that wasn't my decision. I just follow orders. Did my job. I don't hate them. Not anymore at least. Not after what I seen happen [in Vietnam.] I had a job to do. Anyhow, the next day [May 2], Nixon says he was sending troops into Cambodia, and that really lit their fuse. Worse than anything Johnson ever did. They couldn't get to Nixon, so they used us."

"I worked in Operations [at the festival] and I'll tell you this. I didn't hardly crap for a week, it was that bad. I signed up [with Woodstock Ventures] in May [1969] so I was in on some of the early stuff. We worked 80, 90, maybe a hundred hours a week going into the weekend [August 15–17], and just about around the clock that whole weekend. Man, were there problems! Every kind you could think of. We had a whole fuckin' city to worry about. Medical. Sewage. Food. Recreation. Hundred departments all working together. Well, mostly working together. John and Joe [John Roberts and Joe Rosenman, festival directors] took a bath on this one. It was really too bad because they really cared, and all they got for it was a whole lotta shit. Do you know that on Friday [the first day] there were roving bands trying to 'liberate' the Festival by breaking down the fences? They could have easily reinforced the fences, but Roberts decided to take them down and make it a free festival. He was afraid people would get hurt. Now, I'll tell you what others would have done. They would have said, 'Screw you!' But these two birds [Roberts and Rosenman], they still manipulated and wheeled and dealed and tried to make it cool. They cared, and they ate it."

"We weren't too organized at first. Best I could recall, none of us knew what was going to happen. All we knew was we were supposed to protect life and property. Lot of us weren't long out of Basic, but we all worked together, kinda looked after each other. Somehow, we all got it set up and organized."

"I remember the Hog Farm the most. They set up these food tents. Ran 'em just like a business. Most efficient operation I ever saw. They were about the most unselfish people you'd ever meet. Hardly none of us had much cash. We just kinda all drifted out when we heard what was going down. The Hog Farm people, they were there cooking and dishing out food for us. And when we'd have bad trips, they brought us down."

"Bunch of selfish pricks! All they cared about was themselves. Didn't care about no one else. I think about it every moment. Maybe they thought it was cool, maybe *groovy* to shout 'Pigs!' and 'Fuck the establishment!' and go destroying other people's property. They was screamin' and yellin' and actin' just like a bunch of foul-mouthed assholes. Burned the ROTC building, then cut the firehoses. I remember it like it was yesterday. We got hit by rocks and molotov cocktails. Can you fuckin' believe it! They was yellin' for peace, and they was a-throwin' molotov cocktails! I wanted to take one of their cocktails and give them a fuckin' enema!"

"You get half a million people in 35 acres of open field, and I don't care how good you plan, how many johnnies you set up, it's still going to smell like shit. It was hot and muggy, and that made it even worse. They kept digging ditches, but the odor was still there. Not even all the hash and weed in the world could kill it. I never smelled anything as bad since."

"With all that yellin' and screamin', and them sayin' how the country sucks, they were still singin' 'This Land Is Your Land.' Ain't that a riot? They were singin' patriotic songs and torchin' the flag. Not some Commie flag, but our flag. The stars and stripes! Some of the chicks even tried to stuff flowers into our rifles and get us to sing with them. . . . Actually, now that I think about it, it wouldn't have been such a bad idea."

"Man, that music was something else! I mean, like up there in one place was all the best there ever was. [Among them were, The Who; Blood, Sweat, and Tears; Jefferson Airplane; Credence Clearwater Revival.] And there was Janis Joplin and Arlo Guthrie and Jimi Hendrix and Johnny Winter and Joe Cocker and Santana and about 30 bitchin' groups, man. And they was a-shakin' that stage, and you could feel the vibes all 'cross the land, and they got into your soul, man—do you know what I mean?—they got into your soul—and they stayed there. We were singin' stuff from 'Alice's Restaurant,' and 'Sgt. Pepper.' Whole bunch of us was singin' stuff like 'Hey, Jude.' You know, the part that goes, 'Take a sad song and make it better?' And when we got tired of that, we took off on 'Day Dream Believer.' Just over and over. Mostly just the chorus. But it sounded kinda right. Like it belonged."

"Assholes! They don't belong anywhere. Maybe except on a college campus, protected from reality. Anyhow, they was selfish. Didn't give a shit about nobody. Not their country. Not themselves. No one. Year later, I remember what happened, and it ain't been easy. It hurts. It really hurts, and I get these dreams and I can't make them go away."

"They had this amateur stage away from everything else, and anyone could perform. Bands and poets and jugglers and people who just wanted to have their say. Well, Joan Baez—can you believe it, man, Joan Baez!—well, she sees that there are people kinda just hangin' loose, so she does an hour! A whole fuckin' hour on an amateur stage! Know what else? She didn't just go up on that stage. She waited her turn. Must have waited an hour, two hours. No one knew she was waiting, I guess, but she waited her turn, just like everyone else. Was almost late for the main stage. You know what? Best of them all, the very best, that was Country Joe [McDonald]. Now, that's one heavy dude, and that ain't no shit. Y'know, man, like on Friday, they was a havin' trouble getting their shit together. Afraid there might be dead air on stage. Well, they find out Country Joe was there, and they asked him to do a set. Now, he ain't on their program, and he was just kinda like hangin' loose. But, y'know, Country, he just played just about every gig anyone asked him for. Lot of them were for nothing, just to help the cause. Even wrote some good shit, too. Powerful political shit. Well, anyhow, last couple of years, hardly anyone seen him. He'd been lying rather low, like on the decline, and he kinda didn't want to do this gig. Well, they told him they needed him. I mean they really needed him. So, he gets out there and follows Richie Havens. Can you believe that?! Anyhow, there's a whole shitload of us out there. More'n Country's ever seen in his whole freakin' life! And he's scared shitless. And we don't know 'bout Country, him bein' out of circulation so long. But he gave us the Fish Cheer, and we all went wild, just a-yellin' and a-hollerin'. And Country, he was just a whoppin' up there, doin' his thing. I mean, like he couldn't do no wrong. He made it happen, man. But, wait, that's not all of it. When the big rains came [Sunday], and there were electrical lines all over the place, and all of us were scared shitless 'cause we thought we might fry 'cause we didn't think they'd ever turn off all that electricity fast enough, Country [and the Fish] gets up on the stage and they sang to us. Got our minds off things. None of us could hear him. But he was singing for all he was worth! Calmed us down. Sucker sure do know his shit!"

"My unit had been called up for the race riots in Cleveland [1966] and Akron [1968]. But I'll tell you this, I was more scared at Kent than anytime in my life. They was gonna kill us, like thinking that wiping us out would end the war. We was scared shitless, but we was there 'cause we had to be. They should have let us be. They shouldn't have messed with us. We were dressed in full combat gear. Flak jackets. Helmets. Bayonets. Hell, we never even used bayonets exceptin' for training. And the hippies, they thought they'd take us on. . . . I . . . there's . . . I just . . . can't forget what happened that day. Mom's been tellin' me the past year to just put it all behind me. Get on with my life. But, I can't. I can't do it."

"When some people think about Woodstock all they think about is the drugs and nudity. The media focused on that. Sure, we were stoned. Well, most of us anyway. But we weren't hurting no one. Yeah, I went swimming nude. Lot of us did. Some even walked around nude. It was fucking hot, for Chrissakes! Hot and muggy, and we didn't have showers like the vacationers at Howard Johnson's got. It wasn't no giant sex and drug orgy like the papers tried to make it out to be. It was just a lot of people getting tuned up, just groovin' to the music and free of the Man."

"They just shoulda let us be. You can't commit violence without getting some of it back. I didn't like what happened, but it had to happen. They made it happen. We had to fire! We didn't have no other choice. If we didn't fire, we would have sustained heavy casualties. We told them to disperse. We warned them! We told them what would happen but they kept coming at us, trying to surround us. I couldn't see the looie [lieutenant] and Sarge was in the line somewhere, and none of us knew what the fuck was going down, but we had our orders. They told us to return all fire. Then I heard a shot. Then a lot more. I was sure there was a sniper. I'd have sweared to it."

"They hired hundreds of rent-a-cops, told them to protect life and property, but don't hassle us. Kinda just blend in; help out and be cool. Even the cops from all the local towns, they was cool, rappin' with us. It kinda upset the locals, though, 'cause there's these state laws about drugs, and on the grounds, cops were lookin' the other way, except for the big dealers, and you step off the grounds one foot, and they'd bust you. Locals thought they shoulda been bustin' us no matter where we were, but there weren't enough of them, and they knew we weren't gonna cause no trouble."

"They had to be on drugs. All of them. Drugs make you crazy. They was crazy. Destroying everything. Messin' with armed troops at bayonet-ready. No doubt about it, they had to be stoned, otherwise why would they destroy everything. Why'd they try to attack [combat-ready] soldiers? Don't make no sense."

"I was working in Big Pink. That and the White Tent were for the medical problems. The yellow tent was for other stuff. Any time you get close to a half million people together, you'll have problems. We had to watch for hep [hepatitis] because the sewage facilities weren't much better than open ditches, and the stench—man, the stench was unbearable at times, especially after the rains. All the chemicals in the world didn't get rid of that smell. They don't teach you about this in med school. It's a whole different kind of medicine. Almost no injuries caused by fights. But drugs were all over the place. Mostly acid, hash, pot. Problem was that a lot of the junk was bad. Some of the problem was that a lot of them didn't get too much sleep, not much food. That made it even worse. There were always people waiting for treatment for bad trips or cut feet. Humidity was high. Damned near impossible to work. I guess it was like a combat zone, though I never went. And the casualties were coming in all the time. They had to airlift in supplies, it was that bad."

"No, there was no official order to fire. The situation didn't allow it. A Guardsman always has the right to fire if his life is threatened. I didn't shoot no shots, though. My weapon still had its issue [bullets]. Didn't fire nothin' at no one! You gotta believe me on that one. I didn't shoot no one. It wasn't good what happened, but violence isn't the answer. I . . . I don't regret what we had to do. I was just doing my job. You do what you're told. You can't think about the consequences. . . . There was a burst of fire, then it was over. Captain called for a cease-fire almost immediately, but there was still some shooting. Then it was over. 'Ceptin' it's never been over. And it just won't go away."

"Woodstock was a burst of our energy; our music; our spirit. Phil Ochs said it for all of us. He wrote a lot of powerful words. But I cried when I first heard 'I Ain't Marchin' Anymore.' I just sat there and cried. I couldn't take it, it was so powerful, and all I could do was cry. I guess, maybe, that was what Woodstock was all about. It told the world that you could live in peace and harmony and celebrate life and not have to march. And not have to kill. And it's your decision."

"I didn't like what we had to do. There's gotta be something real horrible wrong when we kill our own people. I mean, there we was. Them and us. 'Bout the same age. Next day, it hit me. I just sat down and cried and cried. I couldn't help it. None of us could."

The Monday Night Football Game

The minuscule cocktail tables, red cloths draping their round tops, threaten to tip when pushed; nevertheless, they serve their dual functions as repositories for drinks and cigarettes, and as excuses to cluster chairs.
The semistuffed chairs that surround the tables, however, are sturdy, made with a wood-like veneer for the back and base, and covered with a synthetic something-or-the other that is supposed to look like leather. At the beginning of every evening, four chairs surround each table, making for intimate experiences, but the chairs roll, and during the evening will roll back and forth from table to table.
Along one wall, with its fake fireplace motif, are recently-manufactured Victorian-style couches and high-backed chairs. On the walls are photomurals—one of deer grazing in the field, the other of geese in flight. Near the geese are fake-wood bookshelves supporting *Reader's Digest* condensed books and plants that will never die.
A 60-foot U-shaped bar edged in naugahyde softness, guarded by 25 or 30 fake-oak $80 bar stools, is on the opposite side. Against another wall, not far from wood-panelled restrooms, six

mikes and four speakers quietly frame a Lilliputian bandstand that supports a set of drums and an electronic organ programmed so that anyone who can count to four can play it. On Thursdays, Fridays, and Saturdays, three singer-musicians will have their sounds amplified to the threshold of maybe wilting the plastic flowers. Wood beams and amber chandeliers above, red and black patterned carpeting below. The lights are forever dim. Dim for effect; dim for illusion.

It's now 6 p.m., Monday. There are a few people here, most in their 20s and 30s. At the bar sits a lady, perhaps 25 or 30, maybe older, flanked by two men. The lady could be a secretary or junior executive. Her golden highlighted hair is jelled, curling-ironed, permed, and blow-dried to give her a perfectly natural look. She wears makeup and lipstick; Max Factor on her face, Revlon on her lips. Her fashionably low-heeled pumps add an inch to her height. Her pink silk blouse and tan wool skirt could not have been bought more than a month ago. The two men, also in their late 20s or early 30s, could be lawyers or junior executives or ad salesmen. Suits of blues, ties of red. Modishly-long razor-cut blown-dry hair, as painfully attained as the lady's, covers half their ears. A slight fashion statement, but nothing too extreme. Clean-shaven with a gentle splash of Bijam. Expensive-looking watches and 10-karat gold college rings.

First one, then another, talks to the lady. Then both talk to her. For part of the evening, she'll delight in being in the middle. They'll talk to her and with her; maybe later, about her. But right now, they're both talking with her. About nothing really. They had earlier identified themselves by their occupations; she had identified herself by her astrological sign. Of course, this had meant that the two men had to identify their own signs. Compatibility is important in a place like this.

A man sits nearby, a touch of talcum and after-shave hinting the air, a casual synthetic drip-dry V-neck squeezing what are probably his rock-hard chest and washboard abdomen, drip-dry 501s hugging his waist and thighs, imitation leather shoes caressing feet that have been adequately powdered. A few moments later, another man, almost a copy, but with a golden chain dangling in his 'V'—few men will be bare-necked—sits down. There's now one immaculate lady surrounded by four *GQ*-approved men. To others, it appears that they're close friends—buddies—pals. Singularly, they talk with her. About cars. About careers. They talk about this. And they talk about that. About promotions and job security, racquetball, jogging, or time-sharing. About something each of them read in the *National Enquirer* or *Penthouse*, but which they remember as having read in *The Wall Street Journal*, *Esquire*, or *Business Week*. The high cost of apartments and condos is a major problem. Finding a good CD system or cellular phone for the BMW or Celica is a major problem. Every now and then, there might be a discussion, but never controversy, about the something in the news, their mouths parroting *Time* or *Newsweek*, their concern as deep as cocktail glasses, as lasting as cocktail napkins.

Cocktail waitresses—costumed in black high heels, black-net hose, micro-mini fluffy skirts, push-me-up bras disguised beneath titillating-cut blouses—hustle the drinks while the customers hustle each other. No glass will be allowed to be empty for more than a moment. There's always another drink to be served, another tip to be earned.

At a table, a young man orders a Vodka and 7; at another table, a young lady orders a Vodka and 7. They have something in common. They glance at each other, and away from each other. She gets up, goes to the *hors d'oeuvres* table, and delicately places small carrot sticks, dip, and shrimp puffs onto a small paper plate. It's just enough, but not too much. Must watch that waist. She turns, and almost falls over the gentleman who exchanged glances with her. She apologizes. He apologizes. They apologize. They giggle over their embarrassment of almost falling into each other, begin some small talk, then wander to a table at a neutral site. It's all so superficial, but no one cares. They need to hustle so they can be with someone. So, they'll keep searching . . . reflecting . . . being conversationally attractive.

A pair of "barely-21s," a few months into the work force, enter and sit at a table. She's carded, her ID discreetly checked by a waitress. This is too lucrative a business to be jeopardized by a Liquor Board violation. Her companion, blowing smoke rings from a Marlboro positioned beneath an anemic brown-blonde mustache, is accepted without ID. They order piña coladas and think they're in love.

Two 30ish ladies sit near one of the bookshelves. They talk what must seem to be "girl talk." Two 30ish guys sit near another bookshelf, talking "man talk." It isn't long before there are four people at one of the tables and no one at the other, and God-only-knows what they have to talk about.

The regulars greet each other; the infrequents settle in. Watching. Waiting. Four more razor-cut, blown-dry junior somethings enter, survey the swingles scene, find almost everyone attached to someone else, order Heinekins and Bud, talk, joke, make polite noises, and imagine they're successfully cool.

Near one of the photomurals sits a lady with a vacant sadness in her eyes as she sits alone, reflecting—thinking—maybe waiting. For a friend? Lover? Nevertheless, she's attractive, and probably won't be alone long. Someone will claim to have just the same values she has—and wouldn't she like to go somewhere else?

It's now 8:30. More than a hundred people are here. Talking. Chatting. Discussing. Talking about jobs and vacations, cars and condos. Every day it's the same. Every day the people are the same. And they all talk about never—ever—planning to get into a rut like Jim or Karen or Roger or Maureen. They all reaffirm that although they love their jobs and are more than amply rewarded, soon they'll be promoted or move to something better. There's always something better, whether people or jobs. And they're so busy hearing themselves that they don't know that no one is listening, but they'll be sure to "thank you for sharing that," or letting us know that they "can relate to that."

For the last time this evening, the *hors d'oeuvre* table is replenished, and the price of drinks goes up another 50 cents; Cokes and beer are now $1.50, mixed drinks as much as $4. The sandwich and salad special is $7.95—chips and pickle slices included.

Nine O'Clock. The bartender pushes buttons on a remote control, and from a large-screen television, Eagles and Giants appear. There's noise from the television and noise from the lounge. People are chatting and watching, hustling, munching, and drinking. In their confusion of who they are, and what they want, they'll settle for instant friendships made in front of a cathode ray tube that changes pictures 30 times a second. The Monday Night Football Game is about to begin.

Out of the Closet, and Into the Living Room

By the end of the 1996-1997 television season, just about the only ones who didn't know that Ellen Morgan, bookstore worker on the ABC-TV prime-time sitcom "Ellen," or Ellen DeGeneres who portrays her, were both gay were trappist monks in the Media-Free Zone in Lesotho.

For years, reporters questioned DeGeneres, a stand-up comedian before becoming an actor, about her sexual orientation. For years, she refused to be lured into sensational journalism, her orientation hidden beneath a veil of rumor and innuendo. In March 1994, when "These Friends of Mine," later renamed "Ellen," first appeared in prime time, questions about DeGeneres's sexual orientation again surfaced, but it wasn't until three years later, with "Ellen" no longer in the Nielsen "top 10" and headed into the middle of the pack, that rumors began dribbling out that the show would "out" the character—and, maybe, the star. DeGeneres had wanted the character to declare her sexual orientation, causing innumerable discussions among ABC-TV executives and the Disney conglomerate which not only owns ABC-TV but also distributes "Ellen."

Shortly after the season's premiere in September 1996, the *Hollywood Reporter*, quickly followed by *TV Guide*, had suggested the "coming out" plot line. Hundreds of stories appeared in the media during the next seven months as the "Ellen" publicity mill fed the media frenzy.

During the 1996-1997 season, numerous double entendres snuck into the scripts, while innumerable reporters turned into gossip columnists and tried to get DeGeneres to reveal if either she or her title character were gay. DeGeneres herself flirted with the media most of the season, coyly teasing reporters and TV talk show hosts that the character wasn't a lesbian but a Lebanese, and that the hoopla was a misunderstanding—the lesbian on the show was really a new character, Les Bian.

The Christian conservatives and others who piously proclaimed their belief in "family values," aligned themselves against the suspected "Ellen" plot line. At the beginning of the season, a rather oblique Pat Robertson of the Christian Coalition had said he found it "hard to believe [DeGeneres was gay] because she's so popular. She's such an attractive actress." The Rev. Jerry Falwell called her "Ellen DeGenerate," and the Rev. Fred Phelps in a hellfire and brimstone speech ranted, "It's a sign we're on the cusp of doom, of Sodom and Gomorrah." Thousands of flaming Internet chatters and morally-outraged newspaper readers declared they would boycott the show and its advertisers if either of the Ellens declared a single-sex orientation.

An internal report from the Leo Burnett advertising agency, which represents McDonald's, an "Ellen" sponsor, strongly recommended against buying time on shows with gay characters. The report stated that McDonald's franchise owners in the Bible

Belt could be hurt by such ad placement, especially when confronted by the conservative Christian opposition. McDonald's disregarded the advice, according to *Advertising Age*.

Disney, long identified with "family values," was one of the first major corporations to extend benefits to its single-sex couples. However, the controversy probably backed Disney/ABC into a position that if it didn't approve the "outing," it would be seen as succumbing to hate-mongering and fear. In March, after an entire nation already knew or at least suspected the "coming out" episode was no longer just a rumor, ABC-TV finally announced it had approved a revised script, and that Ellen Morgan would be "outed" in a one-hour special, April 30, during ratings-obsessed "sweeps week." Appearing on that episode would be Laura Dern, Oprah Winfrey, Demi Moore, Billy Bob Thornton, and singers k.d. lang and Melissa Etheridge, both of whom are lesbians. In subsequent episodes, Ellen Morgan would tell her parents and her employer she's gay.

A little more than a month before the broadcast, the religiously fundamental and politically conservative American Family Association (AFA) and Christian Family Network (CFN), which claimed the outing was "attacking the moral fiber of our nation," jointly created the "Ellen" Media Watch, "aimed at bringing about changes in advertising practices and ultimately target changes in offensive programming content." The implementation, housed within a slickly-designed web page, was a massive public e-mail campaign to the corporations which had bought advertising time on "Ellen" during the season.

The counter-attack came from the Gay and Lesbian Alliance Against Defamation (GLAAD) which created a "Come Out With Ellen" campaign that would eventually have parties in seven major cities and 1,500 individual homes the night of the outing.

Chrysler, General Motors, J.C. Penney, and Wendy's eventually chose not to advertise on the "coming out" episode, possibly concerned more about the publicity and controversy surrounding the show than in any biases. Microsoft and Intel said they'd remain, no matter what the public said. The other scheduled advertisers at first said they would see what happens, but eventually stayed with the "outing," probably not for any principle other than recognizing that a probable spike in the ratings certainly couldn't hurt their sales.

Recognizing the potential audience for the one-hour show, ABC raised its advertising rates from an average of $170,000 for a 30-

second spot to an average of $335,000, according to a report in *Advertising Age*. The network, however, refused to take ads from the Human Rights Campaign and lesbian-owned Olivia Cruises and Resorts, stating it was network policy to reject "controversial issue advertising." Human Rights Campaign, however, bought spots on 33 local affiliates to alert viewers that 41 states allow employers to fire workers for being gay or lesbians. WBMA-TV, Birmingham, Alabama, rejected the program entirely.

The episode, possibly the best-written and acted one in "Ellen"'s history of lame scripts, had killer numbers. The show scored a 23.4 rating (the percent of all television homes that watched the show), a 37 share (The percent of all television homes that had their sets turned on at the time and watched the show), and an estimated audience of about 42 million, making it the top-rated show that week. The season's average for "Ellen" was a 9.6 rating and a 16 share, placing it 37th of all prime time television series during 1996–1997.

Shortly after the episode was filmed during the first week in March, DeGeneres herself had playfully told a media awards dinner sponsored by GLAAD that she spent a lot of time doing "research" for her character. However, by then most of the entertainment industry already knew she was gay, some knowing for as long as 20 years. A month later, two weeks before the overhyped broadcast, she stated the reality to *TIME*—which had previously run stories in three other issues— then to dozens of newspapers, magazines, and TV shows. ABC's "20/20" ran the first part of a two-part interview on Friday, April 25, after the network moved the interview from "PrimeTime Live" two days earlier to take advantage of higher ratings and the beginning of the May sweeps. The second part ran on "PrimeTime Live" in the hour following the "outing."

During the past four decades, several dozen TV series have broadcast episodes with gay characters, usually in minor roles, and often in contrived variations of a plot line where a pretty female character has a crush on a handsome athlete whom she later learns is gay.

Possibly the first episode with a gay plot line was "The Eleventh Hour" (1962–1964), an NBC medical drama which had a secondary story line on one episode in 1963 that centered around an actress and female director. Four years later, producers were brave enough to again introduce a gay character on prime time television when "N.Y.P.D." (1967–1969) debuted on ABC with a one-episode story line about a group of hoods who blackmailed gays. Four years after that, President Nixon told the nation how disgusted he was that CBS had broadcast a segment of "All in the Family" that showed the bigoted Archie Bunker questioning his own beliefs when he learned a friend is gay.

In 1972, ABC risked viewer and advertiser antagonism when it slid past two socially-restricted barriers. "The Corner Bar," which included a swishy set designer, became the first American series to include an openly-gay character in a recurring role. "That Certain Summer," a two-hour character study of a gay father who tries to explain his sexual orientation to his son, was probably the first TV movie with a gay theme. Written and produced by Richard Levinson and William Link, the movie featured an all-star cast of Hal Holbrook, Martin Sheen, Hope Lange, and Marilyn Mason.

The 1975 series, "Hot l Baltimore," was the first to show a gay couple. Other series that included gays or lesbians in recurring roles were "The Bob Newhart Show" (1972–1978), "Ball Four" (1976), "The Nancy Walker Show" (1977), "Mary Hartman, Mary Hartman" (1975–1978) "Soap" (1977–1981), "Dynasty" (1981–1989), "St. Elsewhere" (1982–1988), "Hooperman" (1987–1989), "Heartbeat" (1988–1989), "Doctor, Doctor" (1989–1991), "Anything But Love" (1989–1992), "Sisters" (1991–1996), and "My So-Called Life" (1994–1995).

The basis for the ABC sitcom "Three's Company" (1977–1984) was that a straight man pretended to be gay in order to fool a prudish landlord and be allowed to share an apartment with two women.

"Roseanne"—which set new standards in realism before ending a nine-year run in 1997—alone had four continuing gay characters, including her boss, mother, a close female friend, and the friend's girlfriend. "Star Trek," which boldly explored social issues other series wouldn't touch, featured a provocative lesbian relationship in 1996 in a "Deep Space 9" episode.

"Northern Exposure" (1990–1995) was set in the fictional town of Cicely, Alaska, founded by lesbian lovers. An episode of "Northern Exposure" in 1994 included a gay wedding; the following year, "Friends" had a lesbian wedding.

There currently are almost two dozen gay characters in recurring secondary roles on prime-time television while Hollywood, which once banned gay roles as well as gay actors in any role, openly flirts with yet another prime-time way to draw sexually-explicit ratings. In "Hollywood Chic," gays may be represented in television in numbers far greater than in society's realism.

However, the networks have been cautious about open sexuality involving gay issues, although the soaps and a few prime time series have tread close to soft porn on man-woman sexual themes. In 1989, ABC stated it lost about $1 million in advertising when it broadcast a "thirtysomething" episode that showed two gay men in bed. That episode was not included in the rerun schedule. ABC allowed a teacher on the daytime soap "All My Children" to be gay during the 1995–1997 seasons, but forbid any on-screen single-sex romance.

However, in a handful of extraordinary instances, networks have allowed female petting and kissing. The first on-screen lesbian kiss, according to GLAAD, was on an episode of NBC's "L.A. Law" in 1991, followed by a kiss two years later on the CBS comedy-drama "Picket Fences." ABC in 1994 forbid a lesbian kiss on "Roseanne" until Roseanne and Tom Arnold used their considerable ratings clout to demand the network permit it. "Relativity," an ABC drama which had a slobbering lesbian kiss in January 1997, was a marked exception to most standards.

The networks, usually playing it relatively safe in controversial issues, slowly advance story lines only when it seems the public would accept such issues. In relatively sluggish delayed increments, the networks brought gay issues to the public, first in a one-episode secondary theme about a lesbian relationship, then in a made-for-TV movie, followed by a primary drama, minor recurring characters, major recurring characters, and on-air sexuality. The next barrier was now ready to fall.

"Sidney Shorr," an NBC-TV two-hour movie, had starred Tony Randall as an openly gay New York commercial artist. However, NBC-TV refused to allow producers to write Randall's character as gay when the network turned the TV film into a sitcom for the 1981–1983 seasons.

Apparently PBS wasn't as concerned about ratings as the commercial networks. In 1982, the non-profit network broadcast "Brideshead Revisited," a mini-series based upon Evelyn Waugh's novel. The lead character in the series, set during a two decade period in post-World War I England, was bisexual.

In 1984, the Showtime cable network premiered the continuing sitcom "Brothers," the story of three brothers, one of whom was gay. The series, originally rejected by both ABC and NBC, was "one of the first shows on which a major character was gay," according to *The Advocate* which tracks the depiction of gays and lesbians in the media.

"Sara" (1985), the story of a law firm with two male and two female lawyers in San Francisco, survived less than a season on NBC. Bronson Pinchot, portraying a gay lawyer, received fourth billing, behind Geena Davis, Alfre Woodward, and Bill Maher.

In 1994, "Daddy's Girls," a one-season CBS sitcom about the New York garment industry, starred Harvey Fierstein as a gay fashion designer. However, Dudley Moore got top billing. It would be two more seasons, and about 50 years after television became a mass medium, before any network would finally declare a lead character in a successful continuing network show to be gay.

Possibly helping ABC make its decision about "Ellen" was an *Entertainment Weekly* poll that revealed 72 percent of Americans "would not be personally offended if a lead character on a TV show were gay." Disney/ABC undoubtedly did innumerable polls of its own. However, a later *USA Today*/CNN poll revealed that 42 percent of Americans thought there were too many gays and lesbians on television.

The problem isn't that Morgan or DeGeneres are gay, but of the reluctance of the networks and the news media to deal with controversial issues until they determine what the majority, and their advertisers, are willing to support. Then, the networks zealously pursue the "topic of the week," burying the gullible news media under a dumpster of press releases and hype.

Two weeks before the "coming out" episode, *Newsweek* and *TIME* each ran seven pages on "Ellen," Ellen, and gay issues in American media. Neither ran anything that week about the devastating floods of the upper Midwest that would force the evacuations of more than 100,000 people, and cause about $1 billion damage to homes, farms, and businesses.

Give the publicists for "Ellen" and Ellen DeGeneres hefty raises; they did their jobs well. Give the media a slap upside the head for pandering, and to both the media and the public for failing to realize there are other important issues in the world than one's sexual orientation.

Swifter, Higher, Stronger . . . Greedier

Tabitha Matthews, a 15-year-old honors student, is one of 300 volunteers the Atlanta Committee for the Olympic Games (ACOG) selected to work at the softball competition in Columbus, Georgia. In exchange for two nights of training and 20 hours of work in the information booth, she is being paid . . . nothing. She receives no benefits, not even a pass to any of the games.

Each of the five days she works, her mother must drive her 30 minutes to Phenix City, Alabama, where she catches the Olympics shuttle that takes an hour to get to the stadium. The Olympics required their volunteers not only to take the shuttle but to pay $5, a fee the ACOG grudgingly rescinded only a couple of weeks before the games.

Not free are the mandatory uniforms. Like other volunteers, Tabitha was required to buy a pair of khaki shorts or skirt of her own choosing, and pay $10 for a T-shirt or $20 for a hunter green polo shirt, each with a swatch of flash red, a yellow star, and block white script that proclaims, "Superstar." She and most of the other volunteers have no idea what "Superstar" means. It's not even an official Olympics shirt. Official souvenir T-shirts go for $18–$25, and baseball-style caps are $15–30.

The sweat and sacrifices of 10,500 athletes from 197 countries is nearly lost amid the commercialism and greed that threads through an Olympian effort to create the 17-day competition. Just a few other items . . .

Each of the torch carriers who ran, biked, wheeled, or jogged a few minutes of the 84-day circuitous 15,000 mile trip from Los Angeles to Atlanta may buy their own torch for $275.

Tickets for the four-hour opening day ceremony were $636. However, having money didn't guarantee anyone a seat. Of more than 200,000 who wanted to attend, the ACOG selected only 15,000. The other 60,000 who vaulted past the fans were special Olympic friends, officials, and high-rollers, most of whose corporations pay for the ticket, then deduct it from the taxpayers.

Synchronized scalpers are expected to reap as much as ten times face value for single event tickets. Not to be left out of the dash for dollars, the ACOG added a $1 per ticket "fulfillment fee," a $10 one-time account set-up fee, then tried a gold-medal scam.

A seasonal pass in a nice section of the stadium for all track-and-field events cost $1,779. But, the cost of individual tickets to all events would have been only $1,196. The official ACOG response was that a 50 percent surcharge wasn't unreasonable since the Committee is "entitled and empowered to offer ticket packages and price them as we see fit." However, the ACOG reconsidered the price, and refunded a lot of money to several hundred angry spectators when it became apparent it may have violated the state's two-year-old law against ticket scalping, a law the ACOG had vigorously supported.

Fortunately, there are other ways to make money.

Parking runs about $25 a day, with the closest lots a mile or so from the stadiums.

The average temperature in Atlanta in late July is about 88 degrees, with humidity matching the temperature most days. Every few minutes an announcer tells spectators in the 83,000-seat open air track-and-field stadium to avoid dehydration by drinking a quart of water an hour. The only food and drink spectators can bring into the Olympics are plastic containers of water. Those who don't wish to pay inflated prices at the local stores can wait until they get to the stadium to buy a pint of Olympic-approved water for $2.75 from official sponsor Crystal Springs. If they haven't mortgaged their house for water, fans can eat a junk-food lunch of emaciated hamburger ($4.25), soggy fries ($3.25), and 50-cent peach pie, now priced at $2.25.

Fans who want to go all out and have a Coke for that special sugar kick will spend $3.25, about twice the cost at professional sports stadiums, according to *Team Marketing Report*. But, Atlanta-based Coca-Cola needs to make money; it paid 40 million tax-deductible dollars to be an exclusive official sponsor.

Corporate tents, each bearing logos of official sponsors, cover Centennial Olympic Park, built over what once was a section of flophouses.

Official sponsors and ticket sales account for most of the $1.7 billion budget. The international radio and television media paid about $900 million for broadcast rights, but no one paid more than NBC which decided it could still rake in a profit after paying $456 million, then budgeted $100 million for production costs.

Several dozen advertisers see no problem in helping NBC recover their investment, knowing that 200 million Americans—and a world audience of over a billion—plan to watch at least one day of the coverage. Spread over 171½ hours of the telecasts are about 1,500 advertising minutes, each going for about $500,000.

Even "average" Americans can make money off the Olympics. Some enterprising Georgians at the ACOG request decided to rent out their houses then leave the area for three weeks. The average cost per night for a nice three-bedroom split-level is $750–$1,000, with two and three-week minimums. However, for only $100–$200 a night, visitors can rent a room in the house—refrigerator extra. Several regulations kept hotels and motels from price gouging, so they are charging only about twice the normal July rate.

Other enterprising Georgians—and quite a few carpet-baggers—are hawking overpriced food and souvenirs from plywood stands that line the roads leading to the stadiums.

During the 1960s, the establishment freaked when they spotted "hippies" wearing jeans patched by 3-by 5-inch American flags. Today, we are inundated by an overpriced collection of stars-and-striped dishrags, women's panties, shoes, ties, blouses, mugs, and watches, as well as several dozen official Olympic trinkets that include thimbles, playing cards, and sunglasses. There's even an official money clip for spectators who have any money left. About $5 billion in merchandise will be sold by the end of summer.

Finally, the official underwear sponsor is Hanes whose Olympic slogan could be the theme of all concessionaires—"Just wait'll we get our Hanes on the Games." [*July 1996*]

Conventional Fund Spending

In the same month Philadelphia opened its $522 million 1.3 million square foot convention center, the most expensive public works project in the city's history, the Philadelphia school district ended its year having had to make $60 million in personnel and program cuts.

The civic center cheerleaders cite numbers to show how beneficial the center is to the people. The average attendee at one of the trade shows will stay three nights in Philadelphia and leave $1,040; the average attendee for one of the 120 conventions will leave behind $688, and even the locals, defined by the center as "leisure travelers," will leave behind $75 when they attend a trade show, convention, or meeting, according to the International Association of Convention and Visitor Bureaus.

The Center says 6,000 new permanent jobs, about 80 percent

of them in the lower-income service industry, will be created by the end of the century. And, they proudly point to a $10 million decade-long education program that will train persons in four to eight-week programs to be entry-level service industry employees who will become the chambermaids, waitresses, cooks, and desk clerks at the Center and hotel to assure a permanent low-income staff.

And, say the cheerleaders, most of the $522 million cost of the center hardly costs anything since the state provided $185 million of the cost, the city floated bonds for another $277 million, and the rest is being repaid from hotel occupancy taxes.

Here's a few more numbers that the cheerleaders don't mention. Had the 3,000 persons who attended a $250 per person black-tie opening night dinner, and the 10,000 who attended a $25 "Fun-Conventional Fling" decided to stay home and donate the $1 million cost of their tickets to the school district, quite a few teacher jobs could have been saved. Had just half the $2 million spent for artwork in the new center been donated to the school district, creative arts programs could have been significantly expanded. Had just half the $3.6 million 11-day opening promotion budget ($1.1 million provided by the state) been given to fund cancer research at the Temple University medical school, perhaps we would have a major advance within the year.

Had the state's $185 million construction share been used for existing state programs, it would have funded about half the annual budget of the State System of Higher Education or two-thirds of the PennDOT budget. It could have funded almost the entire health department or Department of Environmental Resources budgets. At today's costs, it might have funded any of the following—the state police for almost two years, the labor and industry department for the next four years, the state's share of helping the homeless for almost 12 years, the literacy program for 26 years, or either the emergency management program or the Scranton School for the Deaf for the next 37 years. Or, it could have been used to help improve the lives and programs for the elderly, disabled, and homeless.

In 1993, Philadelphia was on the verge of bankruptcy, and responded by slashing budgets from all departments, and severely cutting back on libraries, fire stations, and homeless shelters. Those cuts have not been restored. Had the city's share been spent on the city's 5,000 homeless, half of them in the city's excellent shelter program that sustained heavy financial cuts, perhaps there wouldn't even be any homeless today.

In Atlantic City, an hour by expressway from Philadelphia, the state of New Jersey built a $268 million 1.2 million square floor convention center, with 500-room hotel. But, the Center will primarily help corporations, conventions, and maybe the 31 million "visitor trips" the casinos will record this year. As for the people of the city, poverty and urban blight, marked by gutted stores and abandoned houses, stretch from Route 87 to the Boardwalk.

Seattle completed a $158 convention center in 1988. Five years later, Boeing, the largest employer in the city, began laying off 38,000 workers, 25,000 of them in Seattle. In Manhattan, which has almost 50 million square feet of vacant office space, the $486 million Javits Center, with 720,000 square feet of exhibition space, is less than a decade old.

Convention centers have recently been built on South Padre Island, Texas ($10.5 million), Moline, Ill. ($33.4 million), Austin, Texas ($50.4 million), Mobile, Ala. ($52 million), Columbus, Ohio ($94 million), Charlotte, N.C. ($141 million), and Providence, R.I. ($290 million). We are told these centers benefit all the people. But, the homeless, unemployed, and low-income Americans usually don't attend conventions.

Our environment reeks of decades of abuse, we still haven't found cures to the health care crisis, more than 8.8 million Americans are unemployed, another 250,000 are homeless, and almost 25 million low-income Americans, about one-tenth of our population, are receiving foodstamps. The money spent for convention centers could be spent on a massive jobs program that trains people not for "service" jobs that benefit the few, but for entry-level training in the health professions and environmental planning, social work, transportation, and labor education. But we're building convention centers, and the conglomerate-owned media have become the biggest cheerleaders. Something just doesn't seem right.

For Casinos, 'Six-Hour Visitors' Make a Full House

She's a 77-year-old slightly overweight white-haired widowed grandmother from northeastern Pennsylvania who has worked the past 15 years for the state at a minimum wage "Green Thumb" job. But five or six times a year, she and two of her closest friends pay $22 to a bus company that hauls passengers the four hours to Atlantic City.

"I can't afford not to go," Gloria Adams says with a twinkle. Depending on which casino the bus goes to, and which day of the week it is, each bus rider receives $10–$15 in tokens from the casino, usually another $3–$5 good for the next trip, and a $5–$10 meal credit. She can choose from any of 92 restaurants or 80 cocktail lounges; if she eats at one of the lower-priced buffets, her meal is almost free.

To lure 81 million "visitor trips" a year, one-third of whom come by bus, casinos spend about $800 million a year, one-fourth of their revenue, on promotion. For most senior citizens, the $15–$25 worth of "comps" is sufficient. But, for the late evening "high-rollers," the ones who think nothing of dropping a few hundred every Black Jack hand or roll of the craps dice, the casinos will provide free limousine or helicopter service, luxury suites, food, beverages, show tickets, myriad trinkets from keychains to suits, and just about anything a loser could want.

Every day, about 800–900 buses, each carrying 30–45 passengers, most of them women over 55 years old, pull into the casinos, stay six hours, then leave. With travel time, combined with limited bus parking, the casinos figure that six hours is the "right" time for the "low-rollers."

On the casino floors the senior citizens scramble to their favorite slots—they have more than 33,000 to choose from—and most won't leave for three or four hours, just shoving coin after coin into the machines, watching the dials spin, and hoping for a jackpot. They'll crowd the nickel slots first; few ever try one of the 46 $100 slots. They'll put in five coins, get a cherry, and win two coins which hit the metal coin tray and boldly announce yet another winner. Sometimes, they'll get mini-jackpots of five, ten, even twenty times what they shoved into the slot. But, they'll recycle the change, hoping for the Slotbusters payoff that will give them and their grandchildren an income for life. Sometimes, even if there are people waiting, they will play two slots at once; if one doesn't pay, its neighbor will—at least that's what many figure. And most go home with less money than they came with. It's not unusual for bus travelers to drop $100 in their allotted six hours at the casino. A few have dropped most of their entire month's social security checks.

For their part, the casinos tell their players—in TV commercials, on all the printed literature, even in frequent announcements beamed from concealed loudspeakers—to "bet with your head, not over it." But then they put an acre of machines, tables, dealers, and provocatively-dressed hostesses into an air-conditioned room that has no windows or clocks, and entice their victims to sign up for plastic card memberships that, when inserted into slots, record the number of times a coin was dropped, and lead to even more trinkets to lure them back into the casino.

The casinos also send employees around to convert currency into coins, and provide free drinks for parched throats that yell encouragement to the machines, and "wipes" for fingers that become dirty handling all those winning coins. For those who have arthritis or don't have the energy to pull a lever, the slots even have push buttons. The casinos want their victims to sit there, in one spot, and lose. If they could figure out a way to catheterize the players so they don't even have to go to the bathroom, they would.

Gloria Adams often comes back with more than she began with. "I know my limits, and I don't go over them," she says, emphasizing that unlike some players, she never uses a MAC card to get "just a little more" playing cash, just in case the "big one" is on the next slot pull. It doesn't upset the casinos. They like it when people win. Nothing entices other people to lose money like the ching-chang of coins dropping into slot trays, and the excited boasts of winners back home. But, most of the gamblers are supposed to spend the freebies, then gamble some more. It has worked very well for more than 15 years.

According to the Casino Control Commission, the "handle," the amount of money bet, since the first casino opened in 1978 is about $361 billion, with slots now accounting for as much as 75 percent of all betting and 60 percent of all revenue. Last year alone, the revenue, the amount of profit prior to expenses, was about $3.2 billion. By law, each slot machine must pay back at least 83 percent of its take; most now pay up to 90 percent. The Casino Control Commission even makes public which casinos have better payoffs and which groups of machines pay better than the others. But, few study the numbers, and none of the casinos see any reason to post them.

The first of the 12 casinos went into business in 1978 following a statewide referendum to allow gambling in a city that had combined Miss America, salt water taffy, rolling wicker chairs, a four-mile boardwalk—and a deteriorating downtown, tenement housing, and the state's highest violent crime and poverty rates.

Atlantic City was incorporated in 1854, about a half century after first being settled, as a summer resort on a 3.9 mile long coastal barrier island. In 1870, the city built the boardwalk, and private companies added numerous businesses and amusements, including the Steel Pier, site of innumerable headline acts. The first modern Miss America contest was held in Atlantic City in 1921; the city built a center eight years later to lure innumerable conventions to the city.

During World War II, the military took over the beach front hotels and turned the city into one of the nation's largest training camps and rest-and-rehabilitation (R & R) sites. However, the war also brought an end to the prosperity. For the next three decades, Atlantic City declined as a resort; the rich moved onto other places; the poor remained. The city's population, infrastructure, and tax base declined. During the mid-1930s, the population peaked about 66,000; by the mid-1970s, it was about 46,000; by the mid-1990s it was about 38,000.

And then came what the state called "a unique tool of urban development." Legalized gambling will save the city, proclaimed voters, legislators, and even businessmen who planned to mine the East Coast, smugly knowing that one-third of the nation's population live within six hours driving time of Atlantic City and could easily be lured to a gambling empire that promised instant wealth.

By the mid-1980s, speculators and the casinos had gobbled up all available land in Atlantic City, expecting as many as 35 casinos to rescue the city. Only when it appeared there would be a saturation of 12 casinos could the school district (which for the 1996–1997 school year received almost $37 million of its $73 million budget from the casinos) finally buy enough land to relocate its high school. But, the taxpayers of the $81 million 470,000 square foot high school still had to pay $9.7 million for 48.8 acres, a lot for a school district but less than the $4.6 million the Showboat spent in 1995 for three acres so it could add 200 more hotel rooms.

Since 1975, the casinos have paid about $6 billion in regulatory fees and revenue, property, corporate, local, state, and federal taxes. About 8.1 percent of the state's budget is a result of casino taxes.

For its part, the state of New Jersey has been so appreciative of receiving money, it built a 43-mile long expressway from Philadelphia directly into the Boardwalk. To lure even more middle- and upper-class marks to the casinos, in 1997 the city and state completed a $268 million 1.2 million square floor convention center, with a 500-room hotel, then added a $100 million three-block "corridor" to link the center with the Boardwalk. City officials are thinking of turning the 380,000 square foot convention center on the Boardwalk, site of the Miss America contest, into an entertainment and shopping complex, and arena for sporting events and concerts.

By 1999, the city will triple its hotel rooms to 27,000, and there will be six more casinos, built for $3 billion, to make sure there's enough gambling and hotel rooms for the conventioneers. For those who want a break from gambling and GP-rated evening shows, the city is building a $12 million 6,000-seat minor league baseball stadium, financed primarily by casino taxes, plus $3 million worth of city bonds. Casino taxes are also paying for $30 million in road improvements around the casinos, a $13 million casino area beautification plan, and 192 new jitneys that will carry gamblers and conventioneers throughout the developed part of the city any time of day or night.

Not benefiting from the taxes and handouts have been the city's permanent residents. In 1996, the state's legislature authorized that $175 million from casino taxes, meant to aid the urban poor, be directed back to the casinos to allow for their expansion. To make sure there's enough land for the casinos, the city and the Casino Reinvestment Development Authority have been using the power of the eminent domain to condemn and then seize homes, businesses, and land in the way of the casinos' expansion plans or in the route of improved streets going into the casinos. Most of the property condemned in the past few years, often against the will of the owners, isn't run-down or boarded-up; most are well-maintained, with a presence in Atlantic City several decades longer than the casinos.

Although city officials are now proudly proclaiming a renaissance for the ocean front resort, which has received about $500 million in property taxes from the casinos since 1978, about 69 percent of its property tax base, they are also faced by the blemish that four of the past six mayors were indicted on a variety of malfeasance and criminal charges, the downtown has deteriorated even further, population has declined 14 percent since the first casino opened, there has been an increase in violent crimes and prostitution—and poverty is still the way of life for a large chunk of the 38,000 residents who live in a city with no theaters and only two supermarkets, one built as part of a $100 million strip mall for tourists. So deteriorated has Atlantic City become, even with its proposed massive revitalization, that most of the 50,000 casino employees won't even live in the city where they work.

Nevertheless, no matter what the city's problems are, the buses still come to Atlantic City, and senior citizens flood the casino floors by day, while the high-rollers take over by night. And the ching-chang of coins continues to lull Americans into believing the good dream belongs to them.

"Gloria Adams" is a fictional name for the lady who asked that she not be identified.

There She Is, Miss-Representing America

It's time for the annual Miss America Pageant, and once again America will probably be represented by a never-married 21-year-old college student who's 5-foot-5, 119 pounds, believes in God and family values, and claims she wants to save the whales and protect the homeless. The only thing we don't know about her is what shade of blonde she'll be.

The contestants all say they're in the pageant to earn a college scholarship and, since they're so beautiful, they want to become broadcast journalists. No one says she wants to be a waitress, small business owner, auto mechanic, or even to meet some hard-body with perfect razor-cut hair, get married, and have 2.3 genetically-perfect children.

In 1881, the *Police Gazette*, a cross between the *National Enquirer* and *People*, reported that following a nationwide search Louise Montague, a burlesque actress and singer, was awarded $10,000 after being judged to be the most beautiful woman in America. She was described as having "a beautiful light complexion [with] a mass of wavy dark chestnut hair." The magazine also reported she was "of medium height [with] a full and symmetrical figure. Her weight is 147 pounds." At the turn of the century, America's sex symbol was singer/actress Lillian Russell. She weighed almost 200 pounds. Margaret Gorman, who was named the first "official" Miss America in 1921, had a rather flat 30–25–32 figure. By today's Miss America beauty standards, none of them would have made it into the finals of the local Miss Rutabaga contest.

Although swimsuit and evening wear competition each count for only 15 percent of the total, it seems the contestants spend 90 percent of their time perfecting, sometimes with collagens, the pouty-lip look that is "in," and spend hours applying makeup to every available millimeter of emaciated skin. There's vaseline to glisten, tape to firm up, and rhinestones for reflection. In 1994, for the first time, the contestants had to do their own hair and make-up. As important as these skills are, it might have been more impressive if they went to the flooded Midwest and stuffed sandbags along the Mississippi.

There was a new wrinkle in the swimsuits that year. Instead of being honest and saying that American men want to see women in swimsuits, the organizers claimed in a puffed-up news release that the swimsuit competition is to allow judges to determine "each contestant's perseverance and self-discipline in maintaining a physically fit and healthy body." Maybe, the contestants might run laps, or be required to submit results of blood tests and X-rays. Perhaps, psychologists and physicians will replace the celebrity judges. Nevertheless, just so we can see those physically fit bodies, the contestants wear one-piece suits that firm and raise—but not too much; after all, we don't want to offend Aunt Myrtle and the Citizen Decency League. Those swimsuits are as much designed for splashing in the ocean as mackerels are meant to wear lipstick and eye liner.

In an inspired moment of public relations, Pageant officials in summer 1995, declared they would allow the American people to vote on whether to keep the bathing suit competition. It was a no-lose plan. No matter how the public voted, the timorous officials could merely claim they were following the will of the people, while reaping the PR deluge that fell with the creation of the contest. On the night of the Miss America Pageant, almost one million viewers called in to one of 11,000 phone lines. By a 4–1 margin, to no one's surprise, they said they wanted to keep bathing suits in the competition.

For 1996, jubilant over their mock audience participation the year before, Pageant officials deluded Americans into believing they were actually voting for Miss America. For a 50 cent call to a 900 number, voters in 40 states—residents in the ten states represented by one of the semifinalists were disenfranchised—could determine who they thought should become one of five finalists. In reality, the majority vote counted only as *one* of eight votes to move five of the ten semi-finalists into the finals. Celebrity judges determined the rank order of the final five.

Because they've become sensitive about image, the organizers tell us, trying to keep from smirking, that the mind and talent are the most important parts of the pageant. And, to prove it, the organizers even programmed their telephones to answer, "Miss America Scholarship Program," apparently to make us believe that beauty has brains and will shortly complete that doctorate in biochemical engineering.

At least half the contestants in the 70,000 or so preliminary beauty contests sing "The Impossible Dream." What's impossible is they actually believe they can sing. If they don't sing, they play the piano, violin, or flail their arms and legs and pretend it's "modern dance." A few even pretend they're actresses and read a monologue from a play they never knew existed until someone from the pageant told them they had to develop a talent real fast or else lose the right to publicly proclaim they believe in the environment.

What we don't see are writers, artists, or sculptors; we see no one who can make quilts, design dresses, or is a fine comedian. If the organizers truly believe that talent is 40 percent of the score, then why weren't Bette Midler, cartoonist Cathy Guisewite, comedian Rita Rudner, or even Grandma Moses ever in the finals?

Now, just in case they have little talent, contestants can redeem themselves in interviews. The organizers proclaim that the "newly expanded private 12-minute session," worth 80 percent of the total, is to evaluate contestants on "such subjects as world affairs, state and local politics, personal interest" and, of course, "interpersonal relationships." During interviews, the contestants recite carefully prepared speeches, sweetened by voice coaches who have studied interpersonal communications, and can now cover any possible question with the same prepared answer.

Because this is a pageant, not a beauty contest, Miss America contestants must present their "platforms," their goals to change the world should they be elected beauty queen for a year. In fact, the Miss America mandate, say the organizers, is to "encourage young women to explore the relevant social issues of their times and to excel in arts, science, communications or any area of inquiry that inspires their interest and devotion." But, how many contestants are going to be allowed to have pro-choice or pro-life platforms? How many will forcefully argue that corporations are exploiting foreign labor? Know anyone past preliminary contests who contends that lesbians should be allowed to serve in military combat units?

It took the organizers more than a half-century to figure out there were Blacks, Hispanics, and Asians in America. Until the organizers recognize that beauty comes in many packages, then no matter what PR and glitz the organizers use to sugarcoat their contest, the reality is that it's still just another beauty contest that excludes most women from consideration.

The Day the Circus Came to Town

The circus came to town the other day, quietly and without fanfare. There was no mile-long parade with animals and bands, for the circus had snuck in on RVs and 18-wheel semis. No barefoot boys, their faces sunburned from the summer, were idling by the gates hoping to be asked to water the elephants and camels in exchange for an admission. No one sold cotton candy or pink lemonade, for the menu was overpriced hot dogs, hamburgers, candy, heavily salted but unbuttered popcorn, and ice-laden carbonated soft drinks, all of them huckstered throughout the show.

No one tried sneaking in under the main tent, for there wasn't one, just an impersonal green-tinged concrete-domed auditorium that also hosted farm shows and rock music acts. People no longer flocked to the sideshow because this time even the sideshow wasn't there—perhaps a tribute to mankind's sensitivity to human concerns, perhaps because the circus could still sell tickets without having to display society's "freaks."

The ringmaster, a hired actor wearing a tux—not even shiny black hip boots and a scarlet red coat—stood just outside the center ring, commanded the attention of his appreciative audience, and with a flourish blew his whistle and called out the acts.

First into the show was a trainer and some lions. The trainer snapped his whip, and fired a pistol loaded with blanks and special-effects smoke. The lions got up on stools, executed marching maneuvers—and yawned, undoubtedly wishing that the afternoon whistle would blow so they could quit work, go home, drink some beer and watch TV, or whatever it is that lions do when they're not working.

A couple of elephants and a half-dozen ponies ran around the center ring, stood up, bowed, and did tricks. All circus animals do tricks. Somehow, we believe that taking animals out of their natural environment, then forcing them to conform to what humans think is cute, is something to be applauded.

It costs a lot to feed and care for circus animals and the people who perform with them, rent auditoriums, buy newspaper ads, print tickets, hire a half-dozen local musicians, and pay the prodigious costs of liability insurance. In a wood-panelled board room in a steel-and-glass building far from the smell of sawdust, a group of directors, undoubtedly guided by a CEO advised by a gaggle of MBAs and lawyers, none of whom have the talent to do anything more than pick up after the elephants, may have determined that to maintain the price-to-earnings ratio, and to be able to continue to make quarterly dividend payments to its vaporous plethora of stockholders, this business had to cut a few animals from the show, maybe also cut back on some acts and support staff.

Far above the grey concrete floor sprinkled with sawdust, above the safety net held by a dozen hefty roustabouts, swung the aerialists, their split-second movements drawing appreciative gasps. After them, an illusionist made doves appear and a tiger disappear.

Between acts came the clowns, a half-dozen of them prancing, chasing, falling to the syncopated rataplan of their own drummer, now throwing a bucket of water, now a bucket of confetti, blowing whistles and honking horns, bobbing and weaving and ducking. Once the highest form of comedy, clown comedy is dying. Instead of wearing fright wigs and red-bulb noses, baggy pants, floppy shoes, and polka-dotted stuffed shirts, today's upwardly mobile comedians wear designer jeans and theatrical makeup; instead of perfecting pratfalls, their managers help them perfect stock portfolios.

The show ended 90 minutes after it began. The actors returned for a mini-revue, then went to their RVs. The audience quietly walked out, past the entrance where they could still purchase circus T-shirts, programs, and recorded calliope music, assuming they didn't buy any during the dozen or so times vendors walked the stands just to make sure everyone who paid the $8 admission didn't have anything left in their wallets or purses.

The acts that were seen only a couple of times in a lifetime now flood the television screens, and it's far easier at the end of a day just to stay home and push buttons on a remote control box.

But the circus is our reminder of a childhood when we didn't worry about mortgages and the languid economy, when our lives weren't complicated by problems with the environment, street crime, or if we could scrape up enough money for an overpriced prescription. As with all things, we matured, and the circus matured, its freshness left for the young who will have their memories, and for the elderly who have everything to remember—and, maybe, for the dreamers who, like the clowns, will find their own drummers.

'And Now a Word From Your Local Sponsor'

In the *Police Academy* movies, Michael Winslow portrays a rookie cop who baffles and harasses the bad guys by imitating the sounds of helicopters, machine guns, and even the high-pitched sirens of police cars. Naturally, the 60 trillion or so people who have seen the movies know *Police Academy* is a comedic exaggeration. Unfortunately, the nation's military and paramilitary agencies haven't yet figured this out.

In 1990, the Army set up loudspeakers to blast rock music at opera-loving Panamanian dictator Manuel Noriega, figuring that no one could withstand "Voodoo Child" and "You're No Good" for long. During the Gulf War, the Army set up speakers to transmit sounds of tanks to make Sadaam Hussein believe an invasion was imminent. Since Sadaam isn't cooperating with us, we may never know if the deception led him deeper into his bunker. In Waco, the Bureau of Alcohol, Tobacco, and Firearms and the FBI bungled their way into a two-month-long stand-off when they tried ousting Wakko David Koresh and his Branch Davidians from their fortress by using psychological warfare. The Feds shined spotlights into the compound, and set up a ring of loudspeakers. They recorded a high-pitched screech from an off-the-hook telephone, cranked up the decibels, and beamed that noise into the compound. They also blasted Christmas carols, chants from Tibetan monks, military bugle calls, and rock music at the man who believed he was a prophet, a savior or, depending on the tide, the son of God. The spotlights and rock music didn't seem to affect the Davidians. The only ones affected by the psychological warfare were the Feds, a third of whom are now in rest homes.

Although it didn't work in Panama, Iraq, and Texas, the use of media to force surrenders shouldn't be abandoned. For unlimited torture, the kind that Amnesty International would surely oppose, I'd set up large-screen TV sets. I believe I have the ultimate "surrender-at-any-price" programming.

I'd open the broadcast day with a sermonette by rocker David Lee Roth, followed by a 15-minute quick-cut montage of politicians and government officials saying, "Trust me." Next up would be two hours of clips from each of the 15,000 celebrity exercise videos currently on the market, followed by an hour of clips of "Stupid Funny Home Video Tricks," and two hours of afternoon soaps, featuring actresses who can't act, woodenly reciting words from writers who can't write.

Next up would be a rerun of the deservedly-defunct musical TV series "Cop Rock" followed by music videos of Ratt, Twisted Sister, and Nine Inch Nails. In between the programming, we'd beam endless commercials of Sally Struthers blathering about correspondence courses, some bald-headed guy telling how to restore hair, and Ed McMahon telling every known life form that it *could* be a winner.

About 6 p.m., bring on the local "Happy-Time News," with Susie Sweetwater's big scoop on who she thinks will win the next Miss Rutabaga contest, Harry Handsome's biting feature about the county's largest cucumber, and Darla Dormant's questions to local residents—"How do you feel about being wiped out by a flood?"

If that doesn't cause him to surrender, unleash the "Big One," guaranteed to bring anyone to his knees to pray for eternal salvation from TV—four hours of reruns of Jenny Jones and Ricki Lake.

Kernels of Truth

It was an important news day. The massacre in Rwanda, which followed a period of stability following a three-year civil war, continued with no hope for peace, and would claim 500,000 more lives. In Somalia, warlords were still fighting small battles for political control. In Haiti, soldiers murdered two dozen fishermen. Serbian artillery was still hammering targets in Bosnia. South African politicians were campaigning for office in the country's first election in which all citizens could vote. And, in America, thousands still weren't receiving adequate health care, President Clinton called for Social Security to be taken out of the Department of Health and Human Services and become an independent agency, and Americans were planning to go to Yorba Linda, California, to pay tribute to former President Nixon who had died only a few days earlier.

But, the most important news story, the one CNN and the networks pumped all day, the one that was splashed in inch-high type across six columns on newspaper front pages, told a shocked America that theater popcorn was dangerous.

The Center for Science in the Public Interest told reporters that a medium bag of popcorn, popped in coconut butter, had more fat than a day's menu of a bacon-and-eggs breakfast, a Big Mac and large fries lunch, and a steak dinner with baked potato and a mound of sour cream. Add a few wisps of butter, and you need a Roto-Rooter to clean your arteries. The Council claimed that theater owners use coconut oil because it gives popcorn a unique theatrical flavor that the almost-healthy corn oil or air popping can not.

After learning that cigarette smoke is dangerous, thousands of Americans stopped smoking after sex. But, because of AIDS and other venereal diseases, they also decided to abstain entirely. So, they went to R-rated movies, but now we learn they can't even munch popcorn, and must now practice Safe Kernel.

Because about 90 percent of all movie house revenue is from food sales, the impact could force theaters out of business. If attendance at movies drops because of a drop in popcorn sales, then thousands of actors, costumers, and film projectionists will be thrown into the unemployment lines. There's nothing more pathetic than seeing Clint Eastwood whimpering to an unemployment clerk about how hard he tried that week to get a decent minimum-wage job that would make his day.

Those addicted to popcorn might be able to smuggle in a bag or two. Naturally, to preserve their dwindling profits, theaters would have to hire popcorn police to make sure that didn't happen. Since there's no ban on assault weapons, the Kernel Kops could spray a few thousand rounds of 9 mm. cholesterol pellets against popcorn sneakers.

Some government body somewhere will soon prescribe there must be separate sections of the theater for those who eat popcorn and those who don't. After all, secondary popcorn smell can be almost as devastating as drinking a gallon of coconut oil. At the very least, there'd have to be warnings on popcorn bags, like, "Eating too much popcorn can make you go blind" or "Making noise while eating popcorn can injure your eardrums and annoy that spike-helmeted biker nearby."

Based on the evidence, Congress will convene a special select subcommittee to analyze the impact of popcorn on society. The first witnesses, of course, will have to be Orville Redenbacher and that Howdy Doody grandson of his. Certainly, in our gold-chained society, anyone who wears bow ties must be suspect. If the Cold War still existed, the Popcorn Potentate would probably have been a Communist. After all, doesn't the name "redenbacher" really mean "Commie backer"?

Recently, a cigarette company executive, with straight face, told a Congressional Committee that cigarette smoking is no worse than eating Twinkies. If he had said that cigarette smoking wasn't as bad as munching theater popcorn, he'd probably be a hero of the industry by now.

Of course, producers will continue to churn out R-rated movies with 62,000 violent acts per hour, and feel rather safe about their Constitutional license to practice freedom of celluloid.

The Hustle

The hustle had begun less than six hours after they buried the producer when the production manager on a 30-minute "infomercial" decided he wanted four times more money since he figured it was now more difficult without the producer.

The widow, who had been in "The Industry" for 17 years, said there wasn't that much money, especially since the production manager had taken it upon himself that evening to hire not only another production assistant, but also a script clerk whose only talent seemed to be that she smiled a lot at the production manager.

But the production manager knew there was now no way production could be completed without him—and his friend. The friend was a salesman who somehow had become the star's agent, then decided to become a producer. After all, with his gold-color Cadillac, $150 shoes, open shirt, and three golden chains strung around his neck, he looked Hollywood.

In his best macho voice, the salesman–producer proclaimed to cast and crew, "We'll do whatever is fair." He decided it was "fair" for everyone, including him, to get more money. Naturally, the additional expense would come from the widow's pocket—and from the "star" who was convinced that "good" production needed even more money. Well, thought the widow, at least she could count on the Russians not doing anything stupid. She was wrong.

The "Russians" were two Russian immigrants who had been neophyte film makers in the Soviet Union, but who had defected because they were denied "artistic freedom." Neither was political; they just wanted a chance to get more work.

The now-deceased American producer–director had been the

only one who had given the Russians film work in more than three years. When the producer–director died, the Russian first assistant director became the director at twice his original salary. Within hours, he claimed the American director of photography didn't know what he was doing, and gave control to the other Russian who had originally been hired as a production assistant.

The day after the producer was buried, the Russians demanded even more money. Naturally, the salesman–agent agreed; it was, as he proudly proclaimed, "only fair." Then, a young assistant cameraman decided that twice his contract rate was "only fair." And someone else submitted an expense voucher for eight hours driving time for a hundred mile trip.

Next, the salesman-agent who thought he was a producer decided the script needed changing, so he changed it without consulting the writer or director, and set back production another two days and several thousand more dollars. Then it was time to tell the film editor and sound engineer they weren't competent, and to dismiss both of them, although the film editor had taken numerous productions through final edit during his three decade career.

When the unions started questioning some work rule violations, the salesman-agent tried "sweet talking" them—he called it PR—and handed out some "gifts." Only because the now-deceased director-producer had such a good working relationship with the unions, and because of concern for the widow, did they return the gifts and decide not to shut down the production and bring the amateurs up on numerous charges, including stupidity.

So now, "The Magnificent Four"—the production manager, the director, the cinematographer, and the salesman-agent—were going to edit the film—if they could just get it out of the lab.

"The film won't cut," the widow had been saying all along, knowing that the way it was shot after her husband's death was so scattered that scenes didn't match, and that an editor would have an impossible time putting it all together.

"You're crazy!" they told her, and kept shooting fill-in scenes.

"You don't have a film," she now firmly told them to their sarcasm. But, when they tried to get the negative out of the film lab, they were told that, indeed, they didn't have a film. By law, the widow was the only one who could release the negative; after all, she was the one who had previously paid for it.

For the next six months, the four would-be film makers, their lawyers and cronies, tried every trick they could to get the film. None succeeded.

"Buy me out," she said cooly. They had no other choice. But at least they were now "Hollywood," and could use their production credit to convince other companies to invest in making infomercials, even if they didn't air except at 3 a.m.

Creating a Best-Seller

Nothing is more pathetic than an author sitting at a card table surrounded by unsold copies of his latest book while watching humanity pass him by in front of a book store in a crowded mall.

For several weeks, I have been pathetic.

Potential readers turn their eyes away, picking up their pace as they jog past the card table, avoiding me as if I were the lead locust in the upcoming 14-year plague. With humor, sarcasm, even pleading, I call to them. Most have innovative reasons why they don't want to enter the bookstore. "I don't got time to read" is one of the more popular ones.

To accommodate them, publishers have condensed about 25,000 books and placed them onto two-hour audio cassettes that allow almost-readers to shove a tape into a car cassette and do auto-aerobics in morning rush hour traffic.

More than 90 million American adults are functionally illiterate, according to a U.S. Department of Education study in 1993. That same year, the United Nations determined that the U.S. literacy rate is now 49th of 158 nations. There may be no correlation here, but the average time in front of a TV set is about seven hours a day; the average time reading a book is about seven minutes.

But people do wander into bookstores. By the year 2000, consumer spending for books designed for pleasure reading is expected to be about $17.9 billion, up from $10.3 billion in 1990, according to the Book Industry Study Group.

Fixing my targets, I cheerfully ask what kind of books they like, pitching my book to fit their needs. Usually they ask for directions to the cookbooks. *In the Kitchen With Rosie*, by Oprah's chef, has sold six million copies. *The Bubba Gump Shrimp Co. Cookbook*, hyped by ads in all major newspapers and on the 10 million *Forrest Gump* videos, hit more than 700,000 in sales. *Entertaining With Regis & Kathie Lee*, as syrupy as you'd expect, was also a big seller. Even *Menus for Entertaining*, by flighty Martha Stewart who once told America to leave an inch of snow on the ground to beautify their estates, made it onto bestsellers lists.

Once, I tried to explain to a 30ish woman covered by peroxide and makeup that my book of short columns was a humorous look at some serious social issues, but she slapped me with reality—"Oh, no! I wouldn't be able to sleep if I read your book. Those kind make me so upset."

"Go ahead, try it!" I implored. "I've even read it twice myself." When there was only a blank look, I sent her into the romances.

Romance readers, led into illusory bedrooms by Danielle Steele and Janet Dailey, spend about $1,200 a year on their bodice-ripper tales of poor writing told by women with Anglicized bylines who can follow a lame plot formula and write quickly—or, if you're Barbara Cartland, dictate three to four books at a time to secretaries. Overall, about 1,500–2,000 romances are published just in the United States and Canada, accounting for about 42 percent of all mass market paperback fiction sales, according to Barnes & Noble, booksellers.

Romance readers are often soap watchers. A book about what goes on behind the scenes at TV's "General Hospital" made it to the racks in time for a hefty Christmas sale in 1995. However, one of the most popular books in 1995 was a diary by a soap character—not the star who plays her, but the character herself. *Robin's Diary*, more lurid and as superficially revealing as anything on daytime TV, easily outsold *The Diary of Anne Frank*.

Also outselling Anne Frank's diary is *The Sensuous Woman*, by "J," which has seduced more than 10 million Americans since 1971, well ahead of any book by a Nobel laureate. When William Faulkner won the Nobel Prize for Literature in 1948, every one of his novels, none of which had sold more than 2,000 copies, was out of print. In 1995, *Beavis and Butt-head's Ensucklopedia* sold more than 400,000 copies, more than books by Peter Benchley, E. L. Doctorow, Joseph Heller, Jack Higgins, John Irving, James Michener, and Herman Wouk.

Readers want to buy books from people they know, or think they know. Books by actor-comedians Ellen DeGeneres, Paul Reiser, and Tim Allen, and singer Dolly Parton have each had sales of more than a million copies.

On a day when I was selling a handful of books in Wilkes-Barre, Pennsylvania, cross-dressing radio shock jock Howard Stern was two hours away in Philadelphia deluged by 15,000 sales of *Miss America*, significantly ahead of Colin Powell who managed a one-day sale of almost 3,500 copies, and Newt Gingrich whose best one-day sale was 1,800 copies, still about 50–100 times more than the average writer sells at a bookstore stop.

Because author personality is often more important than substance, authors fine-tune a "spiel" and hit the radio and television book circuit. Appearances on major talk-shows, even if for only a few minutes, can generate more than 2,000 to 10,000 sales. It isn't too unusual for an appearance on "Oprah," the leading spot for authors, to generate more than 20,000 sales. Radio interviews conducted by phone allow authors to sit at home or in the office and spout witticisms half a continent away. Authors don't even have to be present in TV studios. With satellite technology, authors can show up at their publishers' or publicists' offices, step before a camera in a mini-studio, and be seen instantly on any TV station in the country. Often, a best-selling author will spend an entire day in a studio, being interviewed by one host after another, each TV station claiming an "exclusive" interview.

Rush Limbaugh's *The Way Things Ought to Be*, hyped by its author's national book tour and never-ceasing mention to his 18-20 million daily radio listeners, spent 52 weeks, beginning September 1992, on the *Publisher's Weekly* best-sellers lists. His followup, *See, I Told You So*, with sales of about 2.5 million, hit the list for 13 weeks, beginning the end of 1993. Al Franken's somewhat humorous reply, *Rush Limbaugh is a Big Fat Idiot*, became a best-seller in 1996.

Politicians, political advisors, and political criminals also get big advances because their books get big sales. Almost all the Watergate crowd made money off book deals. Dick Morris, one of President Clinton's senior advisors, resigned during the August 1996 convention and became known throughout the nation. As a political advisor, he was known only in political circles, and would not have received more than a couple of hundred thousand dollars for his memoirs. As someone who visited a prostitute, shared White House secrets, and made the cover of the tabloids, he got a $2.5 million advance.

Books by athletes also hit best-sellers lists. In the summer and fall of 1996, basketball superstar Dennis Rodman, aided by a seven-figure advance, fluorescent-hued hair and multibody tattoos, outdid even Howard Stern by wearing a dress and feather boa in Detroit and a wedding dress in Manhattan to promote his autobiography, *Bad as I Wanna Be*. The book hit the *Publisher's*

Weekly best-sellers list at Number 1 the week it was released, and stayed on the list 19 weeks, selling more than 750,000 copies. His publisher was so pleased with the public response that it offered Rodman another seven-figure advance for two more books, one of which is a picture book of his tattoos.

Name recognition also extends to former family members, even ones who may have little writing ability. Rodman's ex-wife, Anicka, got a six-figure royalty advance from Dove Books to write *Worse Than He Says He Is*, published in spring 1997.

If it's a diet-and-exercise book by a TV or film star—Suzanne Somers, Jane Fonda, and even Angela Lansbury have told us how to look wonderful—bring out the SuperCray megacomputers to figure the sales. The books don't even have to be well-written to make the lists. Robert James Waller's *The Bridges of Madison County,* which could have used a covey of copyeditors, sold more than six million hardcover copies and stayed on the *Publishers Weekly* best-sellers list for 161 weeks. Books by and about O.J. Simpson also hit best-sellers lists between 1995 and 1997, making millionaires of lawyers, plaintiffs, cops, friends, and hangers-on whose prose fit literature as badly as undersized gloves. Even ex-girlfriend Paula Barbieri bared her soul for a $3 million advance.

A weak book can even get prime display in bookstores if the publisher or author wants to rent space. In the Barnes & Noble chain, $1,500 gets positioning in the "Discover Great New Writers" spot, as well as a favorable review in a store brochure. For authors and publishers who want even better exposure to the public, and a chance to hit the best-sellers lists, $10,000 gets one-month rental of a "dump," a stand-up cardboard display near the front of the store. Can't afford $10,000? For only $3,000, Barnes & Noble will put the books in a display at the end of the aisle. It's no different at other major chains. "Original Voices" books at Borders costs the publisher between $1,500 and $2,500 a month. The thinking, of course, is that people see a lot of books in a favorable spot and will buy because they think others are buying.

Some books don't get seen. Books that criticize conglomerate bookstores—if anyone has written such a book—probably won't get bought by the chains. And, Americans have a strange sense of what's proper. *Huckleberry Finn*, which innumerable literary organizations regard as the finest American novel, is also the nation's most banned book. Also on the list of banned books—censured by people on school boards who appear to be afraid of ideas—are *The Dairy of Anne Frank, Of Mice and Men, Catcher in the Rye,* and *To Kill a Mockingbird.*

Fortunately, many well-written best sellers by authors—not athletes and movie stars—aren't banned. With a first printing of 2.8 million hardcover copies, John Grisham's *The Rainmaker* set an industry record. Not far behind was Michael Crichton's *The Lost World.* However, the average first novel sells 2,000–4,000 copies, not enough for either the author, who earns about 10 percent of the book price, or publisher to make any money. The break-even point for most publishers is 5,000 copies, with New York publishers now looking at 10,000 copy break-even books.

With the industry spending seven-figure royalty advances and six-figure promotion budgets on just a few authors, most of the rest of us don't even get a chance to see our books published, no matter how well written and insightful. Those that are published are usually buried in a promotion budget the size of a business executive's conscience. It's just a matter of economics in an industry that has seen conglomerates cannibalize each other, and just 10 publishers place 94 percent of the year's best sellers. All that matters is the bottom line—"Can it sell?"

In 1960, William Jovanovich, chairman of publishing giant Harcourt Brace Jovanovich, said, "The day it gets to be a choice between manuscripts and the balance sheet, I'll get out of publishing." He was forced out in 1990 in a hostile takeover.

Once, mass market books got three or four months before they were returned to the publisher. Now, in most cases, it's only four to six weeks as book sellers don't want books cluttering up their stores.

Would-be writer Chuck Ross, who believed he was a better writer than his rejection pile indicated, scammed the book publishing mentality. He retyped word for word Jerzy Kosinkski's *Steps,* which had won a National Book Award. Thirteen literary agents and 14 book publishers, proving they often buy manuscripts on the basis of name recognition and other factors, rejected Ross's manuscript. Even the ones who wrote semipersonal replies stated that the book wasn't to their standards. Among those which rejected the retyped *Steps* was Random House, which like the others not only didn't recognize the manuscript, but had been the company that first published it.

From mall-sitting, I realized that the peroxided, made-up 30ish lady was right. The public wants books about social issues about as much as the impoverished living in tenements want roaches. What the people want are how-to, self-help, and celebrity tell-all books, as well as books about cooking, computers, diets and exercise, and sex and intimacy. I'll soon be starting my next book, a guaranteed best-seller, *How to be Your Own Best Friend While Using the Internet to Sensually Bake Diet Pornographic Cookies with O.J. and Bill Clinton.*

Liner Notes on an American Future

At 11:10 a.m., every third Thursday of the month, Betty Fodness of Millville, Pennsylvania, walks into a 24-foot-long-blue-and-white bookmobile of the Columbia County Traveling Library and checks out 10 to 15 books from a traveling collection of about 2,500.

"I'm there right on the button when they get there," Fodness says. By now, the county librarian knows what Fodness likes to read and often has four or five books already picked out.

Each month, the bookmobile visits 50 sites in the rural northeastern Pennsylvania county, stopping about an hour each at preschools, day care centers, nursing homes, senior citizen centers, and public schools, as well as relatively isolated communities in the county. Last year, the library checked out about 30,000 books, almost 200 to Fodness alone.

Millville is an agrarian community of almost 1,000 people. It once had its own library on the third floor of the local bank. But accessibility problems and a general lack of interest by local residents forced the all-volunteer library to close about a decade ago. The nearest library now is ten miles south in Bloomsburg, the 12,000-population seat and geographical center of Columbia County. There are only three public libraries and two bookstores in the county.

"I used to go into Bloomsburg," Fodness says, "but parking is a problem." Another problem is snow during the winter which makes parts of the two-lane Route 42 hazardous.

"When you're a widow, you need a little getaway," says Fodness whose getaway is through literature. She reads a lot—"always have"—but doesn't rent videos or watch much television. "Too much sex and violence," she says.

However, entertainment and information for Millville residents tends to be stuffed within VCRs and broadcast on television sets. On the four blocks that intersect to form Millville's downtown are three places where residents may rent videotapes. Between 50 and 150 persons a day rent tapes from The Fireside Video; on busy weekends, rentals approach 500. Nearby, the Quakerette, a restaurant, rents about 25 videos a day. Even Pop's IGA, a supermarket, rents out five a day. About 18 percent of all videos are rented in supermarkets.

Millville's glut of video isn't unique in America. About 87 percent of America's 96 million households have a VCR, up from only 10 percent in 1984, says research firm Paul Kagan Associates. Of 35,000 libraries in America, only about 9,000 are public libraries, with a funding of about $5 billion a year. In contrast, Americans paid about $11 billion to rent 4.1 billion videos, and about $9.7 billion to purchase 682.9 million prerecorded tapes from about 120,000 places, including 27,000 video stores in 1996, according to the *Hollywood Reporter*.

In a world dominated by the visual media, sale of videotapes has often been the key to guaranteeing a profit for the studios. Home video sales accounted for 57 percent of all revenue for the major Hollywood studios in 1995; theater bookings accounted for only 23 percent, according to the Goldman Sachs Research Report.

Video stores purchase 300,000 to 700,000 copies of blockbuster hits, and 100,000 to 300,000 copies of films that have box office sales of $10–$30 million. Retailers often pay $40–$60 for home videos, renting them for $2–3 a day. The sale price often drops to about $20 within a year of release. A few blockbusters, including *Jurassic Park* and *Pulp Fiction,* have topped $20 million in sales to rental stores and consumers. Disney's *The Lion King*, with sales of 30 million videotapes, and *Snow White and the Seven Dwarfs*, with 25.5 million, both issued in 1995, are the two biggest selling videos of all time, giving Disney a $2 billion sale in videos that year, up from $1 billion just three years earlier.

At one time, direct-to-video releases were considered inferior to movies shown in theaters. However, the quality of production has improved significantly, and studios no longer need theater releases to guarantee high video sales. About 95 percent of all videos—from "how-to" tapes to the O.J. nonconfessional tape to major feature releases—have never been seen in a movie theater. It isn't just smaller studios making money on direct-to-video. Disney's Aladdin was released to theaters; its two sequels were released directly on video.

Cable systems, pay-per-view, and digital satellite broadcast systems have given the studios even more opportunities for distribution and the opportunity to show profits; Direct TV shows

55 separate films every night in prime time.

Betty Fodness doesn't have satellite TV, seldom rents videos, but will continue to go to the bookmobile and read 10-15 books a month. Ironically, she now has more books to choose from. In 1995, the Frank Laubach public library in Benton, located in the northern part of Columbia County, closed. Its 2,500 books were transferred to the Traveling Library's permanent collection of 17,000 volumes. Laubach, a Benton resident, was the founder of the "each one teach one" literary movement that brought significantly increased literacy throughout America and the world. In the future, literacy may more appropriately be defined as the ability to read the liner notes on video boxes.

Fantasy Week at Walt's

Some people think columnists spend all morning lying around on the couch, surrounded by beautiful women while contemplating outrageous things to write, then the afternoon writing it up in an opulent office funded by a consortium of lobbyists.

All of that is true, of course, but that still leaves the evening when we're expected to incessantly grill our sources until they admit to having shot the Easter Bunny so we can justify writing our 700-word pack of lies. The result of all that writing is that I have tendinitis in my shoulder.

First stop, my family physician who said if I'd lose a ton, I'd feel much better. Of course, he also believes that being hit by a truck is good for you since you can lose weight in the hospital by drinking dinner through an IV.

Next stop, an orthopedist with tendinitis. He said he couldn't prove I became lame because of writing, but that he got his injury at Baseball Fantasy Camp.

For $4,000, you can spend a week in Florida training with the Phillies, and even get to play in a game with the veterans. It's an opportunity for social workers, speech pathologists, fire fighters, cancer researchers, and others to actually do something with their lives instead of wasting it away helping humanity. By hitting a home run and possibly getting that $3 million contract and $10 million in endorsement fees next year, they qualify for front-page news coverage and the right to do 30-second TV commercials that tell us how important Nikes and Coke are in our lives.

While on the Columnists Injured List, taking drugs and lifting weights like all athletes, I figured I'd go into coaching. For $4,000 each, I'll let a couple of readers follow me around all week. I'll even bring in a strength conditioning coach; after all, you have to make sure those fingers and eyelids are in top shape.

You would stay in a 110-square foot spare bedroom in our house in a quiet rural working class neighborhood. During work breaks, you'll have a chance to play with two overtly friendly German Shepherds and a miniature pot-bellied PWA—Pig With Attitude.

For meals, you'll have a choice of raiding the refrigerator or dining out at any of the exclusive Route 11 fast food restaurants. After a hard day's thinking, you could experience part of the columnist's fast-lane entertainment lifestyle by watching TV and falling asleep in the recliner or chatting with any of my neighbors, all of whom know I'm a journalist, yet still talk to me.

At the end of the week, just as in Baseball Fantasy Camp, you'll get a chance to write a column. As deadline approaches, you'll get exclusive tips on how nationally-syndicated columnists check e-mail and play card games on the computer to avoid writing. Sunday night, hours before the deadline, you'll panic and ask my wife for an idea. Since she's a labor relations specialist, she'll even advise you on contracts and how to earn that $3 million a year as a star advice columnist.

Monday morning, with an 8 a.m. deadline, you'll get up at 7 a.m., and dash off 700 words that you swear is the best lexical effort since Noah Webster walked the earth, but for which some readers can prove their letters to Aunt Matilda are better written and more thought-provoking.

Now, before you rush off to your bank and take out that $4,000 in small unmarked bills, it's only fair to warn you that you'll have to read a half-dozen newspapers, watch two or three TV newscasts, and listen to the radio and CD player a couple of hours every day, as well as read a half-dozen magazines during the week to find not only the news, but how the media cover the news. This much exposure to the media could result in a mental meltdown.

But, it's all worth it since writing a weekly column isn't much harder than getting a major league hit. As for that opulent office with the dancing girls—you'll have to sign-up for Advanced Columnists Week. It's only $8,000, and I'll guarantee you'll have a better batting average than the Phillies' starting pitching staff.

About the Author

Dr. Walter M. Brasch is a professional writer-journalist and college professor. He was a newspaper reporter and editor, magazine writer, book publishing company editor-in-chief, and a writer-producer of multimedia productions.

He is the recipient of numerous writing awards for his newspaper column, including awards from the Society of Professional Journalists, National Society of Newspaper Columnists, National Federation of Press Women, Pennsylvania Press Club, Pennsylvania Women's Press Association, International Association of Business Communicators, Pacific Coast Press Club, and Press Club of Southern California.

Dr. Brasch is the author of ten books, two of which were named by *Choice* magazine, published by the American Library Association, as Outstanding Academic Books in communications during their years of publication. He is also the author of about 200 magazine and journal articles, 25 multimedia productions, and has worked in both the television and film industries. Dr. Brasch is also a public information specialist for nonprofit disaster relief organizations and a consultant in crisis public relations.

Dr. Brasch earned an A.B. in sociology, an M.A. in journalism, and a Ph.D. in mass communication/journalism. He is a member of the national scholarship honor fraternities Kappa Tau Alpha (journalism), Phi Kappa Phi (general scholarship), Alpha Kappa Delta (sociology), and Pi Gamma Mu (social sciences).

He is listed in *Who's Who in the East*, *Who's Who in the Media*, *Directory of American Scholars*, and *Contemporary Authors*.